RICHMOND
UNCHAINED

RICHMOND UNCHAINED

THE BIOGRAPHY OF THE
WORLD'S FIRST BLACK SPORTING SUPERSTAR

LUKE G. WILLIAMS

ORIGINAL ILLUSTRATIONS BY
TREVOR VON EEDEN

AMBERLEY

For my wife Kemi, without whose love and support I would never have started writing this book, let alone finished it ...

First published 2015

Amberley Publishing
The Hill, Stroud
Gloucestershire, GL5 4EP

www.amberley-books.com

British Library Cataloguing in Publication Data.
A catalogue record for this book is available from the British Library.

ISBN 978 1 4456 4489 9 (paperback)
ISBN 978 1 4456 4509 4 (ebook)

Typeset in 10pt on 12pt Sabon.
Typesetting and Origination by Amberley Publishing.
Printed in the UK.

Contents

... and it was now too late and too far to go back, and I went on. And the mists had all solemnly risen now, and the world lay spread before me ...

Charles Dickens, *Great Expectations*

Author's Note

In this book I have preserved numerous eccentricities of grammar, capitalisation, italicisation and spelling from original sources, save for the old-fashioned abbreviation of L for pound sterling, which I have replaced with the symbol £. The surnames I have used match the most common versions used in modern sources, for example, 'Richmond' rather than 'Richman' (a common way of spelling Bill Richmond's surname in his early career), 'Cribb' rather than 'Crib' and 'Molineaux' rather than 'Molyneux', 'Molineux', etc. However, I have preserved these variant spellings where they have been utilised in original sources.

Prologue:
The Coronation of
George IV, Westminster,
London, 19 July 1821

George IV's coronation was a lavish affair. Partly this extravagance was a result of George Augustus Frederick's natural inclination towards profligacy, a characteristic that had earned him much public opprobrium since his teenage years. However, the decision to host an elaborate coronation, complemented by a series of public celebrations including a fête in Hyde Park, was also borne of political expediency. As an unpopular and widely mocked member of the Royal family, it was in George's interests to create a self-consciously colourful event that might infuse the public with feelings of patriotic fervour and loyalty towards their new monarch.

Ten years earlier, George had been appointed Prince Regent, parliament having concluded that his father, George III, was unfit to rule, languishing as he was in Windsor Castle, his decaying body wracked with rheumatism and his mind beset by mental illness. Rather than acting as a signal for his son to assume greater responsibility and frugality, the Regency merely served as an inducement for 'Prinny' – as he was popularly known – to continue the lavish spending and obscene consumption for which he had obtained notoriety as Prince of Wales. In contrast to his modest, dutiful father, the Prince Regent cared more about the trappings of power and fashion than matters of state. While Britain faced a series of seismic political and military challenges throughout the Regency, from the assassination of Prime Minister Spencer Perceval to continuing war with Napoleon and France and the Peterloo Massacre, Prinny was more concerned with masquerade balls or with John Nash's redesign of the Royal Pavilion in Brighton.

It was hardly surprising, therefore, that when the eighty-one-year-old George III finally died on 29 January 1820, his son eagerly began preparations for the most expensive coronation in British history. Determined to mount an event that made Napoleon's elaborate 1804 coronation as Emperor of France look like a minor village fête, George succeeded in securing the staggering sum of £243,390.6s.2d[1] from parliament to satisfy his desire for opulence – £100,000 in the form of direct parliamentary funding while the remainder was creamed off from payments made by France as part of the terms of the 1815 Treaty of Paris following Napoleon's defeat at Waterloo and second abdication. No item of expenditure was too extravagant for the soon to be crowned King; £8,205.15s was spent on providing foreign ministers attending the coronation with gifts of ornate snuff boxes, crafted by jewellers Rundell & Bridge for example.

When George arrived at the West Door of Westminster Abbey at 11 a.m. on Thursday 19 July 1821 for the ceremony, he was clad in sumptuous robes with a 27-foot-long crimson train made of the finest velvet and generously decorated with gold stars. Meanwhile his crown, specially designed and customised, sparkled and shimmered with 12,314 hired diamonds and was described breathlessly by one newspaper as 'larger, loftier, and more magnificent, than the former Crown', and therefore 'more appropriate to the dignity of the British Empire, and the splendid taste of the sovereign'. Later that afternoon, coronation formalities complete, the massed ranks of invited peers, bishops, archbishops and foreign dignitaries surged into Westminster Hall for a coronation banquet, all eager for a glimpse of the new King, as well as the chance to feast on meats, pies, fruits and other rich delicacies that had been prepared for their delectation.

Amid this dizzying panoply of extravagance, pomp and luxury, stood an unlikely figure. Bill Richmond was no more than 5 foot 9 inches tall and was already fifty-seven years old but, in contrast to the corpulent, sweating King (who was just one year his senior), Richmond was still in magnificent physical condition, without an ounce of fat on his defined and wirily muscular frame, which had been once been described by an admirer as 'a study for the sculptor'. It had been seventeen years since Richmond had first ventured into the glamorous but dangerous world of the London prize ring and he was now retired, but his achievements as a bare-knuckle boxer, or 'pugilist' to borrow the Georgian term of choice, were impeccable. Only two men had ever beaten him in competitive combat: the legendary Tom Cribb and the burly George Maddox. Maddox had paid for his impertinence in humiliating an unprepared Bill in nine rounds in January 1804, by being soundly beaten in a brutal fifty-two-minute rematch five years later, a contest that ended with both of Maddox's eyes closed, Richmond having administered a fearful and prolonged beating.

Dressed as a Royal page in the retro Tudor-Stuart finery that George had personally selected to create the aura of 'Olde England', Richmond stood proudly alongside seventeen other prominent pugilists. It was a somewhat incongruous group of men to find at the coronation of the monarch of arguably the most powerful nation on Earth, yet the unlikely presence of these men had been on the specific orders of George himself. The new King's unpopularity, coupled with the fact that his estranged wife, the uncrowned Queen consort Caroline of Brunswick, was expected to try and gatecrash the coronation had, understandably, made George nervous. He hoped that the forbidding presence of a group of loyal toughs would deter any troublemakers and ensure order. An enthusiastic patron of the prize ring in his youth, George had therefore turned to the country's greatest fistic heroes for protection. It was an astute and symbolic gesture, for pugilists were widely seen as the living embodiment of English manhood and the foremost possessors of pluck, grit and guts – or *'bottom'* as the Georgians termed it. It would also not have escaped George's attention that the presence of these pugilists would add a layer of celebrity stardust and a *soupçon* of notoriety to the normally staid coronation proceedings.

Even within this surreal tableau, though, something dramatically differentiated Richmond from his pugilistic comrades and the ranks of nobility in Westminster Hall – namely, the colour of his skin. For unlike the rest of the assembled masses, who were uniformly white-skinned, Richmond was a black man. Even more remarkably, he was a black man who, less than six decades earlier, had been born into slavery in America, a country which, even as the coronation was taking place, continued to bear witness to the horrors of slave auctions and was still forty-four years away from the Thirteenth Amendment to the constitution that would finally banish the hateful practice to the history books.

By the time of George IV's coronation, Richmond had, metaphorically and literally, undergone a remarkable journey, travelling 3,500 miles to escape life as a slave in a Staten Island parsonage and carve a life of freedom, glamour, and social acceptance in London. The prospects for a black child born into slavery in America in the eighteenth century were bleak indeed, but through the considerable force of his personality and his unerring eye for social advancement, Richmond had – like a real-life version of a protagonist from a Charles Dickens novel – hauled himself from a potential life of grinding and condescending servitude to sample the rarefied heights of elevated upper-class English society, becoming, in the process, one of the most prominent 'men of colour' of the Georgian era.

One of the defining characteristics of great men or women is their ability to transcend the capricious historical contexts within which, by some infinitesimally unlikely cosmic happenstance, they find themselves living. By making the absolute most of the opportunities that, by chance or design, fall into their paths, they thus ensure their place in history. By this definition, Richmond was indisputably great; for a black man to achieve any level of prominence, let alone 'celebrity', during the early nineteenth century was a rare feat. Although the British Slave Trade was abolished by parliament in 1807, slavery would not be banned in the British colonies until the 1830s. Moreover, British society's attitude towards black people was broadly characterised by ignorance, mistrust and prejudice. This was still a society where it was possible for the *Encyclopaedia Britannica*, in 1810, to describe 'negroes' thus:

> Vices the most notorious seem to be the portion of this unhappy race; idleness, treachery, revenge, cruelty, impudence, stealing, lying, profanity, debauchery, nastiness and intemperance, are said to have extinguished the principles of natural law, and to have silenced the reproofs of conscience. They are strangers to every sentiment of compassion and are an awful example of the corruption of man left to himself.

It is also hard to forget the words of the philosopher David Hume, a leading figure of the Scottish Enlightenment, who in 1753 summed up the prevailing presumption of superiority among white society: 'I am apt to suspect,' Hume declared, 'the negroes and in general all other species of men, to be naturally inferior to the whites ... There are negro slaves dispersed all over Europe of which none ever displayed any symptoms of ingenuity.'

On many occasions after moving to Britain, whether in the boxing ring, while walking the streets or while tending the bar at his public house the Horse and Dolphin, Richmond suffered abuse because of his ethnicity. The bravery he demonstrated to overcome these taunts and live a professional and public life was considerable. Furthermore, Richmond's pugilistic exploits caught the imagination of the public and were regularly recounted in exhaustive and precise detail in the pages of national and local newspapers, and this at a time when most newspapers ran to only four pages in length. Richmond's speed, skill and punching power were held in high esteem by members of 'the Fancy', the cognoscenti of the pugilistic arts, such as John Wilson, who wrote approvingly of him in *Blackwood's Edinburgh Magazine*:

> ... it is evident, that at Oxford he would have been a first-class man; and at Cambridge, probably senior wrangler. We scarcely see on what principle he could well be beat. His activity is miraculous. His bounds are without bound, boundless. His right arm is like a horse's leg; that is, it's blow like a kick of that quadrupled. So what boxer, pray, seeing it is impossible to hit him, and impossible to avoid being hit by him, could with any safety be matched against the Lily-white?

The term Lily-white was a popular Georgian epithet for chimney sweep, and was typical of the sort of patronising language that even Richmond's admirers used to describe him. He was also referred to variously as 'the black', 'Mungo', the founder of the 'sable school of pugilism' and a 'black devil'. Despite such casually demeaning language, Richmond nevertheless became hugely famous and respected, not only as a fighter but also as a trainer and tutor of both professional and amateur pugilists. For example, he gave lessons to the brilliant essayist William Hazlitt, who admiringly referred to him as 'my old master', while Lord Byron was also said to have been one of Richmond's eager pupils; the fact that the Romantic poet was a Richmond admirer can be ascertained from his presence among the pugilists whose images comprised an extravagant collage which decorated one side of his beloved *découpage* screen (theatrical stars such as Edmund Kean, featured on the reverse).

The extent of Richmond's considerable fame can also be measured by the fact that artists of the period produced prints of him, such as Robert Dighton's *A Striking View of Richmond*, an original of which can still be found in the archives of the National Portrait Gallery in London. Furthermore, the coronation of George IV was not his only encounter with royalty, for when Frederick William III of Prussia visited London in 1814 Richmond was one of the 'celebrated professors of the fist' who was commissioned to spar in front of him and other assorted royals and nobility.

Remarkably, given his reputation for athleticism, Richmond spent the entirety of his boxing career, perhaps even his life, labouring under the handicap of a defect in one of his knees, most likely the right one, which, as can be seen in Dighton's etching, was somewhat unusual in its shape and angularity.[2] The Revd J. Richardson provided more detail about this 'deformity', remarking that Richmond's 'lower limbs were the reverse of symmetrical; one leg being bent inward at the knee, and acting as a prop to its companion, which, when the owner was in "attitude" for either assault or defence, it appeared to support, as what is termed a "spur" does a ricketty post'. Despite this considerable physical disadvantage, Richmond's agility was so 'extraordinary' that he once deputised for an unwell acrobat at Astley's famed Ampitheatre on Westminster Bridge Road.

As well as his pugilistic and gymnastic excellence, another remarkable characteristic of Richmond was that he was as far removed from the common stereotype of the monosyllabic pugilistic thug as it was possible to be. Those that met him frequently referred to his excellent manners, witty conversation and intelligence, as well as his ability to tell amusing 'milling anecdotes' – a series of qualities that put paid to the bigoted but widespread perception that black people were intellectually inferior. Pierce Egan, the legendary writer whose journal *Boxiana* was one of the key factors in popularising the exploits of Georgian pugilists for the wider public, wrote at length about Richmond's intellect in an extensive profile of his career in the first volume of *Boxiana*,[3] declaring,

... we cannot omit stating of our hero that he is intelligent, communicative, and well-behaved; and however actively engaged in promulgating the principles of *milling*, he is not so completely absorbed with *fighting* as to be incapable of discoursing on any other subject; in fact he is rather facetious over a glass of noyeau,[4] his favourite *wet* with a SWELL ... His experience in LIFE has taught him to be *awake* to the tricks of it; and there are few subjects upon which he suffers himself to be *lulled to sleep*.

In the second volume of *Boxiana*, Egan would reinforce his positive impression of Richmond's charisma by declaring of him that 'a merrier man ... I never spent an hour's talk withal'. In addition to his engaging personality, Richmond was also endowed with the keen business sense and altruistic spirit of a social entrepreneur. For young black men in London during the early nineteenth century boxing was one of the few routes (albeit a dangerous one) to paid and independent employment and Richmond would often tutor such men. One of his pupils was another former slave, Tom Molineaux, who Richmond mentored and trained for his famous English Championship contests against Tom Cribb in 1810 and 1811. These were arguably the two most significant sporting occasions of Georgian times, attracting huge crowds and unprecedented press attention and Richmond was a key figure in brokering and promoting both bouts.

Given the wide scope of his accomplishments, Richmond has a good case to be recognised as the first black sportsman of national fame and international significance, the trailblazer in a long, illustrious and socially significant line that eventually stretched to include the likes of Jack Johnson, Jesse Owens, Jackie Robinson and Muhammad Ali. Richmond wouldn't have known this in 1821, of course, but as he stood at the heart of the coronation festivities – a black man thriving within a bastion of white privilege – he could have been forgiven for pausing to reflect just how far he had travelled, and how remarkable a life and career he had already led. Exactly how he earned the admiration of his peers, the respect of royalty and the adulation of the public to become a popular hero of the Georgian age is a story that is as astonishing as it is unlikely.

I

The Strange Mystery of Bill Richmond's Birth

Several myths, counter-myths and mysteries exist surrounding Bill Richmond's early years. Documented details of his birth and parentage have proved persistently and frustratingly elusive, while the story of how and why he was released from slavery has also been the subject of conflicting accounts. There is also the intriguing claim to consider that the thirteen-year-old Richmond served as the hangman for the execution of the American revolutionary hero Nathan Hale on 22 September 1776.

Richmond's early life is inexorably linked to the history of slavery in the United States, a subject that remains an uncomfortable topic for many Americans, even today. The issue of slavery, and its links to the Episcopalian church – specifically the parish of St Andrew's, Staten Island, where Richmond's life began – was examined in 2008 by Geri Swanson, a deacon in the Episcopal Diocese of New York, in a disarmingly honest article entitled *Reflections on a flawed past*. Swanson described how the process of researching her family tree had revealed a hitherto unknown and unacknowledged familial connection to slavery. She wrote candidly of her shock on discovering that a branch of her family from Long Island had been slave owners and that 'any wealth they accumulated had been bought with the labor of people held in involuntary servitude'. Swanson went on to pose a challenging but pertinent question, which many people in the USA and UK are still nervous of addressing, namely, 'If my own family history bared the ugly head of slavery, how many other families and institutions would also yield hidden histories that had scabbed over?'

It's a question that must be addressed if we are to gain a full appreciation of the social, historical and cultural context from which Richmond emerged, for in order to understand the early years of his life it is essential to understand the context of slavery in the northern United States at the time of his birth in the mid-eighteenth century, as well as the complicity of the Episcopal church and individual parishes such as St Andrew's in the slave trade.

Northern slavery is an often neglected and misunderstood subject. Although emancipation for northern slaves occurred gradually after the end of the American War of Independence in 1783 (and before the Emancipation Proclamation of 1863 that legally freed 3.1 million of the USA's remaining 4 million slaves), the extent to which the foundations of economic prosperity within the northern states were established using forced labour cannot be exaggerated. Edgar J. McManus made the crucial point that

> Northern slavery was far more varied and complex than its Southern counterpart. Unlike the South, which used slaves primarily for agricultural labor, the North trained and specialized its slave force to meet the needs of a mixed economy. From the seventeenth century onward, blacks could be found in virtually every field of Northern economic life.

New York City, in particular, was a bastion of slavery during colonial rule. In 1703, 42 per cent of New York households owned at least one slave, while census figures for 1771 indicate that nearly 20,000 blacks lived in New York, the majority of them slaves. Aside from Charleston, South Carolina, there were more slaves in New York in the eighteenth century than any other American city and slavery was thus the bedrock of the city's rapid development. It was slaves who built the original wall that gave Wall Street its name and it was slaves that built the forts, bridges, mills and houses that sprung up around colonial New York. Furthermore, as historian Philip Papas explained, slavery was also 'a common and visible institution' on Richmond's birthplace of Staten Island, where the 'economy relied considerably on slave labor'. In 1771, of Staten Island's total population of 2,847, a staggering 594 were slaves and, according to Papas, 'ordinary white Staten Islanders owned from one to three slaves, and the more affluent owned between five and ten'.

It remains an uncomfortable truth for the Episcopalian tradition that the church consistently neglected to assume an abolitionist stance towards slavery, largely through fear of provoking institutional division. As Gardiner Shattuck observed, the church abhorred the prospect of 'ecclesiastical schism more than the suffering of the people held in bondage'. The church was hostile in its prejudice against blacks, even in death, for example, in 1697, after Trinity Church in Manhattan was established, a resolution was passed which forbade the burial of any 'negroes' within 'the bounds and limits of the churchyard', forcing the establishment of the 'Negroes Burial Ground' in Lower Manhattan. Although some individuals within the church condemned slavery, many ministers owned slaves – the Revd Richard Charlton, rector of

St Andrew's, Staten Island from 1747 until 1777, was one such minister, and Bill Richmond was one of his slaves.

The parish history of St Andrew's is steeped in slavery; the land on which the church was built was given to the church by William Tillyer, a local slave owner, and the church itself was established in 1708 by the Society for the Propagation of the Gospel in Foreign Parts (SPG), a section of the Church of England focused on converting slaves to Christianity, prior to being chartered by Queen Anne in 1713. The SPG, like the Episcopal church as a whole, saw no hypocrisy or contradiction in seeking to convert slaves while simultaneously neglecting to challenge the institution of slavery itself or, indeed, in owning slaves or employing ministers who owned them. Charlton was far from the only minister at St Andrew's who owned slaves. When wealthy congregation member Ellias Duxbury died in 1718 he left 'his negroes' to then minister Revd Aeneas MacKenzie. The second rector of St Andrew's, the Revd William Harrison, was also a slave owner, specifying in his will that his executors should 'sell all ... my negroes'.

Revd Charlton, who had been born in Longford, Ireland in 1706 and was educated at Trinity College, Dublin, came to America via the Leeward Islands with the stated mission of catechising slaves. Prior to becoming rector of St Andrew's, he had been attached to Trinity Church where he ran classes of Christian instruction for slaves. In 1740 the SPG proudly boasted of Charlton's work 'that the number of his Catechusans increases,' and that the 'Spiritual Knowledge of some Negroes who attend him ... might make many White People Blush'.

According to anecdotal accounts within his own family, as described by his descendent John R. Dungan, Charlton was 'pompous, red-faced and strictly Anglican'. A somewhat rambunctious figure, when Charlton took his 'fowling piece' hunting he would roll up his sermons and use them as 'wadding' for the gun, boasting that he 'already knew what's in 'em'. Despite owning slaves, Charlton was, in an indication of the bigotry of the time, considered moderate in his views due to the fact he considered blacks worthy of conversion and education, if not freedom. Dungan also recounted that Charlton's reputation within the family was that he was 'not unkind' to his slaves and gave them instruction in how to read and write. Unlike many ministers, Charlton also recorded some slave baptisms in the parish records, Swanson having uncovered eight such occurrences between 1768 and 1773 in the St Andrew's archives.

Unfortunately, there is no trace of Bill Richmond in the St Andrew's birth or baptism registers. The details of his birth that have long since entered into popular consciousness originated not in Staten Island but from the pen of Pierce Egan who, in the first edition of *Boxiana*, informed his readers that Richmond 'was born at Sturton Island, at a place called Cuckold's Town' on '5 August 1763'. This statement demands close attention; Egan was a wonderful stylist but an inconsistent historian and the aforementioned sentence rings alarm bells as far as reliability is concerned.

For example, 'Sturton Island' is a pretty poor approximation for Staten Island (perhaps, in fairness, Egan's misidentification was a simple typo or transcription error, rather than geographical ignorance). Secondly, 'Cuckold's Town', widely cited since as Richmond's birthplace, never existed – there was once a Coccles Town in Staten Island, named in recognition of the abundance of oyster and clam shells to be found in the waters of the Fresh Kills estuary, however, by 1763 Coccles Town had been renamed Richmond town, which makes it clear that Richmond was named after his place of birth and not his parents.

Assuming that Egan's source for this birth date was Richmond himself, who he knew well, and presuming that the errors of nomenclature discussed above were merely a product of journalistic sloppiness, there is no reason to doubt that Richmond himself believed he was born on 5 August 1763. Sadly, that is perhaps the closest we will ever get to the truth, although when pondering the reliability of this date, it is hard to forget the haunting words of Frederick Douglass, author of a famous first-person 'slave narrative': 'I do not remember to have ever met a slave who could tell of his birthday.'

The question of Richmond's parentage is similarly mysterious. Many sources assert, with no evidence beyond the unsubstantiated or anecdotal, that his parents were Georgia-born slaves who somehow drifted north, or that his mother was one of Charlton's slaves. However, there is also another possibility, which circumstantial evidence supports, that must be acknowledged, namely, that the Revd Charlton could have been Bill's father. Egan states that Richmond was born 'under the auspices of a reverend divine of the name of Charlton' and this somewhat ambiguous statement could be interpreted in many ways. 'Auspices of' is a phrase that in modern usage refers to a sense of patronage or protection. However the term 'auspice', in its more archaic usage from the sixteenth century onwards, can also be interpreted as meaning 'a divine or prophetic token'. Might, therefore, Egan be implying that Charlton's relationship was more than merely that of a master and his slave – a 'divine' birth if you will?

It's a theory that was alluded to during Richmond's lifetime. In *Blackwood's Edinburgh Magazine* in 1820, the respected writer and moral philosophy professor John Wilson (who was one of the journal's editors under the pseudonym Christopher North), reflected that Egan's use of the phrase 'auspices of' was 'an ambiguous expression, which leaves us in our simplicity, doubtful whether Dr Charlton acted on the occasion as father, clergyman, or accoucheur'. Wilson, who was clearly unaware of Charlton's background, went on to speculate: 'Was Dr. Charlton, if really the father, a black – or is Richmond a Lily-white by his mother's side?' Wilson also drew attention to the further 'ambiguity' caused by the 'unfortunate juxtaposition' of Egan's description of Richmond's birth with the place name of 'Cuckold's Point',[1] which possesses a sexually transgressive subtext. No sooner had he raised this issue, though, than Wilson coyly resisted further speculation by 'endeavouring to forget this perplexing passage', although he does refer to Richmond later in the same passage as 'Dr. Charlton's son'.

Wilson knew Richmond and corresponded with him, mentioning that *Blackwood's* had 'several letters ... in our possession' written by the pugilist. He also hinted at a social connection with Richmond by using the phrase 'Richmond has often told us'. Frustratingly, however, Wilson did not use this acquaintanceship to resolve the mystery of Richmond's parentage. Wilson's speculation concerning which 'side' of his lineage Richmond was a 'Lily-white' by is also intriguing. Significantly, it strengthens the assertion made in several later texts that Richmond was of mixed ethnic ancestry, thus increasing the possibility that Charlton, or perhaps another white man in the Charlton household, could have been his father. For example, George MacDonald Fraser, in his novel *Black Ajax*, which contains a fictionalised first-person portrayal of Richmond, works on the presumption that Bill was a 'mulatto', as does boxing journalist Nat Fleischer in his book *Black Dynamite*.[2]

Although historians disagree on how common sexual relationships and abuse were between white male masters and black female slaves, the fact such incidences occurred is beyond dispute. If Charlton was his father, Richmond himself might not have known, although he may have suspected so and even discussed the matter privately hence, perhaps, Egan's ambiguous phrasing and Wilson's speculation. Although no documented evidence exists of Richmond's thoughts on the matter, again the words of Douglass have resonance: 'There was a whisper that my master was my father, yet it was only a whisper.'

If Richmond was Charlton's son, then that would, remarkably, make him the uncle of the widely revered Saint Elizabeth Ann Bayley Seton, Charlton's granddaughter and the first American-born woman to be canonised by the Roman Catholic church.[3] Ultimately, I will leave it to readers to draw their own conclusions as to whether a 'strictly Anglican' man such as Charlton may have secretly fathered a child with a female slave. However, before I do so it is worth pointing out that the most compelling evidence of all that Charlton's interest in Richmond was familial is to be found in the mysterious circumstances that led to him leaving the Charlton household and travelling to England. To examine this episode, we must turn to the turbulent events and varied personalities inhabiting Staten Island during the American War of Independence.

2

'Humanity Adorns All His Actions'

If one man could be said to have transformed Bill Richmond's life that man was Brigadier General Hugh Percy. Without Percy's intervention, Richmond would never have come to England, and may well have remained a slave until his death. Percy probably met the teenage Richmond in the summer of 1776, before persuading Revd Charlton to release him from slavery. Accounts of how and why Percy did this differ, but beyond doubt is that his kindness towards a boy who he barely knew was an act of uncommon compassion.

Yet Percy was an unlikely benefactor for a young black boy, as well as an unlikely soldier. A product of the eighteenth-century English aristocracy, Percy's unprepossessing physical appearance did not suggest the able soldier he would become, or give any aesthetic indication of his kind soul. Thin to the point of cadaverousness, he possessed a bulbous nose and a somewhat crooked face. However, he was one of the few members of the higher echelons of the British Army to emerge from the War of Independence with his reputation enhanced, partly due to the fact he left the war in 1777 (before its disastrous conclusion for Britain in 1783), but also because of the generous way he treated those he encountered or commanded, no matter what their station in life.

Percy's father, Sir Hugh Smithson, had married Elizabeth Seymour, heiress to the famous Percy dynasty, in 1740 and their son, also named Hugh, was born on 14 August 1742. The Percys were northern nobles whose lineage could be traced to William de Percy, a Norman who had come to England with William the Conqueror. When Sir Hugh and Elizabeth married, the male Percy line had died out. However, inspired by his wife's pride in her heritage, Sir Hugh soon resolved to revive the family name and reputation and adopted the surname Percy, becoming Earl of Northumberland and subsequently Duke of Northumberland. A

Knight of the Order of the Garter, Privy Counsellor and MP, Sir Hugh also had a keen eye for aesthetics, acting as a patron to artist Canaletto and architects Robert Adam and James Wyatt.

Young Hugh also adopted the surname Percy and the styling 'Earl Percy' when his father acceded to the dukedom and in 1759, while only sixteen, he enlisted in the army, rising to the rank of captain within four months. It was a challenging period for the British Army whose triumph in the Seven Years' War – rubberstamped by the Treaties of Paris and Hubertusburg in 1763 – had succeeded in largely eliminating French influence in America, securing British sovereignty over the majority of the continent to the east of the Mississippi, as well as pre-eminence over the Atlantic shipping trade. However, with these hard-earned and long-coveted laurels came a burden that would eventually pave the way for the declaration of an independent United States of America by the thirteen British colonies on 4 July 1776. At the beginning of the Seven Years' War, Britain's national debt was £74.6 million, but by the cessation of hostilities this had ballooned to £132.6 million, a consequence of heavy borrowing and the determination of Prime Minister William Pitt to fight with as much manpower as possible in America rather than concentrate on the 'European front'. When parliament sought to tackle these debts with new taxation on the colonies, the seeds of the War of Independence were sown.

One factor amid many in fermenting war was the Stamp Act of 1765, introduced by Pitt's successor George Grenville. The statutes of this act imposed direct taxation on the colonists through legislation mandating that a wide range of material (including legal documents, magazines and newspapers) could only be printed on stamped paper produced in London. The introduction of such direct taxation was viewed by many colonists as an infringement of their rights and as the thin end of the wedge of taxation policies to come. With no direct colonial representation in British parliament, the attitude of many colonists was epitomised by the credo 'taxation without representation is tyranny'.

The introduction of the Stamp Act caused widespread resentment and protests on the streets of many towns and cities, including Boston, Rhode Island and New York. The Stamp Act was repealed in 1766, but Benjamin Franklin's summation that the relationship between the colonies and Britain was 'much altered' proved prescient. Over the next few years tensions simmered: the 1767 Townshend Acts enraged many colonists by levying taxes on various imports, leading to riots in Boston. Meanwhile the Boston Massacre in 1770, when British soldiers fired into a crowd who had gathered threateningly around a sentry, killing five civilians, was a further flashpoint that encouraged revolutionary sentiments. Although parliament later withdrew all taxes, except those on tea, temporarily calming the situation, the Boston Tea Party in 1773, in response to the 'Tea Act', accelerated divisions yet further. A furious British government responded in 1774 with a series of punitive measures against Massachusetts, which American patriots termed the 'intolerable acts'. By February 1775, Massachusetts was in open rebellion and the stage was set for war.

Percy's attitude towards these issues when he departed for America with the 5th Regiment of Foot in May 1774 has been the subject of debate. Charles Knowles Bolton, in his introduction to a collection of Percy's letters, claimed he was 'opposed to the American war', drawing attention to the general election campaign of 1774, while Percy was in America, during which a group of his friends circulated a letter stating it was 'well known his Lordship disapproved those very measures which rendered the present service necessary'. Other historians, however, have pointed out that Percy voted against the repeal of the Stamp Act in 1766, hardly the actions of a Whig sympathiser, although, conversely, in the early 1770s he regularly opposed the administration led by Lord North that introduced the 'intolerable acts'.

Regardless of doubts he may have harboured during the lead-up to war, Percy's correspondence from America makes it clear his loyalty to Britain was absolute; in a letter to his father dated 27 July 1774, soon after he arrived in Boston, Percy commented that 'a change of administration ... would be ... the most fatal thing in the world'. Meanwhile, in a missive to his cousin Henry Reveley in August, Percy made his contempt for the rebels clear, condemning them as 'sly, artful, hypocritical rascals'.

When long gestating tensions in Boston erupted into military confrontation, Percy distinguished himself amid the general ineptitude of the British command with a propensity for decisiveness. During the Battles of Lexington and Concord on 19 April 1775 he was asked to support Lt-Col. Francis Smith's expedition, which had been forced to retreat under heavy fire from Patriot militia. Percy succeeded in skilfully marshalling Smith's demoralised and confused forces to Charlestown, averting disaster and preventing severe casualties. His actions in guiding the troops 'through a severe and incessant fire' were, Lord Drummond declared, an act of 'masterly officership'. Percy admitted that the ferocity of the rebels surprised him, confessing to Gen. Harvey, 'I never believed, I confess, that they would have attacked the King's troops, or have had the perseverance I found in them.' His tone in a letter to his father was rather more triumphal: 'I had the happiness,' he boasted, 'of saving them from total destruction.'

Despite his competence, or perhaps because of it, Percy's relationship with his superiors, notably Gen. Thomas Gage and his replacement Gen. William Howe, was shaky. After the retreat from Lexington, Gage privately admitted that 'too much praise cannot be given to Lord

Percy'. However, although Percy's regiment fought in the next major confrontation of the war, the Battle of Bunker Hill on 17 June 1775, Percy himself was kept out of the action and was made to do line duty instead, a decision which it has been theorised was a result of a dispute with Gage. Without the reassuring presence of their commanding officer, Percy's men were, to his dismay, 'almost entirely cut to pieces'. It was a battle the British won, but it was a hollow victory, failing to severely damage the Patriots or alter the stalemate in Boston.

Bunker Hill also badly damaged British morale, mainly because of the considerable casualties with 1,054 injured and 226 dead, many of them officers. Deciding that the only realistic strategy to quell the rebellion was to abandon Boston and attempt to seize New York, the British, including Percy, withdrew from Massachusetts on 17 March 1776 and headed for Halifax, Nova Scotia, in order to regroup. On 1 June, as he impatiently awaited the order to head towards New York, Percy reflected, with a tone of anticipation laced, perhaps, with a dash of foreboding: 'In about a fortnight … something must pop between us and the Rebels.'

* * *

By the summer of 1776 Bill Richmond was thirteen years old. It was already something of an achievement to have lived so long, for among slaves in New York in the eighteenth century the childhood mortality rate was an estimated 25 percent. Although it has been claimed that his mother was part of Revd Charlton's household, it is also possible that Richmond was separated from her at an early age, as was the case with many slaves. Regardless, in the childhood of a slave there was little room for play or parental interaction; instead Richmond's daily routine would have consisted of a variety of menial tasks: cleaning, cooking, serving meals and suchlike. Although not as punishing an existence as that of a field slave, the hours Richmond worked would have been unrelenting, slaves invariably being the first members of the household to rise and the last to go to bed.

With so many slaves in the Charlton household (the Revd bequeathed a total of thirteen in his will in 1777), living conditions were cramped and basic, and sanitation limited. Whether Charlton engaged in physical punishment of his slaves is not known but, disturbingly, he dismissed the views of those, such as the Revd George Whitefield, who criticised abuse of slaves by their owners. Commenting on a letter Whitefield had written on the subject, Charlton argued that 'imprudence and indiscretion directed his pen', a strong indication that the welfare of his own slaves was not a priority. The possibility of physical punishment for slaves, even in the seemingly peaceful rural outpost of Staten Island, was ever present; near to St Andrew's there was even a 'whipping post' where public floggings took place, not only of black slaves but also of white lawbreakers. In summation, the life of a slave, even in the northern states, was a joyless existence. As Jupiter Hammon, the first published African-American poet and essayist wrote: 'Most of us are cut off from comfort and happiness here in this world, and can expect nothing from it.'

While Richmond led a childhood of monotonous and unremitting servitude, Staten Island was proving strangely immune to the revolutionary sentiments sweeping the rest of the colonies. Indeed, it was so pronounced in its sympathies to the British Crown that Papas later claimed that '99 percent' of islanders 'remained loyal to the Crown'. Significantly, in 1774, when the rebellious colonies arranged the Continental Congress in Philadelphia, all the counties of New York were represented – except for Staten Island, Richmond County having steadfastly refused to put forward a delegate.

Geographically as well as politically, Staten Island was something of an idyll. Hessian soldiers stationed there in 1776 were struck by 'the appearance of wealth and plenty' on the island, as well as its pleasant, cultivated fields, rolling hills and valleys, and the picturesque brooks, streams and coastline where locals would catch fish, oysters, clams and crabs. The predominant industry on the island was farming, aided by the rich and fertile soil. The many comfortable houses, surrounded by lush gardens and orchards and peppered with tracks populated by small red wagons drawn by horses, added to the impression of a prosperous and sedate corner of the colonies.

In June 1776, though, Staten Island assumed vast geopolitical significance. The British forces had identified it as the perfect launch pad for their plan to capture New York and set sail from Halifax to take possession of the island. General Howe landed in New York on 25 June, followed by the awe-inspiring sight of the British fleet, all 130 ships of it, sailing into New York Bay several days later. On 2 July the predominantly loyalist inhabitants of Staten Island gratefully submitted to British control, while the rebel soldiers on the island quickly fled without even a semblance of reluctance. A week later, the Declaration of Independence, adopted by the Continental Congress of the thirteen American colonies on 4 July, was read out to Gen. George Washington's troops in New York, and the next great battle of the War of Independence inched closer.

The arrival of the British fleet must have been a thrilling moment for the young Richmond, who, like many islanders, probably gathered at the coastline in wonder to greet the ships' arrival. Bill may also have been present at a ceremony on 6 July in the town of Richmond itself at which hundreds of Staten Islanders swore allegiance to George III, while Gen. Howe looked on approvingly. Staten Island, previously a sleepy colonial backwater, was now the centre of the military universe; soldiers in their glamorous red coats, with variant headwear depending on regiment and rank, now patrolled the streets and drank in the taverns, swapping excited gossip and speculation concerning military manoeuvres. These plans, plots and rumours must have absorbed the imagination of every man, woman and child on the island, rich or poor, slaves or free men. At the peak of the summer, more than 30,000 British and Hessian troops occupied the island, waiting expectantly for the order to attack Washington's troops, who had gathered in Brooklyn – an order which was finally issued on 27 August.

The presence of the British Army made Staten Island a coveted refuge for many black slaves seeking freedom. The previous year Lord Dunmore, the royal governor of Virginia, had offered freedom to any slaves belonging to rebel colonialists who were willing to enter British military service. As a consequence, hundreds of runaways, emboldened by dreams of freedom and liberty, descended upon Staten Island where they were housed in cramped and segregated quarters and put to work in a variety of roles, including as spies, messengers, wagon drivers and carpenters. For many it was their first ever paid work, so it mattered not that the British decision to welcome them was a cynical move, motivated by political mischief and military pragmatism, rather than humanitarian consideration. Tellingly, runaway slaves belonging to loyalists were not welcome to enlist, indeed if they attempted to do so, they were promptly returned to their masters. This was the fate that befell five slaves who sought refuge on the naval vessel *Asia* that was anchored in the New York Bay; once he became aware of their presence, the ship's captain summarily returned them to their master.

As the slave of a loyalist, Richmond was therefore uncommonly fortunate, or perhaps unusually determined, in managing to turn the presence of the British in Staten Island into a ticket to freedom. The most widespread anecdotal account of how he first met Earl Percy is that Percy was invited to dine at Charlton's parsonage and was impressed by Richmond's manners, conduct and charisma, as well as a toast that he proposed to George III. The fact that Percy was firmly pro-abolition in his political persuasion – as later demonstrated by his willingness to be listed publicly as a subscriber to anti-slavery texts such as Ignatius Sancho's letters (1782) and Olaudah Equiano's memoirs (1789) – also suggests that his willingness to offer Richmond an escape route from slavery was born of an overwhelmingly humanitarian impulse.

However, a contrasting account of Percy and Richmond's first meeting also exists, which was first published in the *New York Daily News* in 2003 and which writer Fergus Gwynplaine Macintyre claimed came from Percy's personal 'dispatches', dated 5 November 1776:

A young Blackamore was ostling the officers' mounts, and fetching water to the horses, when a corporal of the Brunswicke division chaffed the black boy and he did make sport of the ostler's colour. Two more Hessians joined in the folly, and one of them tripping the black boy a-purpose so that he dropped his water-can, spilling the lot. The stable-boy fetched his right hand sidelong to the corporal's great beak of a nose, then he layed into the other two Hessians with both fists set flailing. The three men were taller than the Blackmoor boy, and their arms more prodigious of reach. Still he easily payed them in full for their merriment, and laced his right fist again and once more into their ears and shoulders, his left arm parrying and blocking their efforts to hit him in turn until at the last, two of the Hessian rogues gave flight and ran, as the Brunswicke corporal fell to bleeding hard by the horse-trough. The Blackamore warrior triumphant, he fetched his water-can and went again to his work as if nought had occurred.

It's a wonderfully vivid account, but it's possible that this passage is a fabrication. Macintyre, who died in 2010, was a writer with a propensity for fakery and, despite exhaustive research, the original source for this citation has remained elusive.[1] Macintyre certainly had the literary flair and historical knowledge to construct a plausible fake such as this, even down to the accurate reference to Brunswick Hessians. Macintyre's cited date of 5 November 1776, coming as it does two days after the final published letter contained in the collection edited by Bolton, is also suspicious, originating as it does from a period when Bolton admitted 'we have no letters' by Percy. The lavish, at times melodramatic, detail in the passage also raises doubts about its provenance; to be frank, it reads more like a Pierce Egan fight report than any of Percy's other letters which are, by comparison, restrained and sober. Furthermore, the central conceit, namely that an untrained thirteen-year-old could succeed in beating up three adult soldiers, strains credulity, even taking into account Richmond's later pugilistic prowess. In the absence of independent verification of Macintyre's claim, it remains a more convincing thesis that Percy met Richmond sometime during July or August in 1776 while the British Army were stationed in Staten Island, perhaps at dinner at Charlton's, as the familiar anecdote recounts.

It has also been claimed that Richmond served as a soldier during the war and perhaps met Percy prior to, or after, enlisting. Given the fact he was only a teenager at the time, this seems somewhat unlikely. Nevertheless, examination of muster rolls for the British Army do reveal that there was a William Richmond who enrolled on 25 February 1777 into Percy's regiment, the 5th Foot, and was present in Capt. John Gaspard Battier's Light Co. at the Battle of Brandywine Creek in September 1777. However, this William Richmond was not young Bill, as is proven by the fact that this alternative Richmond was still a member of the regiment when it was stationed in Staten Island in July 1778 – by this time Bill, as we will later see, had already begun his education in England.

Regardless of the date, location or circumstances of their first meeting, Charlton's motives for allowing Richmond to join Percy's service also remain the subject of conjecture. A slave was a valuable commodity, and Charlton was not a sentimental man as far as slavery was concerned, for example, when he died in 1777, he freed none of his remaining slaves, instead bequeathing them to members of his family. Indeed, the details of his will were chilling in their lack of humanity, as his slaves were divided alongside such banal ephemera as sleeve buttons:

> Notwithstanding the above bequests I leave to my granddaughter, MARY BAYLEY, my negro girl Bett, and to her two sisters my negro boy, formerly called Brennus. To my grandson, JOHN C. DONGAN, my negro man, Adam ... To my son JOHN, my negro boy, Titus, my Negro wench, Phebe, and negro man, Carlos, but if said Carlos be disposed of before my decease I hereby give him my choice of remaining servants. To my son JOHN also my gold watch, stock buckles and sleeve buttons, with my silver spurs. To ELIZABETH NICHOLLS my negro wench, Nan, and £30.

How then should we interpret Charlton's willingness to allow Richmond to enter Percy's service? The obituary of Charlton published in the *Gaines Mercury* shortly after his death claims that his loyalty to the British Crown was 'unalterably firm', in which case can his decision to allow Richmond to leave with Percy be interpreted as an act of gratitude or flattery towards an important figure from the British army? Or was there another motive at play? Might, for example, the aforementioned theory that Charlton could have been Richmond's father explain this otherwise random act of kindness? Charlton was seventy years old by the summer of 1776, and aware of his advanced years and declining health, might he have detected in Percy the opportunity to grant his 'secret son' his freedom and the opportunity of a new life, without raising the suspicions that might have arisen if Richmond had received 'special treatment' in his will? The fact that the final version of Charlton's will was dated 23 June 1777, a month after Richmond's date of departure to England with Percy, certainly indicates that the document was rewritten soon after Bill left his household. In the absence of definitive proof, perhaps such speculation stretches credibility and sentimentality too far, but it undoubtedly adds to the aura of mystery that surrounds Richmond's early years.

A further mystery that surrounds Richmond's connection with the War of Independence is somewhat easier to unpick: namely, the oft-repeated theory, frequently asserted as fact, that Richmond was the hangman at the execution of the American spy Nathan Hale on 22 September 1776. Any account of Richmond's life must take this theory seriously. After all, if Richmond was in Percy's service by September 1776, which seems likely given there is little documentation to link Percy with Staten Island after the summer of 1776, then surely it is possible that Richmond could have assisted at a British military execution? Perhaps. Conversely, though, it seems somewhat far-fetched that the compassionate Percy, who was opposed to corporal punishment of his own men and expressed disapproval when his colleague Gen. Richard Prescott beat a patriot prisoner in February 1777, would have consented or encouraged a teenager in his service to have participated in the hanging of a prisoner, even one that was a spy.

The Richmond-as-hangman theory took root due to a coalescence of circumstantial evidence: numerous accounts of Hale's execution feature references to a black or mulatto hangman named Richmond (for example, the 1856 book *Life of Nathan Hale: The Martyr Spy of the American Revolution* refers to the 'negro Richmond, the common hangman'); artwork of the execution published by *Harpers Weekly* in 1860 shows a black man holding the hanging rope; and then there is Richmond's connection to Percy and the British military, as well as the proximity of Staten Island to the site of Hale's execution in Manhattan. Given this series of coincidences, it seems a reasonable enough piece of speculation. However several hitherto ignored sources from the eighteenth century directly contradict the possibility of Richmond being involved. Quite simply, Hale's hangman may have been black and named Richmond, but he wasn't *Bill* Richmond. Rather, as reports in the *Gaines Mercury* and *Royal Gazette* indicate, he was a Pennsylvania runaway with the same surname as Bill who ended up working as the hangman for the notorious Boston Provost Marshal William Cunningham. The hangman Richmond absconded from his duties in 1781, Cunningham offering a one-guinea reward for his return a full four years after Bill Richmond's likely departure for England.

Although it's satisfying to debunk the theory that Richmond was Hale's hangman, I would argue that the residual mystery of whether he first encountered Percy while grappling with Hessians or at Revd Charlton's parsonage is of minor importance in comparison to what Richmond's connection to Percy indicates about his character. For a young slave to have sufficient social confidence to convince an influential man such as Percy that he was worth mentoring was a remarkable feat and suggests that the young Richmond was both conversant with social conventions and also possessed a highly charismatic personality. For a young boy whose ambitions stretched far beyond the limited horizons of life as a house slave, Percy was the perfect mentor; not only did he possess myriad social connections but he also enjoyed a reputation for advancing the careers of young men he believed in. For example, while in Boston, he had taken another youngster under his wing, Roger Sheaffe, son of the deputy customs collector William Sheaffe, at whose boarding house Percy had made his headquarters. Sheaffe was subsequently trained for army service at Percy's expense, and in 1778 became an ensign in the 5th Foot – Percy's former regiment. Thereafter, Percy remained a presence in his life as a sort of 'fairy godfather'.

To reinforce the point of Percy's kindly nature, we have only to study the British newspapers of 1776, which are adorned with numerous accounts of his generous character and good deeds. For example, in the *Newcastle Courant* of 14 September, a British soldier who had recently returned from America recounted an exhaustive log of beneficent acts that Percy had performed:

> After the fatal attack at Bunker's-hill, his Lordship gave to the widow of every soldier of his regiment … an immediate benefaction of seven dollars; he paid their passage home, and ordered five guineas to be distributed to each of them on their landing in Britain. His humanity to the sick and wounded, (sending them wine, fresh provisions &c.) and his generosity to their families during their long stay at Boston, have been mentioned … he had a large tent provided for every company at his own expense, to accommodate their women … Though his regiment is distinguished for its admirable discipline, he never will suffer the private men to be struck, or used in a manner unbecoming Englishmen and soldiers, but endeavours to win them to their duty by generous treatment … he is perfectly adored among them … He is equally beloved and respected by his officers, among whom he lives with all the equality of a brother.

A letter published in the *Police Gazette* the previous month adopted a similar laudatory tone, remarking of Percy that

> I never in my life saw a man more the soldier, more the gentleman, or more the Christian … From the politeness and elegance of his conversation indeed, nobody can suppose him a soldier … He has not the levity of officers in general, but is prudent, temperate, and steady: and humanity adorns all his actions.

Despite his high standing among his troops, Percy's time in America was about to come to an abrupt end. The British campaign in New York had begun promisingly, with victory in the Battle of Long Island, while Percy led his regiment ably when the British took Fort Washington in November. By December, George Washington's forces had withdrawn in disarray to New Jersey, however Howe failed to press his advantage, allowing the rebels to escape to Pennsylvania. At the same time, Percy's relationship with Howe deteriorated rapidly after Percy was sent to command the small force holding Rhode Island, which was interpreted by many as humiliating, particularly given his unimpeachable war record. In a further insult, Howe then requested that Percy send 1,500 of his men to support British troops who were reeling after a counter-attack by Washington's forces in Trenton. Percy did not immediately comply, telling Howe that the menacing gathering of patriot forces in Providence made it, in his opinion, foolhardy to send so many men away from Rhode Island. Infuriated by Percy's failure to obey him without question, Howe threatened to have him court-martialled. A further dispute over provision of hay was, for Percy, the final straw and he promptly asked for permission to return to England, his mother's death in December 1776 acting as a useful pretext. Permission duly granted, the residents of Newport, Rhode Island gathered on 3 May 1777 to mourn his departure, before presenting him with an address in which they praised 'the deep sense of happiness' they had enjoyed under his empathetic protection. Back in Britain, the press eviscerated Howe, condemning his 'jealous pique' towards Percy, while venerating the latter's 'distinguished spirit and military skill'.

And so it was on Monday 5 May, accompanied by Bill Richmond, that Percy left America in the *Mercury Packet*.[2] Neither man would set foot on American soil again and America itself would soon never be the same again, the yoke of colonial rule being shaken off permanently as part of the terms of the 1783 Treaty of Paris.

After twenty-eight days at sea, Richmond stepped onto English soil for the first time on Monday 2 June at the bustling port of Falmouth, Devon. With Staten Island slavery now thousands of miles in his past, the young Richmond had every reason to view his arrival in England as something of a miracle. Percy's humanity had indeed 'adorned his action' in transforming Richmond's life and prospects. With a wealthy and influential benefactor by his side, Richmond, still only thirteen years old, had a life of wonder, drama and freedom lying in wait for him.

3

An Education and
'a Complete Milling'

The immediate weeks after Richmond's arrival in Britain provided him with a kaleidoscope of new sights, sounds and experiences, as well as a taste of the rarefied social circles with which his life now intersected. On reaching London, Percy was ushered into a two-hour audience with George III to discuss the state of affairs in America. Meanwhile, the fall-out from Percy's dispute with Howe continued to attract headlines, with competing accounts of the drama jostling for attention in the ever-excitable British press. 'The ministry are greatly embarrassed how to conduct themselves in the dispute between Gen. Howe and Earl Percy,' the *Hampshire Chronicle* revealed. 'The former must be supported, or there is an end to his command, and the latter is of too great a family to be slighted.' Rumours also circulated suggesting Percy would return to America, possibly within a matter of weeks, but by the end of July, his debriefings in London complete, Percy was back in his native northeast.

When he returned to the 'seat of his ancestors' in the village of Alnwick, Northumberland on 24 July 1777, Percy was treated to a hero's welcome and a series of celebrations, the intensity of which must have taken the teenage Richmond's breath away. 'The joy of the inhabitants was demonstrated by every mark of respect in their power to show,' intoned the *Newcastle Courant* breathlessly. 'The whole town of Alnwick was illuminated, and bonfires were alighted on all the neighbouring hills ... the continual rejoicings and acclamations of all ranks of people, gave a most agreeable welcome to this young hero.' One local resident, a Mr Charleton, summed up the prevailing mood by decorating every window in his house with a tree of flowers full of lights, while a decorative gold message written in his centre window read, 'Long live the British Hero Earl Percy'. Gilded leaves, flowers with bows and forty lamps also festooned the iron railings outside Charleton's house. Meanwhile, in a gesture typical of

Percy's generosity, a guinea was sent to all of Alnwick's thirty-three public houses to provide locals with liquid lubrication to fuel the celebrations.

As Northumberland swelled with pride, it was apparent that Percy's father's mission to re-establish the family reputation had been fulfilled. A series of renovations, begun in 1750, had elevated Alnwick Castle and the surrounding estate to new heights of grandeur and the Percy dynasty had a new military hero to savour, with the *Newcastle Courant* noting admiringly that 'the name of Percy' had been 'restored ... to all its ancient lustre'. The adulatory reception afforded to Percy must have reinforced for Richmond how admired his new patron was, and Percy was to prove every inch the generous benefactor towards his young charge. It had been something of a fashion in England since the end of the sixteenth century for members of the upper classes to own black slaves or employ black servants, who were seen as something of an exotic and ostentatious accoutrement. Lady Raleigh, wife of Sir Walter Raleigh, was one of the earliest society figures to own a black slave and the proliferation of black servants in the eighteenth century is amply reflected in art and engravings by the likes of William Hogarth and Robert Hancock; such representations usually depict black youths in turbans or other exotic clothing performing domestic functions.[1]

However, Percy did not see Richmond as a fashion accessory or menial functionary. Instead, he was determined to give him an education, a trade and the capacity to develop economic and social independence. Pierce Egan, for example, wrote that 'the Duke [Earl Percy] finding Bill to possess a good capacity, and being an intelligent youth, had put him to school in Yorkshire,' while John Wilson claimed Richmond initially worked as a valet for Percy, but was then 'put to school, where he made good progress in his studies, and learnt to write a very fair hand for a black man, as several letters to us ... can testify.'

A receipt located in the archives of Alnwick Castle confirms that Richmond – who is identified as 'the little Black boy' – did indeed receive several months of tuition from schoolmaster Malham Blackburn Newton, from 13 July until 31 December 1778. Although Church of England records state that Newton was later licensed as schoolmaster of Aldbrough School in Stanwick it is probable that Richmond received private tutoring. He may have stayed at the Percy family residence Stanwick Hall during this period, while a further receipt confirms that while he was being educated a local woman named Hannah Winn was responsible for his 'diet'.

Once Richmond was literate, Percy arranged a cabinet-making apprenticeship for him in York, where Egan claimed 'he served his time faithfully'. Exactly when Richmond's apprenticeship began is not clear, but the absence of his name from the Register of York Freemen, as well as the national apprenticeship records held by the Library of the Society of Genealogists, indicates that Percy arranged the apprenticeship via private arrangement, rather than legal indenture. This is understandable, for it was unusual for someone of foreign birth to be legally indentured in the eighteenth century, even more so a black foreigner. For centuries the English apprenticeship system had been essentially xenophobic in nature, for example, from 1483 onwards it was forbidden by the statutes of many companies and city ordinances for 'alien-born' children to become apprentices – a tradition that persisted for many years.

Richmond cannot have been in England for long before commencing his training as a cabinet maker, as the duration of such apprenticeships was seven years and fourteen was the usual age at which they began. Later documentation proves that Richmond had completed his apprenticeship and was working as a cabinet maker in London by the mid-1790s, so it seems likely that his training commenced soon after the end of his education with Newton. Percy was stationed in York for a period from February 1779, just a few weeks after the completion of Bill's schooling, and may have timed the commencement of the apprenticeship to coincide with his time in the city.

The apprentice tradition was a well-established institution that permeated the English lower and middle classes, with only the most privileged sectors of society unlikely to become apprentices and instead continue their education at university or enter the military. The apprenticeship system had its roots in medieval society and by the terms of the Statute of Apprentices of 1563 it was a compulsory process for anyone who wished to adopt a trade to first undergo an apprenticeship. Richmond, like other apprentices, would have been bound to and lived with his master for the duration of his training. A master's authority was absolute and substantial restrictions were placed on what an apprentice could or couldn't do, for example, Richmond may have been forbidden from marrying and it was also commonplace for apprentices to be banned from attending the theatre, gambling or frequenting public houses, lest they develop too licentious a lifestyle.

The discipline instilled in Richmond by the stiff guidelines of the apprenticeship system was, I would argue, a significant formative influence on his personality. Egan makes a point of referring to the fact that Richmond possessed a 'temperate mode of living, preferring exercise to wasting his time, or injuring his constitution, by a too frequent repetition of the charms of the bottle', and it seems reasonable to credit his days as an apprentice as the source of his admirable self-control and relative abstinence, as well as his remarkable work ethic.

Although a valuable educative experience, seven years as an apprentice would also have been a hard slog, with wages either non-existent or merely consisting of the most basic monetary recompense for essential items such as food and clothing. Nevertheless, Richmond must have been aware of the incredibly fortunate position he was in; in contrast to lesser skilled trades, such as ribbon weaving or cotton manufacture, cabinet making was a prestigious profession and considered the pinnacle of the arts of carpentry and joinery. The increasing expansion of an affluent middle class in Georgian Britain, coupled with growing interest in interior design, meant that demand for accomplished cabinet makers was growing. Possession of fine items of furniture, preferably made of mahogany – the *en vogue* wood of the day – and upholstered with fine fabrics and needlework, was seen as a symbol of affluence and good taste.

As demand for quality furniture increased, so the work of prominent cabinet makers became more sought after. One such figure was Thomas Chippendale, who published a collection of his designs in the lavishly illustrated *The Gentleman and Cabinet Maker's Director* in 1754, a publication which soon became an indispensable reference guide for provincial cabinet makers who wished to emulate the styles in fashion in London. Richmond's master might well have possessed a copy of this or similar directories by the other members of the 'big three' of English furniture designers, George Hepplewhite and Thomas Sheraton, and used the designs to help train his young apprentice. In a strange coincidence, Chippendale, like Richmond, trained in the furniture trade in York before moving to London, while his London salesroom, which was maintained by his family after his death in 1779, was located in St Martin's Lane, London, where Richmond would also later open a business.

During his time in York, there were several signs of Richmond's developing pugilistic acumen, as well as evidence of a streak of understandable sensitivity to his unusual position as an educated black man within an overwhelmingly white-dominated society. Although polite and charming, Richmond possessed a steely determination to defend himself verbally and also physically, if necessary, against racial insults. Egan details five fights that Richmond was involved in during his time in York, and states explicitly that three originated from him being insulted. Egan does not specify in two of these instances if the insults were racially motivated, but the sight of a well-dressed and well-educated professional black man on the streets of eighteenth-century York would certainly have attracted unwelcome attention, particularly when seen in the company of a white woman, as Egan notes that Richmond was. Writing in 1906, Henry Downes Miles referred disparagingly to how Richmond possessed a 'childish and nigger propensity for fine clothes'. If his affluence and style could inspire hateful and racist invective at a distance of over a century then it is easy to imagine how negatively many people would have reacted to Richmond in the late eighteenth century.

Local newspapers of the 1780s and 1790s seem to contain no references to these five fights, which is unsurprising given that they were informal contests rather than organised sporting spectacles. It is also impossible to tell to what extent Egan embroidered these accounts, or whether Richmond himself exaggerated them for Egan's benefit. Given that Richmond did not officially enter the prize ring until 1804, it is even possible that these York contests were invented fictions designed to create for Richmond a credible pugilistic background and mystique. Certainly later accounts based on Egan's originals add fictionalised flourishes that are best ignored. Nevertheless, Egan's accounts, whether factual or exaggerated, are fascinating in terms of what they suggest of the motivations and impulses that originally drew Richmond towards pugilism, as well as providing an insight into the everyday challenges he faced growing up as a black man within a white hegemony.

Egan states that Richmond's 'first display in the pugilistic art' was against '*George Moore*, recruit under Capt. Connor, of the 19th Regiment, better known by the name of *Docky Moore* who insulted RICHMOND upon the course at York during the time of the races'. It is not clear what the nature of Moore's 'insults' were, but Richmond's refusal to yield to these barbs demonstrates that he was a man who possessed a level of pride and self-confidence which compelled him to defend his honour when it was threatened. The site of the contest was most likely the marshlands of Knavesmire, a pasture to the southwest of York, outside the city walls. By the mid-eighteenth century Knavesmire was a regular location for horse racing, a sport that had existed in various forms in the area since Roman times. The modern York racecourse is still located there, and for many years the area was also a site for regular public executions, highwayman Dick Turpin being perhaps the most famous victim to be hung there in 1739.

In the eighteenth century, horse racing, like bare-knuckle boxing, was a booming spectator sport. A heady and rowdy mixture of gambling, drinking and socialising surrounded both sports, which enjoyed the enthusiastic patronage of the aristocracy and the working classes alike – the 'Kings, Lords and Commons' as Whyte's *History of the English Turf* put it. Racecourses and race meetings frequently played host to bare-knuckle brawls, whether pre-arranged, such as that between Harry Sellers and Joe Hood in 1777 at Ascot Heath, or impromptu, such as Richmond's contest with Moore. Exactly when the contest took place is unknown, although Nat Fleischer's assertion that it was on 25 August 1791 can be discounted due to the simple fact that by this point Moore was dead, having been arrested and charged with housebreaking in July 1789 and executed in April 1790.[2]

As his criminal tendencies indicate, Moore was a dangerous foe. Originally a blade forger from Sheffield, Egan vividly described his intimidating persona and physique:

> This *Docky* had been the terror of Sheffield, and had ruled the *roast* for some time in that part of the country; in fact, he was elegantly proportioned, possessing considerable strength, and all the necessary requisites for *milling*; in height about five feet nine inches and a half, and weighing fourteen stone.

Given Egan's estimate that Richmond only weighed 10 stone 12 pounds at the time, it is hardly surprising that Bill's friends tried to dissuade him from a 'fight with such a man'. However, in a one-sided contest lasting around twenty-five minutes, 'our hero *punished* Docky so completely that he *gave in*, and was taken out of the ring totally blind'.

Egan reports that this encounter was soon followed by Richmond defeating two soldiers from the 'Inniskilling dragoons', the implication being that the dragoons were military colleagues of Moore seeking revenge against their friend's conqueror. After these contests, Egan claimed that word of Richmond's *'milling* qualities' spread quickly and he subsequently found himself accosted in the streets by a local blacksmith, who 'not only insulted him with opprobrious epithets, but gave him a *kick* on the thigh'. Maintaining his composure, Richmond invited 'this *hammer-man*' to meet him and settle their differences the next day at The Groves, a district to the north of the city centre. Another one-sided contest ensued in which 'this *son of Vulcan* was completely *satisfied*, and acknowledged RICHMOND the best man'.

The fifth of Richmond's early bouts is described in Egan's typically inimitable and entertaining style; on this occasion it is specifically stated that the confrontation originated from racial abuse:

RICHMOND, in passing through the streets of York, one evening, with a female under his protection, was accosted by one *Frank Myers*, with the epithets of *'black devil,'* &c. and who otherwise insulted the young woman, for being in company of a *man of colour*. Bill, full of gallantry, and with becoming spirit of indignation, requested him to desist for the present moment, but to meet him at the *Groves* on the next Monday morning, when they would settle this difference, (the circumstance happening on a Saturday night,) to which *Myers* agreed. This affair of honour being *buzzed* about on the Sunday, a great concourse of people assembled early the next day, to witness the conflict: RICHMOND was there at the appointed hour, and after suffering considerable time to elapse, and *Myers* not making his appearance, the spectators became impatient and it was judged expedient that RICHMOND and his friends should repair to the house of *Myers*, to remind him of his engagement. This *Myers* kept a bagnio, with a woman of the name of *Shepherd*, at Uggleford, to which place they went and found *Myers*, who, after some hesitation, agreed to go to the *Groves*, where he was followed by this *shepherdess* and her *flock*.

The tableaux Egan paints of this contest is a colourful one – from the image of an indignant Richmond defending the honour of a lady in his company, to that of a reluctant Myers cowering in his brothel before finally agreeing to keep the engagement. What a sight it must have been to see Richmond and his friends marching Myers to the Groves, with the brothel madam and her retinue of prostitutes pursuing them, while an excited crowd gathered eagerly, holding their breath and waiting for the violent mayhem to begin ...

Egan resumes his compelling narrative thus:

> The battle now commenced, and raged with fury for some time, but upon *Myers* getting the worst of it, the above coves and her damsels rushed into the ring to prevent their *bully* from being annihilated, and took him away. The spectators interfered, and persuaded *Myers* to return and finish the battle like a man. *Myers*, ashamed of his conduct, agreed to it, when RICHMOND soon taught him very properly to acknowledge, that it was wrong, and beneath the character of an Englishman, to abuse any individual for that he couldn't help – either on account of his COUNTRY or his *colour*. *Myers*, very properly, received a complete *milling*.

The fact that Richmond chose to challenge rather than ignore Myers' racist abuse is hugely significant. Richmond's defiant resistance, within a society where racism was not predominantly seen, as it is today, as the product of a deranged, irrational or bigoted mind but as an expression of the natural order of the universe, is a remarkable symbol of his determination to assert his rights and freedom. For Richmond, physical struggle was an essential expression of his refusal to be negatively defined by others in relation to his colour. Once he was older and became a famed pugilist, Richmond would deploy his physical gifts more sparingly, as befitting his status as a man of refinement with a prominent social position among the first-rank of pugilists. Indeed, he eventually adopted the position that violence should be a last resort, rather than a default position, as Egan explained: 'In being a *man of colour*, from the taunts and insults which he has received upon that account ... RICHMOND must be considered good-tempered and placid, even to a degree that could not be expected.' However, when certain lines were crossed, Richmond would determinedly assert his status as a proud black man, as Egan also recounted: 'In one of those instances of unmerited reproach, his indignation would no longer let him remain quiet, and in a *turn-up* with the young Ruffian, at his own house, he completely *served him out*.'

In his willingness to challenge the casual racism of the age, Richmond proved that his bravery and pride in his ethnic background were beyond question. His admirable determination to live his life free from societal restriction or censure was about to be tested even further when he married a white woman.

4

Black Britain and Bill's Better Half

With a secure trade and the favour of an influential patron, Richmond's existence in England was infinitely preferable to how his life would most likely have unfolded in America. Nevertheless, the frequency with which he was insulted on the basis of his ethnicity raises several vital contextual questions: what was everyday life like for black people during the Georgian era? And what were the historical roots of black people within Britain, as well as their legal status, during the years in which the country was heavily engaged within the slave trade?

As historians Peter Fryer and Gretchen Gerzina have so eloquently explained, the history of black people in Britain extends back far further than the common misconception that Britain suddenly 'became' a multiracial society after the arrival of the Empire Windrush at Tilbury in 1948. Ironically, as Fryer points out, there were actually 'Africans in Britain before the English came here', in the shape of groups of soldiers serving in the Roman army from around AD 210 onwards. Nevertheless, from Roman until early Tudor times, the black presence in Britain largely consisted of individuals or small groups, for example, there were several Africans employed, or more probably enslaved, at the court of James IV of Scotland, one of whom was a drummer and choreographer, while Henry VII and Henry VIII both employed a black musician at their courts.

In the following decades the black British population increased, albeit slowly, and began to build into a nascent community rather than a collection of isolated individuals. By the time of Elizabeth I there were sufficient numbers of black people in England for the Queen to pen an open letter detailing her view that there were 'to manie' black people in England. Dated 11 July 1596, this letter mandated that 'those kinde of people' should be 'transported ... out of the realme'. The declaration had little impact, for in 1601 Elizabeth issued a further proclamation, explaining she was 'highly discontented to understand the great numbers of negars and Blackamoores which ... are crept into this realm'. Dismissing 'said kind of people' with the airy generalisation that 'most of them are infidels', she issued an 'especial commandment' that they should be 'discharged out of this Her Majesty's dominions'.

Elizabeth's antipathy was typical of public attitudes towards black people at this time, which oscillated between amusement, mistrust, fear and dislike. Misconceptions and stereotypes were rife, encouraged by such texts as *A Summarie of the Antiquities, and wonders of the Worlde*, based on the outdated work of Pliny the Elder, a Roman naturalist who believed, among other things, that some Africans had no noses while others could not dream. The predominance of such notions had the attendant effect of dehumanising black people to such an extent that the exploitation of human beings in Africa through the increasingly rapid development of the slave trade was, initially at least, met with little moral opposition. If, as the typical pro-slavery thinking went, black people were a sub-human species closer to animals than humans, then where was the harm in trafficking, selling and treating them like animals?

From the latter half of the seventeenth century onwards the slave trade was dominated by Britain; indeed, it is estimated that three million of the ten million Africans who crossed the Atlantic before 1850 did so on British vessels. The huge increase in slave traffic was largely fuelled by the country's developing taste for sugar, with consumption of the product increasing four times between 1660 and 1700. Sugar was the key component in the development of slavery as a 'triangular' trade, in which goods from Europe were exchanged for slaves in West Africa, who in turn were transported to the Americas to work on plantations. The fruits of this labour, predominantly sugar, but also cotton, tobacco and rum, were then returned to Europe.

Economically ingenious, if morally repugnant, this trade model earned a handsome profit at every juncture and was the predominant tool that helped Britain attain geopolitical pre-eminence by developing the country's economy to dizzying new heights, in turn fuelling rapid industrialisation. To borrow a phrase adopted by the historian Eric Williams, the British economy was 'fertilized' by the profits of slavery – and the profits were mind-boggling in their enormity: figures supplied by the African World Reparations and Repatriation Truth Commission in 1999 suggested that adequate modern-day compensation for the myriad effects of slavery inflicted by the British would run to a staggering £150 trillion.

It is imperative to note that Williams' observation does not represent a politically correct or modern reinterpretation of the economic significance of slavery. During the eighteenth century itself many influential thinkers and organisations were all too aware of the integral role the slave trade played in the British economy. As the economist Malachy Postlethwayt explained in 1745, 'If we have no *Negroes*, we can have no *Sugars, Tobaccoes, Rice,*

Rum, &c ... consequently, the Publick Revenue, arising from the Importation of *Plantation-Produce*, must be annihilated ... ' According to Postlethwayt 'the *Negroe-Trade*' represented an 'inexhaustible Fund of Wealth and Naval Power to this Nation.' The Committee of the Company of Merchants Trading to Africa made a similar point in 1788: 'The Effects of this Trade to Great Britain are beneficial to an infinite extent ... there is hardly any Branch of Commerce ... that does not derive some advantage from it.'

Despite the integral role of slaves to the economy, the legal status of slaves who escaped to Britain or were brought there by force remained a subject of fierce legislative debate, largely because no law had been enacted to establish slavery in Britain in the first place. Lord Chief Justice John Holt stated in 1706, in terms that seemed unequivocal, that 'no man can be a slave in England' and that 'as soon as a negro comes into England, he becomes free'. However this sentiment was contradicted in 1729 by the Solicitor General, Charles Talbot, and the Attorney General, Sir Philip Yorke, who met with a delegation of slave merchants and offered the informal opinion that 'a slave, by coming from the West Indies, either with or without his master, to Great Britain or Ireland, doth not become free ... Baptism doth not bestow freedom on him ... the master may legally compel him to return to the plantations.' To add to the confusion, in 1762 the Lord Chancellor Robert Henley maintained that 'as soon as a man sets foot on English ground he is free,' contradicting the Yorke-Talbot opinion, which Yorke had attempted to reinforce in 1749 after his own appointment as Lord Chancellor by declaring that a slave was 'as much property as any other thing'.

This morass of legal contradictions was partly addressed in 1772 with the celebrated Somerset case, in which an escaped slave named James Somerset challenged an attempt to forcibly transport him to Jamaica. The case was spearheaded by one of the early British abolitionists, a tenacious civil service clerk named Granville Sharp, who had, in 1769, published a book entitled *A Representation of the Injustice and Dangerous Tendency of Tolerating Slavery in England*. This book, and Sharp's attempts to assist slaves in cases against their masters, earned him a reputation as a doughty and principled social campaigner. Lord Chief Justice Mansfield's historic judgement in the case, delivered on 22 June 1772, concluded that Somerset must be freed, and that there was no 'positive law' in place to establish slavery in British law. Although at pains to point out that all his judgment did was to establish that slaves could not be forcibly returned abroad, and that the ruling should not be interpreted as ending slavery itself, Mansfield's decision was a watershed moment for the abolitionist movement. Although there were documented cases of escaped slaves being forcibly returned to slavery abroad after the Somerset case, the publicity surrounding the case enabled the movement for abolition, then in its infancy, to acquire much momentum.

Unfortunately, many of the traditional narratives concerning the abolitionist movement focus almost exclusively on the cause's white champions, such as William Wilberforce, and inevitably overlook the fact that, just as the original impetus for the Somerset case came from Somerset's own determination to secure his freedom, so much of the momentum for the abolitionist movement came from the obstinate campaigning initiated by emerging black voices such as Ignatius Sancho and Olaudah Equiano.

The refined Sancho was a fascinating figure. Commonly recognised as the first black citizen to vote in a British parliamentary election (he cast one of his votes in the 1774 election for Hugh Percy, Richmond's mentor), Sancho was a true renaissance man who turned his hand to acting, writing and composing. He famously wrote to the novelist Laurence Sterne in 1766 in an effort to convince him to support abolition. 'Dear Sir,' Sancho implored. 'Think in me you behold the uplifted hands of thousands of my brother Moors … figure to yourself their attitudes; hear their supplicating addresses! – alas! you cannot refuse!'

Equiano was an equally influential black voice. His 1789 autobiography substantially advanced the case for ending slavery, with reviewers commenting on its timely relevance. Equiano worked tirelessly, sometimes in association with Sharp, to draw attention to cases of injustice against black people, notably the murder of 132 slaves who were thrown overboard from the slave ship the *Zong* in 1781. However, outside of studies dedicated to black history, the names of Sancho and Equiano and other black abolitionists and radicals and their contribution in reshaping the social fabric of Britain are seldom cited in adequate detail; William Hague's biography of Wilberforce, to take one example, contains a mere five references to Sancho and Equiano within its 642 pages.

The abolition debate naturally became more heated as more black people settled in Britain and their voices began to be heard. Nevertheless, exactly how many black people were living in Britain by this point remains the subject of debate. During the Somerset case, Mansfield estimated there were around 15,000 'slaves' in England, therefore by the late 1770s, when Richmond travelled to England, the black population could have grown to somewhere approaching 20,000. These figures swelled further after the conclusion of the American War of Independence, as former slaves who had served in the British Army, Lord Dunmore's promise of freedom ringing in their ears, arrived to claim the prize for their loyal service.[1]

With limited education and employment prospects, though, many of these former soldiers ended up extremely poor, having, in Fryer's words, 'exchanged the life of a slave for that of a starving beggar'. Those black citizens fortunate enough to be employed mainly worked in menial roles as servants, valets, cooks or maids. The remarkable members of the black community who succeeded, against all the odds, in attaining public notice or celebrity both before and after the Slave Trade Act of 1807 were usually radical or campaigning political figures, such as Equiano, William Davidson and Robert Wedderburn, or boxers, such as Richmond and Tom Molineaux. Fryer identified within these vocations a common virtue, namely a determined willingness to fight, both physically and metaphorically:

> The great majority of the black people who lived in Britain were very poor indeed and had to fight, in one way or another, to survive. Daily experience knocked into black people the art of self-defence, with brains for a choice, with fists or other weapons as a last resort. To be a radical or a boxer was merely to apply, at a public level, a lesson transmitted by oral tradition and reinforced on the street every day of one's life.

It certainly cannot be over-emphasised how formidable the powers of determination were that a black person needed to possess in order to thrive in Georgian Britain. First-person accounts from this period provide some moving testimonies as to the prejudices faced on a daily basis by black people, for example, one black settler, Ukawsaw Gronniosaw, who had served in the British Army in Martinique after being granted freedom in his slave master's will, wrote an extensive account of the 'trials and tribulations' of his experiences in England. Gronniosaw had arrived expecting 'goodness, gentleness and meekness', but instead was abused in the streets, conned out of fifteen guineas by an unscrupulous landlady and sunk into poverty. An anonymous letter by a 'free negro' printed in 1788 also illuminates how desperate and lonely many black people felt in the face of societal hostility:

> I am one of that unfortunate Race of Men who are distinguished from the rest of the human Species by a black Skin and woolly Hair: Disadvantages of very little moment in themselves, but which prove to us a source of the Greatest Misery, because there are Men who will not be persuaded that it is possible for a human Soul to be lodged within a sable body.

The letter-writer went on to persuasively adapt Shylock's famous soliloquy from William Shakespeare's *The Merchant of Venice* to promote the idea of abolition: 'Hath not a negro eyes? Hath not a Negro Hands, Organs, Dimensions, Senses, Affections, Passions?' The appearance of such letters, alongside the publication of writings by Sancho and Equiano among others, caused alarm among pro-slavers. For example, the magistrate Sir John Fielding, a younger half-brother of the novelist Henry Fielding, grumbled about the influx of blacks into the country, arguing that 'they no sooner arrive here, than they put themselves on a Footing with other Servants, become intoxicated with Liberty, grow refractory, and ... begin to expect Wages according to their own Opinion of their Merits'.

The increase in the black British population inevitably led to a reactionary rise in explicitly racist sentiments and theories, as pro-slavery proponents attempted to justify their views. Such theories often utilised ridiculous pseudo-scientific arguments which may seem laughable now, but at the time they were given serious consideration. Chief among these theories was the concept of polygenism, namely the idea that the human 'races' derived from separate rather than a common lineage. The Swedish botanist Carl Linnæus, who coined the phrase 'homo sapiens', declared in the 1758 edition of *Systema Naturae* (translated into English in 1792) that there was a hierarchy of races with the white man at the peak, due to his 'gentle manners ... acute judgment' and willingness to be 'governed by fixed laws'. In contrast, Linnæus claimed Africans were 'crafty, indolent, and careless'.

Such ideas were disturbingly commonplace, and not merely the preserve of cranks but prevalent among figures regarded as enlightened intellectuals. We have already seen how David Hume regarded blacks as 'naturally inferior' and his contemporary, the advocate, judge and philosopher Lord Kames, held similar views, declaring, 'the black colour of negroes, thick lips, flat nose, crisped woolly hair, and rank smell, distinguish them from every other race of men'. The physician Charles White was another proponent of polygenism, claiming that white Europeans should be considered 'the most beautiful of the human race', whereas Africans were the 'lowest' and 'nearer to the ape'.

A corollary of the widespread acceptance of inherent white supremacy was a pronounced moral panic surrounding marriage between black and white citizens, commonly referred to as 'inter-marriage'. In 1763, the *Bath Chronicle and Weekly Gazette* carried a startling report, claiming Parliament might be lobbied to prevent a trend for inter-marriage which 'amongst the lower Class, is become everyday more fashionable'. The specific reference to inter-marriage being a problem among the 'lower class' is redolent of the middle and upper classes' fear of both 'foreigners' and also the potentially revolutionary masses of the working classes, a fear that would accelerate as America revolted against British rule and the French Revolution overthrew the monarchy of Louis XVI.

In the wake of the Somerset judgement, public rhetoric concerning inter-marriage assumed an apocalyptic tone. MP Samuel Estwick, for example, articulated his desire to 'preserve the race of Britons from stain and contamination', while Edward Long, a colonial administrator and writer, articulated his fear about the increase in sexual and marital unions between black men and working-class white women. 'The lower classes of women in England, are remarkably fond of the blacks, for reasons too brutal to mention,' he summarised, racism, sexual paranoia and class snobbery all evident in his tone. 'They would connect themselves with horses and asses, if the laws permitted them.' Long warned that the English would end up resembling 'the *Portuguese* and *Moriscos* in complexion of skin and baseness of mind', and fretted about the possibility of eventual black representation in parliament, declaring indignantly, 'complexion will be no disqualification'. Although Long and Estwick's views were extreme, they were by no means minority opinions. Nevertheless one must avoid generalising about attitudes to ethnicity during the Georgian era. Perceptions of black people at this time would have ranged the full gamut from welcome and warmth, through to condescension and grudging acceptance as well as extending to outright hatred and hostility.

All of which contextual pontificating brings us back to Bill Richmond and the fact that when, as a young cabinet maker, he married a white woman, the reaction of his contemporaries would have varied. Some would have perceived the union as peculiar, others may not have cared, while a significant proportion would certainly have found it an unnatural coupling. Having said that, inter-marriage was more common at this time than many modern readers might have thought, one factor being necessity: quite simply, there were far more black men in England than black women, a consequence of the manual nature of slavery, as well as the exodus of male slaves into British military service during the War of Independence. Therefore, if a black man wished to marry it was statistically easier to find a white as opposed to a black mate.

A further aspect of inter-marriage that created discomfort for many was the fact that the offspring of such unions were of mixed ethnic ancestry. Mixed-race children were often regarded with disquiet and disgust. Writer Philip Thicknesse, for example, observed in 1778 that 'in almost every village are to be seen a little race of mulattoes, mischievous as monkeys, and infinitely more dangerous'.

It has long been known that Richmond and his wife had several children; newspaper reports of his funeral in 1830 mention four offspring, although these accounts do not name them or identify their gender. It is also well known that one of his children, a son nicknamed Young Richmond, later embarked on a brief boxing career, of which we will learn more in due course. Although Young Richmond's existence has long been acknowledged, the identity of Richmond's wife has remained a mystery. It has always been accepted that she was white, but her identity and name are not revealed in any contemporary newspapers that detail Richmond's career and, as such, a fair degree of myth making has sprung up around her identity. Egan goes no further than mentioning that Richmond 'had the art of persuasion to get a good-looking white woman for his wife, and several children were the result'. Other more contemporary writers, such as Fryer, have asserted, with no supporting evidence, that Richmond's wife was 'rich', and it was her finances that enabled him to later become the landlord of the Horse and Dolphin, a conclusion that is incorrect.

In fact, as can be ascertained from her death certificate (which lists her as the widow of cabinet maker William Richmond), as well as from other public record sources, Bill's wife was born in Wakefield, Yorkshire in either 1773 or 1774, died on 1 March 1858 aged eighty-four and was named Mary. Her maiden name, in all probability, was Dunwick, as there was a marriage recorded between William Richmond and Mary Dunwick on 29 June 1791 in Wakefield, which is the most likely match for Bill's wedding. Presuming the information on her death certificate is accurate, Mary would have been just seventeen or eighteen years old at the time of the wedding and Bill twenty-eight, although, problematically, their marriage bond lists both bride and groom as being twenty-two years old 'and upwards'. This suggests that Mary lied about her age, raising the possibility that she and Bill married without the permission or blessing of her family – a common occurrence for white women who married black men during the eighteenth century.

The bond also indicates that Mary was from a poor background, as her name is signed with her mark rather than a signature, indicating she was illiterate. Significantly, the bond lists Richmond's profession as cabinet maker, increasing the likelihood that this record is the correct match for his wedding. The witness to the bond and the marriage, one James Musgrave, is also listed as a cabinet maker. Might Musgrave have been Bill's former master, or perhaps his employer or a colleague in Wakefield, where Bill is listed as being resident?

Another possible match for Bill's wedding is a marriage between William Richmond and Mary Earnshaw in Doncaster on 14 October 1793, although in this record William's occupation is not listed. Interestingly, though, Mary Earnshaw's baptism (in Pontefract in 1773) could also match the age of eighty-four given on Mary Richmond's death certificate in 1858. Perhaps this is just a coincidence or perhaps Mary Dunwick died after marrying Bill and he then remarried, to Mary Earnshaw?

Details of Mary and Bill's children are similarly clouded by mystery. On 2 January 1792, records in Wakefield detail the baptism of a boy named Charles Richmond, whose parents are named as William and Mary Richmond, although the absence of any further details means that it cannot be stated with certainty that Charles was Bill's son. By the mid-1790s, it seems that Bill and Mary had moved to London where baptism records for St Andrew's in Holborn suggest they had a child named Hannah, who was baptised on 28 September 1795 (adding to the potential for speculation, Hannah was also the name of Mary Earnshaw's mother). In this baptism record the Richmond family residence is listed as Eagle Street in Holborn, where Charles Booth observed, intriguingly, in his survey of life and labour in London, that there 'used to be boxing … which brought a rough class to the street'. Holborn was also an area where there were many black residents at this time.

Later additions to the paper trail of public records strengthen the above conclusions, eventually proving beyond reasonable doubt that Bill's wife was indeed named Mary. A further baptism record at St Andrew's in Holborn dated 6 August 1797 details the christening of a son named

William Richmond and continues to place Bill and Mary in Eagle Street. However it is a dual baptism on 24 May 1813 at St Martin's-in-the-Field which provides more solid evidence. On this occasion a son named Henry and a daughter named Betsy are listed as the children of William and Mary Richmond, with William's profession listed as a cabinet maker and the family now resident at No. 6 Whitcomb Street, a street where other sources have placed Bill at this time. The identification of Hannah, William, Henry and Betsy as the leading candidates to be Bill and Mary's children is supported by the existence of these four baptism records, and reinforced by later reports of Bill's funeral, which mention four children.

What then of Charles Richmond, apparently born in 1792? If he was Bill and Mary's son then it was possible that he died as a teenager, for a record in 1807 does detail the burial of a Charles Richmond at St Andrew's on 12 April, the same church where Hannah and William were baptised. Charles is listed as a resident of Bangor Court, Holborn, around half a mile from the Eagle Street address where Bill and Mary lived a few years earlier although, frustratingly, the burial record contains no age for Charles or details of his parents. Interestingly, there are very few references to Bill in newspapers in 1806 and 1807, when he also fought no boxing contests, in contrast to the preceding and succeeding years of 1805 and 1808; might a possible explanation for this be that Charles was suffering from an illness in 1806 prior to dying in 1807, and therefore Bill stayed away from the prize ring while his son was sick and his family grieved?

Apart from these few details, little else is known about Bill's family or Mary specifically, although it is intriguing to speculate that perhaps she was the white woman whose honour Richmond defended against Frank Myers in York in the incident detailed in the previous chapter. How the couple met and what Mary thought of Bill's eventual boxing career remain resolute mysteries. Nevertheless, one can certainly imagine the emotional agonies of bringing up several children while living with a husband who was risking his life, health and sight on a regular basis in the prize ring. Mary must have been a patient woman, which might explain why Richmond's rival turned friend Tom Cribb later lauded her as Bill's 'better half'. It also seems significant, as well as deeply moving, that the pair's marriage endured for nearly forty years, despite what must have been, at times, almost unbearable societal prejudice. For Mary to have disregarded the forces of convention, as well as the possible disapproval of her family, to marry Bill marks her out as a remarkable woman, which only makes her unhappy fate after her husband's death all the more poignant.

But that is a matter for later; for now let us return to the bustling metropolis of London in the 1790s, and examine the somewhat circuitous route by which Richmond's life became inexorably entwined with the meteoric rise in public affection of pugilism, as well as his connection to the bizarre life of one of the sport's most enthusiastic patrons – the infamous Lord Camelford.

5

'A Turbulent, Rakehelly, Demented Existence'

It somehow seems inevitable that London would entice a man of adventurous spirit such as Bill Richmond to become one of its inhabitants. During Georgian times the city was without equal in its capacity for wonder, excitement and opportunity, its expansion throughout the preceding century having been both rapid and utterly thrilling. Pierce Egan summed up the city's glorious and infinite variety with his typically idiosyncratic and vivid prose by declaring that London was 'the looking-glass for TALENT', and 'the faithful emporium of the enterprising, the bold'. Richmond, as his future business endeavours and prize-fighting career would amply demonstrate, certainly fits Egan's description of the 'enterprising' and the 'bold'. Perhaps Richmond was drawn to London by the wider opportunities the city offered a trained cabinet maker such as himself, or perhaps he harboured dreams, after his successful 'set-tos' in York, of pursuing a prize-fighting career. Whatever the reason for his arrival he was, as we have seen in the previous chapter, a citizen of the city by 1795, and a resident of Eagle Street, Holborn with his wife Mary and his young family until at least 1797.

It was largely due to the influence and charisma of one man that Richmond would ultimately be drawn away from the career of a respectable craftsman to the more dangerous occupation of a prizefighter; that man was Thomas Pitt, the second Lord Camelford and Baron of Boconnoc, whose short but turbulent life scandalised, entertained and intrigued Georgian society in equal measure. Nikolai Tolstoy, Pitt's biographer, succinctly summarised his subject thus:

> His life was short: only twenty-nine years. But it was full of bizarre incidents. He was responsible for the death of more than one man, and he himself died in violence. He was handsome, athletic, arrogant,

immensely sensitive on the subject of his honour, and, with pistols or swords, ever ready to meet an opponent on a lonely spot at dawn ... Some doubted his sanity, but none his courage.

Lord Rosebery would later reinforce the predominant judgement of Pitt as a worthless wastrel, declaring, 'his was a turbulent, rakehelly, demented existence'. Despite, or more accurately because of, his myriad faults, Pitt was one of the more intriguing figures of the Georgian age. He was born on 19 February 1775, almost twelve years after Richmond's generally accepted date of birth. The two men's upbringings were sharply contrasting; if the circumstances of Richmond's childhood can be said to represent the painful realities of life for the enslaved and dispossessed, then Pitt's background could be said to aptly symbolise the opposite state – namely, a life of upper-class privilege. Yet while Richmond extracted every ounce of advantage from the limited opportunities afforded to him, Pitt was his polar opposite – namely a man who squandered the advantages that were granted him by dint of the good social fortune of his birth.

Yet, for all Pitt's shortcomings, one can understand why Richmond was drawn to him. His complex personality also incorporated a passionate streak of altruism that saw him, throughout his short life, secretly give away thousands of pounds to London's most needy citizens, while the aura of danger that surrounded him made him a glamorous figure. Another aspect of Pitt's appeal, certainly for a social climber such as Richmond, was the fact that an association with him offered a tantalising glimpse of one of the most elevated social circles within England, for the Pitt family was one of the most celebrated dynasties of the age, dominating British politics for the best part of fifty years from the mid-1700s onwards. Thomas's uncle and cousin, William Pitt 'the Elder' and William Pitt 'the Younger' both served as Prime Minister, while another cousin, Lord Chatham, was First Lord of the Admiralty and his brother-in-law, Lord Grenville, served as Foreign Secretary. Even Pitt's father, also named Thomas, was an MP who was once sounded out by George III about becoming Prime Minister, although ill health meant his political career never achieved its potential; instead he was raised to the peerage in 1784, becoming the first Lord Camelford and Baron Boconnoc.

In contrast to his level-headed relatives and art-loving aesthete of a father, the young Thomas Pitt was temperamental and hypersensitive to the point of paranoia. Starved of affection by his formal and distant parents, he was largely raised by servants and tutors in isolation on his family's estate in Cornwall. Sent to school in Switzerland at the age of eleven, Thomas developed an affinity with the writings of Jean-Jacques Rousseau; as Tolstoy points out, the Genevan philosopher's 'persecution mania' chimed with Pitt's own feelings of neglect. Pitt's time in Switzerland was a fleeting period of happiness, which was cut short when his father sent him to Charterhouse school in England, from whose brutally repressive discipline an anguished Pitt fled after just nine days.

When it became clear that the fourteen-year-old would not return to Charterhouse, his father acceded to Pitt's dream of a naval career and arranged for him to join the crew of HMS *Guardian*, under Capt. Edward Riou. With a cargo of convicts, the *Guardian* set sail for New South Wales in September 1789. It was to prove a tumultuous voyage, and one that would fulfil the young Pitt's hunger for adventure on the high seas. The *Guardian* ran into trouble in the Southern Ocean, striking an iceberg on Christmas Eve, which smashed the ship's rudder and tore a hole in the hull. With water levels rising rapidly Riou agreed to let the majority of the crew and convicts – many of them drunk and mutinous – leave the sinking ship in five smaller vessels. Those left behind on the *Guardian* included the young Pitt and an abject fate seemed assured for these unfortunate souls.

Ultimately, only one of the five vessels that escaped the *Guardian* was ever sighted again and Pitt's family, assuming their son had perished, went into mourning. However, sensational news eventually reached England; it transpired that Riou, as well as sixty other men, including one 'Tho. Pitt, Midshipman', were still alive. The patched-up wreck of the *Guardian* had staggered safely into Table Bay after a scarcely believable two-month voyage through freezing and treacherous waters. Pitt, still only fifteen, arrived back in England in September 1790 to a hero's welcome.

Unfortunately, Pitt's experiences on the *Guardian* were a rare highlight of a naval career blighted by controversy. His next engagement, three years on the HMS *Discovery* as part of the landmark Vancouver expedition,[1] was an unmitigated disaster. Several times Pitt incurred the wrath of Capt. George Vancouver, and was punished by being mercilessly flogged. On one occasion, after being accused by Vancouver of sleeping while on watch, Pitt was placed in iron chains for two weeks, before being released from service in February 1794. Pitt was stung by what he perceived as unjust treatment by Vancouver and would nurse a vengeful grievance against his commanding officer for years to come.

In a further blow to his fragile psyche, the news reached Pitt, more than a year after the event, that his father had died on 19 January 1793. Pitt was now the second Lord Camelford, Baron of Boconnoc and the heir to an income of more than £20,000 a year. However, the new Lord Camelford had no desire to take up his place in the House of Lords, instead he was still determined to prove himself worthy of a high naval rank. Therefore, he made his way to Malacca, where he persuaded Capt. Edward Pakenham to allow him to serve on the HMS *Resistance*. Pakenham took a shine to Camelford, and recommended him for promotion to Acting Lieutenant.

However, with the prospects for advancement limited on the *Resistance*, Camelford left the frigate in November 1795.

All the while Camelford's resentment against Vancouver had been festering and, when he arrived back in England in September 1796, the situation spiralled out of control. Camelford prefaced his return by writing to Vancouver demanding that the two men should meet in a duel. By this point, Lord Grenville was Foreign Secretary and Pitt the Younger had been Prime Minister for almost thirteen years, and Camelford's vendetta against Vancouver was causing them no small measure of social and political embarrassment. Vancouver, aided by the interventions of Grenville and the Lord Chancellor, attempted to deflect and defuse Pitt's challenge and broker a peaceful outcome.

However it was to no avail. On 21 September the matter came to a head when Camelford spotted Vancouver and his brother in Conduit Street, central London. An enraged Camelford squared up to his nemesis, striking him several times with a stick. News of the confrontation leaked into the press and, fuelled by the publication by caricaturist James Gillray of a print entitled *The CANEING in Conduit Street*, the incident became a media sensation.[2] Meanwhile Camelford's state of agitation was exacerbated when his promotion to lieutenant was delayed, further fuelling his perpetual sense of injustice and the wilder excesses of his personality. Worse was to come though – in 1798 while in Antigua, where he had been appointed acting Master and Commander of the HMS *Favourite* Camelford quarrelled with colleague Charles Peterson.[3] When Peterson refused to obey his orders three times Camelford shot and killed him, claiming his actions were justified on the grounds of Peterson's 'mutiny'. The resulting court martial acquitted Camelford, but his reputation was terminally damaged.[4]

The inevitable end of Camelford's naval career came in January 1799 when he was arrested after attempting to make his way, illegally, to France, with whom England was at war, while armed with pistols and a dagger. 'It is impossible to account for Lord CAMELFORD's conduct in any other manner than his being insane,' reflected *The Times* of this latest scandal. Camelford's motives for his bizarre attempt to reach French soil were never discerned, although a theory was advanced in the *London Chronicle* that he had been 'prompted by a too ardent desire to perform some feat of desperation, by which … the cause of Europe might be essentially served', the implication being that he had been seeking to assassinate Napoleon or another member of the French administration. Although Camelford was granted a pardon and released from custody, the privy council recommended that it was 'not advisable' that he should be entrusted with the command of any vessel. Enraged that his dreams of naval stardom had been stymied, Camelford resigned his commission.

Some relative calm was restored to Camelford's existence when, later in the year, he embarked on a relationship with his cousin Lady Hester Stanhope, which would last nearly three years. The pair made a handsome couple; Camelford was 'just under six foot two inches in height, with curly brown hair, bold blue eyes, and a lithe and muscular figure', while Lady Hester was renowned for her majestic 'mien' and 'eminently graceful' manner. Significantly, the couple had endured mutually miserable childhoods and they also shared an unlikely passion for helping the poor.

Indeed, Stanhope's recollection of her lover's many kindnesses towards those of a lower social rank provide us with a clue as to how he may have befriended Richmond:

> He would sometimes dress himself in a jacket and trowsers, like a sailor, and go to some tavern or alehouse; and if he fell in with a poor-looking person, who had an air of trouble or poverty, he would contrive to enter into conversation with him, and find out all about him. 'Come,' he would say, 'tell me your story, and I will tell you mine.' He was endowed with great penetration, and, if he saw that the man's story was true, he would slip fifty or a hundred pounds into his hand ...

Although it is unclear how the two men met, one can certainly imagine that the incredible tale of Richmond's journey from slavery in America to a life of educated respectability in England would have captured Camelford's fertile imagination. Richmond most likely entered Camelford's service in 1799 or afterwards, as Camelford was only infrequently based in England before this point. There was certainly a black servant in Camelford's employment by February 1801, as another bizarre incident from his life proves, although whether it was Richmond is open to debate. When Camelford installed his friend John Horne Tooke (a controversial parson who had once been tried for treason) as an MP for the 'pocket borough' of Old Sarum, his plan was met with widespread objections, largely due to Horne Tooke's radical views. Infuriated by this reaction, Camelford told Lord Grenville that if Horne Tooke was rejected than he would instead send 'a black man, referring to a negro servant of his, born in England, whom he would qualify to take a seat'. Richmond, of course, was not English-born, although this does not preclude him from being the servant referred to; in the heat of this display of grandstanding, Camelford may have overlooked the fact of his American birth. The majority of sources for this incident refer to this black servant as being named 'Mungo' – a black character from the 1768 opera *The Padlock* whose name had thereafter came into popular usage as a term applied pretty indiscriminately to any black man; *The Sporting Magazine*, for example, would use it in 1804 to describe Richmond himself.

If there is doubt about whether Richmond was the servant who Camelford threatened to send to parliament, then there is also significant debate about what the nature of his role in Camelford's household was. *Bell's Life in London* claimed Richmond worked for Camelford 'in the capacity of a teacher of gymnastics' rather than 'a menial servant', while other sources have described him as Camelford's valet, footman, minder and even bodyguard. Whatever his exact occupation, it seems that Richmond's first experiences of major pugilistic events, which came as a spectator, were a result of his association with Camelford, who was an enthusiastic patron of the sport. Camelford was frequently sighted at significant bouts, often seated on the top of his carriage and wagering huge sums on the outcomes, such as when he reportedly lost £1,000 to Berkeley Craven on the outcome of the Andrew Gamble versus Noah James bout in July 1800 at Wimbledon Common. Henning, who described Richmond as Camelford's 'faithful mulatto minder' asserts he was in attendance with Camelford at Gamble's next bout, a losing effort against the great Jem Belcher on 22 December 1800, which is the earliest direct reference to Richmond being a part of Camelford's retinue.[5]

Richmond's frequent attendance at prizefights in Camelford's company enabled him to become a recognisable face among 'the Fancy' – the random assortment of enthusiasts and patrons who fervently supported pugilism. However, when the opportunity next arose for Richmond to prove his physical worth, it would not be in the boxing ring. Instead it was in the unlikely environs of Camelford's lodgings at No. 148 New Bond Street, during an extraordinary series of events in 1801 in which Camelford's troublesome nature and his love of prizefighting intersected in tumultuous circumstances. On 13 July, Camelford and Richmond had been present at a contest between Isaac Bitton and Tom 'Paddington' Jones. To the delight of the crowd an unexpected supporting bout took place when Joe Berks, a butcher of imposing stature, emerged from the crowd and drunkenly attacked reigning English champion Jem Belcher, who was among the spectators. An unplanned twenty-minute brawl between the two men ensued, in which Belcher eventually got the better of his opponent by knocking him down, sending blood gushing from his upper lip and nose.

Sensing an opportunity, Camelford promptly offered to arrange a rematch between the men. To the crowd's delight both pugilists agreed and the second Belcher versus Berks contest instantly became one of the most eagerly awaited boxing events in years. Camelford was convinced that if Berks could survive for twenty minutes against the champion when drunk then he had the potential to depose him, so he took Berks under his wing, enlisted former champion Daniel Mendoza to train him and placed the challenger on a strict diet and training regimen. No detail was overlooked, with Berks ingesting 'raw eggs to improve his wind, and raw beef to make him savage'. By keeping Berks' thorough preparations under wraps, Camelford hoped to secure long odds on his charge and make a financial killing when, hopefully, he triumphed. The contest was set for 12 October 1801 at Enfield Wash to the north of London, hopefully out of the reach of the city's magistrates – prizefighting often being frowned upon by the authorities, even if it was patronised by many members of the aristocracy and reported eagerly and exhaustively in most newspapers.

As the fight neared, other matters also jostled for Camelford's attention. The preliminary signing of the Treaty of Amiens, announced on 1 October, had halted the War of the Second Coalition by brokering peace between Britain and France, causing a wave of jubilant celebrations throughout London. Camelford disapproved of the settlement, believing Napoleon could not be trusted. As a consequence, the delight with which the general populace greeted the treaty was a source of great irritation to him. While London rejoiced, Camelford returned to his lodgings in New Bond Street on 7 October, where he was confronted by his landlords who pleaded with him to place lighted candles in his windows, in deference to the illuminations that were springing up across London as an expression of joy with the peace settlement. To not do so, the landlords argued, would leave their property at the mercy of a violent and combustible mob who were circulating the streets enforcing the custom. Camelford scoffed at the suggestion, declaring that he was highly sceptical about the peace settlement (rightly enough as it turned out, for the two countries would be back at war by May 1803). Instead of deferring to his landlords' wishes he specifically ordered his servants *not* to place any candles in the windows of his rooms, declaring he would defend the property himself if necessary.

When the mob arrived at New Bond Street and witnessed what they perceived as Camelford's unpatriotic defiance they laid siege to the property. Accounts vary concerning exactly what happened, but Richmond certainly appears to have been instrumental in defending Camelford from serious injury or even death. *Bell's Life* later supplied an engaging version of how Richmond aided Camelford against the furious mob, admittedly with a few probably fictional flourishes:

In the course of the evening the mob paid him [Camelford] a visit, calling for 'lights,' and ultimately attempted to break his windows. Scarcely, had the first stone been thrown, when out sailed his Lordship, followed by Richmond, who had previously had his *cue* to follow *suit*, Lord Camelford commenced the attack with a broadside; he soon *floored* five or six of the mob, Richmond also dealing out some of Bob Gregson's *cristy casters*,[6] sending his opponents down right and left. A sort of panic immediately seized the mob, and it was the 'devil takes the hindmost,' in the twinkling of a moment.

The more contemporary account in *The Times* did not mention Richmond by name, but did stress the crucial role of Camelford's 'friends' in rescuing him from the mob and prevailing upon him to 'retire' back into his lodgings rather than continue the violent confrontation. Anticipating further trouble the following night, Richmond gathered a series of toughs, several prizefighters among them, from the taverns of London to form a protection squad. Many who enlisted already knew Camelford due to his pugilistic patronage and were happy to offer their services, particularly when 5s and a slap-up supper were dangled as an extra inducement. Around forty or fifty protectors were assembled by Richmond and, as night fell, the mob were duly discouraged from returning. Peace had been restored, although *The Times* noted drily, 'Is it not very strange that the public never hear of a certain Lord but in a riot or a duel?'

The incident also had an unforeseen effect on the Belcher-Berks contest, which was due to take place the following Monday. Camelford complained bitterly about the local authority's failure to protect his lodgings, and was preparing to sue them for the costs he had incurred from his landlords to repair the property. Infuriated by these complaints, the Bow Street Runners decided to vindictively stymie the plans for the fight; they arrested Belcher at Camelford's lodgings on Sunday evening and hauled him before the magistrates the next morning, whereupon he was forced to promise not to take part in the planned contest. The calamitous news only reached Camelford on Monday, as he had spent Sunday night at the Cocoa Tree Club, and it was therefore too late to alert the huge crowd that had assembled in Enfield. Only when Berks was stripped to the waist and ready for combat did spectators realise that Belcher was not present.

Camelford's betting coup would probably have failed in any case, for news of Berks' training regime had leaked, drastically reducing his odds. Besides which, Belcher had his number – the two men would fight four times in all, with Jem victorious on every occasion, solidifying his legend and recognition of his status as champion of England. Sadly, Belcher was forced to retire from the ring after a ball struck him in the eye and 'forced it out of its socket' during a game of rackets in July 1803. Camelford, awed by his achievements and saddened by this freak injury, helped set Belcher up as landlord of a public house on Wardour Street, and even gave him his prized fighting bull and terrier named Trusty, who he had bought from Col. Mellish. It was said that the dog had won 104 fighting contests without a single defeat. Renamed 'Belcher' in the champion's honour, Camelford declared 'two such invincibles would do well to reside together'.

As for Richmond, little is known of what occupied his days or thoughts for the two years after the New Bond Street skirmish of 1801. However the dramas of the prize ring that he had observed during his association with Camelford clearly stirred something in him, namely the more combative aspects of his character, which had lain dormant since those pugilistic encounters in York almost ten years earlier. Having observed at close quarters the vicissitudes and conventions of pugilism for several years, Richmond was keenly aware that, given the right patron and a series of sufficiently thrilling victories, financial riches and public adulation were an inevitability for a top prizefighter.

Weighed against the opportunity for fiscal advantage and sporting glory, though, Richmond also had to consider several other factors before he dared to 'throw his hat into the ring'. Firstly, there was the possibility of severe injury, or even death; as a trained cabinet maker, the risk of damage to his hands must have been a particularly grave concern for Richmond, while as the father of young children the possibility of leaving his wife a widow would also have been an acute worry. There was also the racial factor to consider. Although other black men had participated in pugilistic spectacles in England, the fact was that no black boxer had emerged to make a decent living from the sport.

Then there was the stark reality that Richmond, despite his excellent physical condition, was not a young man. Indeed, by 1804 he was already past his fortieth birthday, which made him a year older, for example, than the former champion Mendoza, who had been retired since 1795. Taking all these factors into account, a less self-confident and ambitious individual than Richmond would most likely have concluded that to embark on a career in the prize ring at such an advanced age was sheer lunacy.

However, Richmond never lacked for self-confidence and his debut in front of the Fancy would finally arrive on Monday 23 January 1804. By the time the sun had set at the end of that fateful day, Richmond had suffered arguably the greatest humiliation of his life, but had also taken the first crucial step on the rocky path to fistic glory.

6

Richmond Is 'Dared to the Field'

Before we turn our attention to Richmond's pugilistic debut, it is necessary to understand the forces that had, by 1804, enabled boxing to establish a significant position of pre-eminence and popularity within English sporting culture. During the latter half of the eighteenth century, the commercialism of sporting activities was advancing rapidly, one force among many that enabled boxing to become one of the cultural phenomena of the age.[1] Pugilism was a sport that united the twin concepts of 'pleasure and business' identified by Pierce Egan as the driving forces of life in Georgian England, with its participants and patrons predominantly gamblers pursuing the adrenaline rush of a successful wager, or thrill-seekers in search of the fame and immortality of sporting glory.

A further factor in the explosion of the sport's profile was the cast of larger-than-life characters who inhabited boxing, the exploits of whom made compulsive copy in the growing number of newspapers which absorbed so much of the typical Georgian citizen's leisure time. The expansion of literacy rates among the English population to an estimated 65 percent by the year 1800 created a huge demand for popular written material and the colourful rivalries that permeated pugilism invariably provided entertaining copy. *The Sporting Magazine*, which was founded in 1792, was the first journal to focus specifically on sporting and leisure pursuits, but virtually all local and national newspapers found space for accounts of pugilistic activities, even if their tone and attitude towards such spectacles was often disapproving.

Egan specifically identified the great rivalry between Daniel Mendoza and Richard Humphries, played out across a trilogy of fights from 1788 until 1790 – as well as in numerous published letters by both combatants – as a key component in popularising the sport. His analysis of this rivalry offers an insight into the confluence of forces that fuelled pugilism's rise:

The abilities of the two pugilists occasioned considerable conversation at that period, both in the BIG and *Little world*. The newspapers teemed with anecdotes concerning them; pamphlets were published in favour of pugilism; and scarcely a print-shop in the Metropolis but what displayed the *set-to* in glowing colours, and portraits of those distinguished heroes of the fist ... Boxing became fashionable, followed, patronized, and encouraged.

Fighting contests, of course, were nothing new. They had been part of the history of human behaviour since time immemorial, either as a means of settling personal disputes or a method by which one man asserted dominance, control or pride over another. However, there was something peculiarly English about the formalisation of the natural human instinct for violence into a sport, complete with its own rules and customs and, before long, recognition of one man among many as the 'champion'. As early as the 1600s impromptu 'boxing' contests on the streets of London had become a common sight, and a custom many foreign visitors found hard to comprehend. For example, the Huguenot refugee Henri Misson de Valbourg, visiting London in the 1680s, declared: 'any thing that looks like fighting, is delicious to an *Englishman*'.

However, it was not until the 1700s, and the arrival of the great pugilistic innovators James Figg and James Broughton, that street fighting began its transformation into the organised spectacle of pugilism. Figg opened the first indoor boxing arena just north of modern-day Oxford Street in 1720, although the contests he promoted and participated in sometimes utilised swords and quarterstaffs as well as bare fists. Broughton, an accomplished waterman who won Doggett's Coat and Badge race in 1730, fought many times at Figg's establishment, before he built and opened his own boxing amphitheatre on 'Oxford Road', not far from Figg's arena, in 1743, aided by patronage from the Duke of Cumberland.

In order to formalise the parameters for the contests that he promoted, Broughton met with several other pugilists to develop a set of rules for bare-knuckle contests, which would become widely accepted, with minor variations, as the standard rules for the majority of contests until the development of the London Prize Ring rules in 1838. The most significant of 'Broughton's rules', as they became known, ran as follows:

THE RING: RULES TO BE OBSERVED IN ALL BATTLES ON THE STAGE
I. That a square of a Yard be chalked in the middle of the Stage; and on every fresh set-to after a fall, or being parted from the rails, each Second is to bring his Man to the side of the square, and place him

opposite to the other, and till they are fairly set-to at the Lines, it shall not be lawful for one to strike at the other.

II. That, in order to prevent any Disputes, the time a Man lies after a fall, if the Second does not bring his Man to the side of the square, within the space of half a minute, he shall be deemed a beaten Man.

III. That in every main Battle, no person whatever shall be upon the Stage, except the Principals and their Seconds; the same rule to be observed in bye- battles, except that in the latter, Mr. Broughton is allowed to be upon the Stage to keep decorum, and to assist Gentlemen in getting to their places, provided always he does not interfere in the Battle; and whoever pretends to infringe these Rules to be turned immediately out of the house. Every body is to quit the Stage as soon as the Champions are stripped, before the set-to.

IV. That no Champion be deemed beaten, unless he fails coming up to the line in the limited time, or that his own Second declares him beaten. No Second is to be allowed to ask his man's Adversary any questions, or advise him to give out.

VII. That no person is to hit his Adversary when he is down, or seize him by the ham, the breeches, or any part below the waist: a man on his knees is to be reckoned down.

As can be seen from their minimal references to what violent actions were and weren't allowed in the course of a contest, fans of modern boxing would scarcely recognise pugilism as the same sport later practiced by the likes of Jack Dempsey, Joe Louis and Muhammad Ali. Not only did early pugilists fight without gloves, but practices outlawed in modern boxing, such as shoulder-charging and hitting on the back of the head, as well as a wide variety of wrestling holds and throws, such as the 'cross-buttocks', were all regarded as legitimate tactics. It was even considered acceptable to hold your opponent around the neck with one hand while hitting him with the other, a manoeuvre known as a 'chancery suit', a somewhat unsubtle dig at the notorious reputation of Chancery Lane lawyers.

Although Broughton's rules did little to make pugilism safer or its violence less extreme, they did at least provide a clear regulatory framework regarding timings and how fights were to be concluded, which immediately made the sport a more attractive prospect for gamblers as well as spectators, in much the same way that the formation of the Jockey Club in 1750 had lent a more consistent structure to horseracing. As the gambling culture surrounding the sport grew throughout the latter half of the eighteenth century, so too did pugilism's popularity, which, in turn, led the sport's legality and morality to become hotly debated. There existed a considerable body of opinion that pugilism was not merely a fleeting amusement and sporting pleasure, but a 'worthy' pursuit that elevated and enhanced the national character. The radical journalist William Cobbett was one such figure. In *Cobbett's Weekly Political Register* he frequently wrote or published articles defending the sport, one of which argued that 'nothing could be more injurious' to England than 'utterly eradicating' pugilism. The parliamentarian William Windham, who served as Secretary at War between 1794 and 1801, was another boxing enthusiast, arguing that pugilism was a crucial force in restricting the rise of 'effeminacy'. Windham often wrote or spoke in defence of 'manly sports', both in public and in private correspondence. For example, in a letter to James Boswell he argued that 'the manly and honourable spirit of our common people' was 'in great measure' produced by pugilism.

To the likes of Windham, pugilism was not just a sport, but also an essential method by which Englishmen were readied for combat with other nations, particularly France, with whom England was regularly at war throughout the latter half of the eighteenth century and the first fifteen years of the nineteenth century. Such patriotic rhetoric was also a key component of Egan's endorsement of pugilism; he argued that the sport was an expression of England's natural superiority, as well as an activity that tended to 'invigorate the human frame, and inculcate those principles of generosity and heroism, by which the inhabitants of the English Nation are so eminently distinguished above every other country'.

Simultaneously, though, pugilism was also an activity whose legality was questionable and whose morality was frequently questioned. Many members of the middle and upper classes were alarmed by the rise in popularity of boxing and other pursuits which they regarded as inherently frivolous. The Revd Edward Barry, in an influential 1789 pamphlet, argued that boxing was a 'direct violation of every law, of humanity, and common decency', and railed against its 'scandalous popularity'.

Objections to pugilism were not merely moral, but in some quarters were founded on concerns about the sport's economic and social effects, particularly on the 'lower classes'. Fears that activities such as boxing would encourage drinking, gambling and rowdiness were reflected in 1787 by a Royal proclamation issued by George III, endorsed by William Wilberforce among others, which sought to discourage 'excessive drinking, blasphemy, profane swearing and cursing' on Sundays, as well as 'dissolute, immoral or disorderly practices'. In the 1790s, with the frightening spectre of the events of the French Revolution hanging over the higher echelons of British society, it was inevitable that any activity that resulted in large gatherings of common folk, such as pugilism, would cause substantial societal unease.

However, contrary to popular myth, pugilism was not, in itself, technically illegal, there being no specific law explicitly prohibiting it. Nevertheless, it was the case that zealous magistrates opposed to the sport could, and on occasions did, prevent prizefights from taking place and brought cases to court in which pugilists were charged with 'breach of the peace', 'unlawful assembly', 'riot', 'fighting a duel' or 'assault'. Furthermore, any pugilist unfortunate or brutal enough to kill their opponent risked a charge of manslaughter. One famous case in 1803 saw Jem Belcher, Joe Berks, Joe Ward and Henry Lee hauled before the courts on various charges including 'breach of the peace'. Lord Chief Justice Ellenborough's summing up at the end of the case represented a succinct summation of polite society's main objections towards pugilism:

> This [boxing] is a practice certainly which must be repressed. It is infinitely mischievous in its immediate effect to the limbs and life of the combatants themselves. It draws industrious people away from the subjects of their industry. And when great multitudes are so collected, they are likely enough to be engaged in broils. It affords an opportunity for people of the most mischievous description to collect.

Such prosecutions were comparatively rare, however, and it has been estimated by Adrian Harvey that of the 500 or so prizefights that took place between 1793 and 1815, only fifteen were halted or prevented by the intervention of the authorities, although many more were forced to switch venues, or take place in secretive conditions in order to prevent magisterial interference. Some magistrates even turned a blind eye to pugilism completely and openly attended fights themselves, as Sir Henry Hawkins remarked: 'Society loved a prize-fight, and always went to see it, as Society went to any other fashionable occasion.'

Pugilism's contradictory status as both a celebrated and reviled pursuit was symbolised by the hypocritical attitude of many newspapers towards the sport. For example, *The Times* in 1790 went to great lengths to criticise the sport as 'barbarous and unnatural', ignoring the inconvenient contradiction that commercial pressures often meant they featured lengthy accounts of bouts in their own pages. In its previous incarnation as *The Daily Universal Register*, the journal had been more honest in its approach admitting 'this amusement is not of the most humane kind; yet, as a *fashionable sport*, it demands our notice.' Pugilism was most certainly fashionable; Egan noted that among its 'numerous splendid patrons' were 'the Prince of Wales, Duke of York and Clarence, Duke of Hamilton, Lord Barrymore, Alderman Combe, &c.'

Alongside horseracing, pugilism was the most popular sporting spectacle of the age, albeit a polarising activity within a society wracked by huge contrasts in wealth, status and moral attitudes. In *Life in London*, Egan frequently drew attention to the 'extremes' and 'contrasts' of Georgian society, particularly within London, remarking that the 'contrasts are so fine and delightful – so marked with light and shade.' It's an apt metaphor to describe England at this time, but it is also a description that we can apply to Bill Richmond's life and career, within which the opposing forces of respectability and civility, on the one hand, and sensation and disorder, on the other, constantly vied for supremacy. As an educated and well-spoken former protégé of an English nobleman, with a secure trade as well as an abstemious personality, Richmond was in many ways a respectable member of society, albeit something of a novelty due to his ethnicity, white wife and mixed-race children. However, within his character there also existed a wilder, more violent side, which drew him to pugilism, a sport that existed in the shady margins of society, in the murky intersection where the highest and lowest of social classes rubbed shoulders in mutual pursuit of pleasure, financial advantage and physical adventure.

By 1804, having accompanied Camelford to several prizefighting spectacles, Richmond's curiosity had been piqued and he harboured a desire to test his physical mettle in the ring. That day finally arrived on Monday 23 January 1804, while Richmond was in Camelford's company at Wimbledon Common for the contest between Henry Pearce and Joe Berks.[2] A typically huge and rowdy crowd had gathered that clear and crisp winter's day in anticipation of a feast of pugilistic activity. The *Ipswich Journal* estimated that there were around 5,000 spectators in attendance, a remarkable figure considering the location of the fight had only been determined at 11 p.m. the previous evening in an attempt to avoid possible interference from magistrates. The *Oxford Journal* set the scene for the day's proceedings masterfully:

> Every avenue to the scene of action was thronged with travellers of various descriptions; coaches, chaises, curricles, tandems, and buggies, were opposed by land carts, dust carts, mules, asses, and donkies; the finest flowers of road rhetoric were culled during the expedition; and had Demosthenes been living, the roaring of the sea could not have afforded him so fine a lesson of mob elocution ... The gentlemen who were so happy as to occupy a front row were compelled to sit down - the second row knelt - the third, fourth, fifth, &c. stood, all with hats off; next came the horsemen, and afterwards the carriages, universally covered with out-side passengers.

The excitement surrounding the Pearce-Berks fight was unsurprising, for it was a significant contest which most observers recognised as being for the Championship of England. With Belcher having retired, Pearce and Berks were the most logical contenders to tussle for the vacant crown;[3] the former was, like Belcher and future title-holder Tom Cribb, of solid Bristolian fighting stock. Nicknamed the 'Game Chicken', due to the fact his Christian name was often shortened to 'Hen', Pearce was a formidable fighter who had enjoyed considerable success in the West Country before heading to London. Egan assessed his strength as 'almost Herculean', while his stamina was 'truly excellent'. Although 'very illiterate', Pearce was renowned for his good nature and was 'generous to an excess'. He would later succumb to the temptations that have befallen sporting heroes for generations – namely 'copious libations at the shrine of Bacchus, added to the fond caresses of the fairer sex' – but would also prove his bravery when he risked his life to drag a servant girl from a burning building in 1807.

That was all in the future though; right now, in 1804, Pearce was at the peak of his pugilistic powers. Belcher had encouraged Pearce's claim for the title, most likely out of a sense of Bristolian loyalty, however Berks, by dint of his ferocious battles against Belcher, was also viewed as a top contender. A low-key and unsatisfactory contest between the two men in a private room in London had gone Pearce's way, but true supremacy could only be settled in public in front of the Fancy.

In the event, it was a dreadfully one-sided contest. During an hour and twenty minutes of fierce combat, the agile Pearce gradually gained the upper hand over his one-dimensional, albeit spirited, foe. By the twenty-fourth round 'streams of blood' were flowing from Berks' face 'as from a bullock' and by the twenty-sixth his condition was even more sickening, red blood staining his body, while both eyes were closed, his nose cut and his arms and ribs lacerated. Pearce bludgeoned his increasingly forlorn opponent for another two rounds, whereupon Berks was finally persuaded by his seconds to yield, and a jubilant Pearce celebrated his triumph by performing two somersaults and vaulting into a Hackney coach.

The bloody contest had exerted a magnetic hold on a rapt crowd, despite its one-sided nature. 'So great was the anxiety of many females,' remarked the *Kentish Gazette*, 'that they actually stood on the tops of coaches to witness the scene.' There was then a bonus for spectators as a second contest was brokered between George Maddox and Seabrook, a 'dustman' and, it was said, a former Berks victim. Maddox was a well-seasoned pugilist 'of fighting notoriety,' who, although nearly fifty, would the following year tussle with rising talent Cribb, giving him all the trouble he could handle. In the approximation of Egan, no less, Maddox was one of the finest pugilists to never win the English title. He was certainly far too accomplished for the over-matched Seabrook. In the third round, the Dustman was poleaxed by a massive blow to the stomach, whereupon he unconvincingly claimed his arm was broken and conceded defeat.[4] In the wake of Seabrook's abject surrender, it did not escape many spectators' notice that, despite his injury claims, he 'could count his money very well'. When he smiled at several of his friends in the crowd it was the final insult for many angry fans. Deprived of a bloody spectacle to rank alongside the Pearce-Berks battle, the Fancy made vocal their displeasure.

At this point, Richmond entered the day's drama. Distinctly unimpressed with Seabrook's efforts, he offered some 'warm observations' about the quality of the fight that had just unfolded. Maddox was somewhat put out by this intervention and, adrenaline still coursing through his veins, he immediately 'dared *Richmond* to the field'. A six-guinea-a-side purse[5] was hastily assembled, possibly on the promptings of Camelford, who most likely put up Richmond's stake.

Richmond quickly and eagerly stripped to the waist and entered the ring. If he was nervous he did not let it show, but he must have known that the odds were stacked forbiddingly against him; his minor skirmishes in York a decade previously were not, in any way, adequate preparation for a contest against an opponent as accomplished as Maddox. Richmond also knew that, at the very least, he needed to give a brave account of himself if he was to escape the opprobrium of an already inflamed crowd, for whom his black skin made him an easy target for jeers and catcalls.

Although not all contemporary reports made negative mention of Richmond's ethnicity, The *Oxford Journal*'s prose was noticeably tinged with racially charged sentiment, remarking that 'there was a singular contrast in their [Richmond and Maddox's] skins,' which were 'black and white, like the keys of a harpsichord'. The writer also commented on the temerity of a black man in daring to take on a white, noting that 'the indignation of the women was particularly roused on seeing a black man fighting a white'. *The Sporting Magazine* was similarly derogatory, refusing to refer to Richmond by his name, but instead using the racist appellations 'Massa' and 'Mungo'.

Despite Richmond's inexperience, it proved a keenly fought contest with both men, in the approximation of *The Times*, displaying 'a great deal of science'. The early rounds were tight, and distinguished by 'very sharp fighting' with both pugilists alert and quick-fisted. In the fourth round, Richmond gained the upper hand, connecting with a severe shot to Maddox's collarbone and knocking him down heavily. The *Oxford Journal* seemed particularly perturbed by Richmond's reaction to this, noting that 'the sable warrior smiled, and seemed to exult extremely over the other'. Such behaviour was not only contrary to the English liking for modesty and fair play, but would have been regarded as particularly impertinent coming from a black man involved in a contest against a white.

Richmond also knocked Maddox down to the end the fifth round, at which point the ringside betting odds were two-to-one in his favour. However, Maddox was nothing if not determined. His 'firmness of resolution and activity of body' enabled him to rally, forcing Richmond on to the retreat and, at the end of the sixth, Maddox nearly secured victory, when a 'cruel blow' to Richmond's stomach 'laid him down for dead'. Richmond only just staggered back to 'scratch' within the appointed time and the momentum was now firmly with Maddox. For the next two rounds Richmond was forced on to the back foot, while the more experienced man punished him severely.

In the ninth round the outcome of the fight was ultimately settled by two punches. Firstly, Richmond found a way 'between [Maddox's] hands', with a vicious and chopping shot which sent blood flowing from his opponent's forehead. Sensing the prospect of a sensational victory, Richmond momentarily lost focus; it proved a fatal error as Maddox steadied himself and countered with an extraordinarily vicious blow, which smashed into Richmond's forehead with destructive effect, opening a deep and dangerous cut over his left eye. Unsurprisingly, Richmond fell, 'clapped both his hands to the eye, and gave it in', probably fearful of the consequences for his eyesight if he continued. *The Sporting Magazine* delighted in Maddox's triumph, declaring tastelessly: 'Mungo could not endure any more *tumpers*; and, though he commenced as a *black*, was compelled to retire with a tinge of the *blue*.'

Richmond's dramatic gamble had failed. He had not only lost, but had also managed to squander a potentially winning position through an inexperienced over-eagerness to close out the contest. In an added humiliation, he had been defeated in front of both his employer and a hostile crowd. The courage Richmond had shown in recovering from a heavy knockdown in the sixth round, and the fact he had competed on even terms throughout with a much more experienced foe, were of scant consolation.

As the crowd rose to acclaim him, an excitable Maddox bellowed for a third opponent, but no one was brave enough to step forward so the day's pugilistic proceedings broke up amid typical chaos, with the restless crowd overturning a gig and cart before relative order was restored. As afternoon turned to dusk, the roads to London were blocked for several hours with the detritus of departing spectators, allowing Richmond plenty of time to reflect as he slunk home nursing his physical scars and wounded pride. He would have been forgiven for never returning to the prize ring again, however the sensational events of the next few months would turn his world upside-down, removing his livelihood and making a return to the ring, no matter how risky, a raging necessity.

7
Exit Camelford, Enter Cribb

With his first foray into the prize ring having ended in failure, options for Richmond within the field of pugilistic endeavour were limited. One significant obstacle was that black pugilists traditionally found it hard, if not impossible, to attract the wealthy patrons who could broker big fights and substantial purses. An illustration of this can be found if we turn to the *Daily Universal Register* of 27 April 1786, which carried an account of an unnamed black pugilist, identified only as a 'black stripling' and former 'servant of Mr. Katterselto', who defeated five men in a week, despite the contests being against 'young men of superior strength'. A white boxer who achieved such a remarkable feat would doubtless have advanced rapidly to a high-profile boxing career, but of this early and promising black pugilist no other references seem to exist.

It would take more than a spirited defeat against Maddox for Richmond to become the first boxer from a black background to break through the unofficial but still discernible 'colour barrier' of English pugilism. Even Richmond's social connections did not seem to offer much prospect of further patronage: Percy was too much of a humanitarian to ever become a patron of the prize ring and as for Camelford, he may have put up the modest stake that Richmond fought for against Maddox, but it was unlikely that he entertained the notion that his forty-year-old black employee might have a lucrative pugilistic future. Whether Camelford might have backed Richmond in any future sporting endeavours is a purely theoretical speculation, however, for less than two months after the events at Wimbledon Common, he was killed in a duel with Capt. Thomas Best – a dreadfully inevitable conclusion to his life given his hot temper and unyielding obsession with personal honour.

The circumstances by which the duel and Camelford's death at the age of just twenty-nine came about were ridiculous, even by the standards of surreal absurdity that characterised his short life. Best had been a close friend of Camelford's for several years and was a keen womaniser. One of his former conquests, Fanny Loveden, had subsequently become Camelford's mistress, without any apparent rancour between the men. In 1803, Fanny had married another of Best's friends, named Simmonds. The newlyweds had departed for the West Indies but Simmonds found his wife's conduct so 'unmanageable' that he summarily sent her back to England, where she once again became entangled with Camelford. By March 1804, Camelford was no longer romantically involved with Fanny, although he was still, with characteristic generosity, supporting her financially.

The events directly leading to the duel were ignited in an intense period of less than five days. On the evening of Saturday 3 March, Fanny ran into Best at the opera and asked him to 'accompany her home'. When Best refused, an outraged Fanny warned him that she 'would set Lord Camelford on his back'. The matter might have rested there, but Fanny decided to recount the incident to Camelford, emblazoning her account with fabrications and exaggerations; she claimed, for example, that Best had propositioned and insulted her, and that when she had invoked the name of Camelford for protection he had uttered the words: 'Lord Camelford may be damned!'

Predictably, Camelford's ever-present sense of self-righteous indignation was duly inflamed and he subsequently confronted Best at a coffee house on 6 March, accusing him of 'traducing my character'. Such conduct, Camelford maintained, led him to conclude Best was a 'damned scoundrel'. By this stage, Best's patience was exhausted and he was in no mood to apologise for things he hadn't said or done. Therefore, instead of attempting to broker some sort of peace, he challenged Camelford to a duel. It was a challenge Camelford readily accepted, despite Best's reputation as one of the best shots in England. Interestingly, *The Times* recounted that the two men had once had a wager that had rested on Camelford's skills as a marksman; Best had challenged him to extinguish a lighted candle at a distance of 10 yards by shooting a pistol. Although one shot had broken the candle, Camelford had lost the bet, a lack of pinpoint accuracy that proved a harbinger of events to come.

Absurdly, it was a duel neither man wanted or relished, but they continued to be propelled towards their violent destinies out of hot-headed stubbornness. Camelford was soon privately admitting that Best's claim that the contretemps was a devious manufacture on the part of Fanny was probably accurate (although for what purpose, aside from pure mischief, remains unknown).[1] However, ever conscious of his reputation, he believed that to withdraw would see him lose respect. Faced with a choice between possible death or being branded a coward, Camelford, without hesitation, opted for the former.

So it was that the two men met in the early hours of 8 March in the village of Kensington, near Holland House. Camelford was 'attended by [his] servants on horseback', although whether Richmond was among them is unknown. The servants of both men were soon ushered away to look after the horses, while Best and Camelford dismounted and wandered off down a country lane with their respective 'seconds', a Mr Nihell and Camelford's close friend Henry Devereux, to find an appropriate field in which to conduct the duel.

Twelve paces were duly measured out; the men took up their positions and the duel began. Camelford fired first but missed, his shot flying past Best's ear. In contrast, Best's aim was true and the 'instant [he] fired Lord Camelford fell at full length'. The guilt-ridden Best immediately ran towards the stricken Camelford. 'I hope you are not seriously hurt?' he asked, his concern reinforcing the futility of the whole enterprise, but it was too late – Camelford was seriously injured and already faint from substantial loss of blood. The coroner would later specify that Best's shot fractured a rib and passed through his right lung before becoming lodged in his spine. Despite being in considerable pain, Camelford reassured Best that he forgave him and believed his account of the incident with Fanny. With several concerned passers-by having arrived at the scene, Camelford then urged Best to flee.

For several minutes, Camelford languished on the ground, waiting for the medical attention he required. It was an inglorious but appropriately surreal endgame to a turbulent life; heavy rain had made the terrain swampy and wet, and Camelford's clothes were soon soaked, while water flooded his boots. A group of gardeners hauled him into a wheelbarrow and he was taken to a nearby house and laid in bed. When a surgeon finally arrived, Camelford's physical state was pitiable, but his spirit remained unbowed. He looked squarely at the surgeon and stated, plainly and without self-pity: 'I know I am a dead man ... tell me how long I have to live.'

With characteristic tenacity, Camelford clung to life until Saturday evening, when he finally died. Due to a codicil in his will added the night before the duel forbidding any of his relations or friends from pursuing a prosecution, Best escaped punishment for his role in the affair, although it was said that he was never the same man again after slaying Camelford, and that until his death in 1829 he habitually wore black gloves as a mark of his grief and regret.

Camelford's funeral took place early on 17 March. His body was placed in an elegant coffin, lined with white satin and covered with crimson Genoa velvet, before being deposited in the vault of St Anne's church, Soho after a procession through the streets of central London. It is reasonable to suppose that Richmond was in attendance as the sombre cortège made its way through the streets of Soho, which were still blanketed in darkness. Perhaps he was one of the principal domestics in the leading coach of six, or perhaps he was one of the two servants who followed the deceased's carriage on foot. Or maybe Richmond was just another anonymous face in the crowd, lost amid the multitude of mourners who gathered in the narrow streets to watch the sad procession, content to pay silent tribute to the man whose wild lifestyle had catapulted him in to the world of pugilism.

As *Bell's Life in London* later suggested it was a considerable blow for Richmond to have lost such a 'valuable friend', while Camelford's death also removed his main source of income and security. Suddenly and unexpectedly, he therefore faced an uncertain future. Surprisingly, given his frequent charitable endeavours, Camelford did not explicitly provide for his servants in his will, although it was reported that he had 'recommended [them] in a very particular manner to Lord Grenville' who had 'undertaken to provide for them'. There is no evidence that Richmond ever entered into Grenville's service or protection though. Instead, in the months after Camelford's death, Richmond's presence seems to have eluded the public record.

He emerged again in January 1805, working as a second at a boxing match between newcomer Tom Cribb and old foe George Maddox. Richmond's role at this contest suggests either that he was sufficiently impoverished to return to pugilism or that, having had an intoxicating taste of life amid the Fancy, he could not resist giving the sport another shot. Whatever his motives, it is probable that between January 1804, when he fought Maddox, and January 1805, when he seconded Cribb, Richmond was a frequent visitor to the Fives Court in Little St Martin's Street, the legendary venue just off Leicester Square which served as pugilism's unofficial headquarters.

With its high ceilings and capacity to cram around 1,000 excited spectators into its bricked interior, the Fives was where both prospective and renowned pugilists sparred, trained, issued challenges to each other and brokered deals for upcoming bouts, often under the watchful eye of 'Gentleman' John Jackson, the former champion and unofficial elder statesman of the sport, who was described by Egan as being 'the LINK' which kept the 'CHAIN of pugilism together'. Jackson maintained well-regarded training rooms at No. 13 Bond Street and it was apparently his idea, in the early years of the nineteenth century, to arrange displays of sparring with gloves at the Fives. Three shillings secured a standing ringside view for spectators, while more affluent visitors paid a guinea to sit in the gallery with the benefit of soft seating. As the bouts were exhibitions rather than competitive contests, they could take place free from any fear of magisterial intervention. To some, the Fives, which also played host to tennis and Eton 'fives', was a den of vice and iniquity; to others it was the most fashionable sporting venue of the day and a compulsory destination for anyone seeking to make a splash in pugilistic circles. Sparring against the wide range of opposition who populated the court, from great champions to novices, allowed a pugilist to fine-tune their skills and tactics, as well as increase their level of public recognition.

By the end of his life, Richmond had boxed for hundreds of hours at the Fives, honing and perfecting his skills, particularly his ability to box on the back foot and avoid the lunges of his opponents, whose larger statures often dwarfed his slender frame. Richmond built and consolidated his reputation at the Fives, and also proved himself an astute innovator of the conventions of the venue. Egan later credited Richmond with being the first pugilist to spar at the Fives while stripped to the waist, as well as suggesting he was responsible for the decision to place the ring on a raised platform so spectators had a better view of proceedings.

Exactly when Richmond suggested these innovations is unclear, but it is evident that throughout 1805 he was making a studied attempt to relaunch his pugilistic career and ingratiate himself within the Fancy. Initially, he focused his attention on building his reputation as a 'second', namely a trainer and corner-man, for other pugilists. Something of a natural at analysing fighters' respective techniques and at explaining the intricacies of the pugilistic arts to others, Richmond's services were soon in demand and he seconded Tom Cribb on two occasions – against Maddox in January and Tom Blake in February.[2] These contests allowed Richmond to observe at close quarters the unquestionable toughness and considerable 'bottom' of the man who would go on to become perhaps the most celebrated English fighter of the bare-knuckle era, and a man with whom Richmond would cross swords on many occasions.

The conventional interpretation of Cribb and Richmond's relationship is that it was mutually antagonistic from beginning to end, however this is not accurate: early in 1805, Cribb and Richmond worked together with notable success, as Cribb successfully won his first two bouts with Richmond in his corner. It was only later in the year that a rift seems to have opened between them, which was sealed by the bitter contest between the two men at Hailsham in October, and accentuated by the events surrounding the controversial Cribb-Molineaux contests in 1810 and 1811, for which Richmond was Molineaux's trainer and mentor. However, as we shall see, the animosity that built up between the men was later buried and they ultimately became close friends.

At which point, it is imperative for us to understand a little more about the mysterious background of Cribb, and how he rose to become one of the most feted boxers who ever lived. Like many of his pugilistic contemporaries, Cribb hailed from the environs of Bristol, a rapidly expanding industrial city and therefore the ideal breeding ground for powerful and hungry young men who wanted to fight their way out of poverty. Of humble birth, Tom was one of seven children born to George and Hannah Cribb in the mining village of Hanham on 8 July 1781. Little else is known of his early life, although it is generally accepted that he made his way to London as a teenager, whereupon he trained briefly as a bell-hanger and then worked as a coal heaver.

At this point two incidents apparently occurred in which Cribb demonstrated the resolve that would later be his abiding characteristic as a pugilist. Firstly, he was nearly crushed between two coal barges after falling between them, only to haul himself to safety and, secondly, he survived an accident when a 500-pound crate of oranges fell upon his chest. After the latter incident it was said he spat blood for several days. Subsequently, Cribb served for a time in the Royal Navy, although exactly where and when has never been definitively established. Whether any of these events actually happened, or were later embroideries of the Cribb legend once he became a national hero, it is hard to say. We can, however, state with certainty that it was in deference to his coal-heaving days that he acquired his famous nickname of the 'Black Diamond'.

By late 1804, Cribb had come to the notice of the Fancy, possibly after an exploratory visit to the Fives. His youth, fitness and muscular bulk attracted the excited interest of several patrons and he was provisionally matched with Joe Berks. When that contest fell through, Cribb was paired with Richmond's wily nemesis Maddox instead, despite the apparent conflict of interest aroused by the fact Cribb had at one point been trained by Maddox, the *Morning Post* even describing him as the 'pupil of his antagonist's'.

When he squared off against Maddox, Cribb was, like Richmond the previous year, a substantial underdog. He may have possessed a stout frame and imposing build, but he was unknown to the wider public and his pugilistic skills utterly untested. Despite his rapid crash course in boxing basics, most observers thought Maddox would prove too stern a test. Certainly, the majority of the established pugilists in attendance were keen to see Maddox triumph against the young upstart. 'All the pugilists of the old school backed him [Maddox],' noted the *Morning Chronicle*, [and] did every thing in their power to assist the veteran, and try to make him win.'

Such favouritism also extended to the rabidly pro-Maddox crowd who gathered at Wood Green, near Highgate on 7 January 1805. The majority of spectators had no idea who Cribb was and it was perfectly natural that they overwhelmingly favoured Maddox who was, after all, much beloved by the Fancy. There was, however, a small body of support for Cribb in the form of 'a few gentlemen of skill' who fancied that 'the youthful constitution and weighty arm' of the debutant might prove decisive, although, as the *Chronicle* noted, this band of men were 'too wise to lay odds' on a Cribb victory.

Cribb was undoubtedly grateful for the presence of Richmond in his corner. Despite the eighteen-year age gap between them, the two men had much in common; they had both overcome tough circumstances of birth to make it to the streets of London and were united by an ambitious desire to forge their reputation, and make their fortune, in the prize ring. Ironically, it was the black Richmond whose background had been the more privileged, given his association with Percy, whereas the white Cribb had grown up dirt poor and uneducated. Nevertheless, the union of two unknown novices who were both looking to gatecrash the pugilistic establishment made perfect sense. Neither, it should be noted, was Richmond's colour any sort of bar or disincentive for Cribb, whose conduct over the years would frequently and amply demonstrate that it made no odds to him what the colour of a man's skin was. There was also, of course, a sound tactical reason for Cribb to seek out Richmond's advice; the fact he had already fought Maddox, and given him considerable difficulties, meant that he was ideally placed to advise Cribb about the veteran's respective strengths and weaknesses.

As it transpired, Richmond's presence in Cribb's corner proved critical to the outcome of the fight. For an hour-and-a-half, in driving rain that soaked the combatants and the hardy spectators in attendance, the contest was desperately tight, with neither man asserting dominance. Cribb was the more frequent aggressor, although his blows were largely ineffective due to Maddox's defensive prowess; for example, the *Morning Chronicle* noted that 'though the coal-heaver made the most desperate heavy body blows at Maddox, he evaded the force of the greater part of them'. Maddox also landed his fair share of weighty shots though and – at first gradually and then more rapidly – these took a fearful toll on Cribb's face; one of his eyes began to swell and close as early as the fourth round and, when it subsequently closed completely, Cribb was forced to fight 'one-eyed' for around twenty minutes.

At this point, the contest took a potentially decisive turn; the force of a series of further Maddox blows 'closed up the other eye of his opponent', and suddenly Cribb was effectively fighting blind. The prospects for a Cribb victory now looked bleak and most spectators swiftly wrote off his chances, with the *Chronicle* declaring 'it was supposed by some that this [injury] must shortly terminate the battle'. It was here that Richmond proved his considerable worth; in between rounds, he furiously worked on Cribb's eye, succeeding in reopening it so that he could continue to fight. The *Chronicle* made it clear that Richmond's medical intervention was decisive in swinging the contest in Cribb's favour, noting admiringly that 'the exertions of the black recovered the sight of the first eye so completely, that Crib attacked the almost worn-out veteran, and put an end to the battle by repeated heavy body blows'. After nearly two hours of combat, Cribb was triumphant and Richmond's skill in marshalling his man to the finishing line did not go unnoticed among the admiring throng of the Fancy.

When Cribb returned to the ring the following month, on 15 February at Blackheath, it was no surprise that Richmond was once again in his corner. This time Cribb was taking on the sturdy Tom 'Tough' Blake, for an appetising purse of 40 guineas. After another hard-fought contest, Cribb was once again victorious, this time surmounting the considerable handicap of an injured right arm within the first fifteen rounds, which meant that thereafter he had to rely almost solely on his left arm. Blake was 'beaten pretty severely' and the contest in general, as well as Cribb's bravery, elicited admiring notices in the press: in the estimation of the *Morning Chronicle* 'few men have ever shown so much game as both parties did on this occasion'. Cribb was now the toast of the Fancy and a strong contender to face Pearce for the title. Since defeating Berks at Wimbledon Common the previous year, the Game Chicken had been active socially but absent in pugilistic terms. The *Hampshire Chronicle*, for one, reckoned that only Pearce could provide Cribb with a worthy challenge, declaring:

> Since young Crib gained the victory over Blake at Blackheath ... he has been looked up to as the champion of the day ... The only man who is thought able to cope with him is Pearce, the Game Chicken, who has received a challenge.

Talk of a Pearce versus Cribb bout ultimately came to naught though; Pearce instead defended his crown against Elias Spray in March and Tom Cart in April, contests which he won comfortably. In the meantime, if later sources are to be believed, Richmond also returned to the ring in April for his first outing since the Maddox defeat, winning a contest in just ten minutes against 'Whipmaker' Green in Islington Fields to the rear of White Conduit House on 12 April. Sadly, no descriptions of this fight seem to exist, save for these bare facts.[3] Of more certain provenance was Richmond's following contest, which came about on the same bill as Cribb's bout on 21 May against Isaac 'Ikey' Pig,[4] a Jewish boxer who had been billed, somewhat hyperbolically, as the 'Jewish Ajax'. Cribb, for this somewhat bizarre inter-faith battle, was described, courtesy of the *Morning Chronicle*, as the 'Ulysses of the Christians'. Given the success of their previous two collaborations, it is somewhat surprising that for this contest Richmond did not act as Cribb's second. Perhaps the two men had, by now, fallen out, or perhaps, now that he was a highly touted prospect, Cribb was seeking to surround himself with better-connected members of the Fancy than a relatively unknown black American. This latter theory gains some weight when you consider that, for his contest against Pig, the experienced pugilist and expert second Tom 'Paddington' Jones was in Cribb's corner, while other influential members of the Fancy, such as the wealthy Scottish patron Fletcher Reid and former champions John Jackson and Jem Belcher, were also in attendance at Blackheath to run their expert eye over Cribb's form.

If Cribb did dispense with Richmond's services it would have been natural for the American to harbour some resentment given the key role he had played in Cribb's first two pugilistic triumphs. Such a theory might go some way to explaining what happened next: Cribb duly defeated Pig, but only after twelve unsatisfactory rounds when the Jewish fighter quit, citing a sprained wrist, despite the fact he had just knocked Cribb down. The crowd were disgusted, and jeered their disapproval; in particular 'those who had laid money on the Jew' were 'very much dissatisfied at his giving in at a time when he had knocked down his antagonist, and was able to walk in a strong, upright manner out of the ring'.

Despite winning, Cribb's image as the new force in bare-knuckle boxing had taken a considerable knock. At which point, with boos still echoing across Blackheath, Richmond put himself forward to take part in a further contest against another Jewish boxer, named Youssop. Exactly how the contest was arranged is unclear, but we can assume that the opportunity to upstage Cribb was too delicious for Richmond to pass up. A small 10-guinea stake was collected and, surrounded by the great and good of the Fancy, as well as a disgruntled Cribb, Richmond stripped to the waist and prepared to fight.

For a wide range of reasons – including his loss against Maddox, the recent death of Camelford, the hostility of the unsettled crowd and the widespread presence of pugilistic royalty at ringside who could make or break his career – it was a fight that Richmond quite simply could not afford to lose.

8

'The Crowd Were Very Clamorous Against the Black'

As Youssop and Richmond stepped into the roped area on Blackheath and appraised each other it was obvious that the crowd's sympathies overwhelmingly rested with the former; the *Morning Chronicle* report makes this clear, declaring that 'though the fight was very fairly and impartially managed by those who had management of it, the crowd, both Jew and Gentile, were very clamorous against the black'.[1]

The fact that the crowd's anti-black sentiment was stronger than their anti-Semitism is telling. Anti-Semitism was fairly commonplace in Georgian England; indeed, Jews had only been informally welcomed back into the country by Cromwell in the 1650s, having been expelled by edict of Edward I in 1290.[2] However, although Jewish people living in England were often treated with suspicion and labelled with centuries-old stereotypes, the majority possessed a higher status than most black citizens. The resettlement in London of many wealthy Jewish traders and financiers from cities such as Amsterdam had ensured that Jewish settlers in England were able to form a more cohesive community than England's black citizens.

It undoubtedly helped that there were no legal grey areas when it came to the status of Jews who arrived in the country, unlike the uncertainties that many blacks had faced, even in the wake of Mansfield's judgement in the Somerset case. As Todd M. Endelman explained: 'Jews born in England or her colonies were considered citizens of the state; those born abroad enjoyed almost as many rights. Granted, they suffered from some political and civil disabilities, but their legal position was not much worse than that of other non-Anglican minorities.' There was even an established boxing tradition among the Jewish community – the former champion Daniel Mendoza, for one, was Jewish, and from the reports of the Youssop versus Richmond fight it is clear there were many Jewish fans in attendance at Blackheath that day.

In contrast, no reference is made to there being any black fans present to support Richmond. Once again, newspaper coverage of the fight also revealed substantial prejudice against Richmond, who the *Star* newspaper labelled as 'Blacky' and 'Mungo'. If Richmond was to defeat Youssop, the intimidating and uncomfortable truth was that he would not only have to overcome the personal demons and doubts engendered by his reverse against Maddox, but he would also have to do so in the presence of an unremittingly hostile crowd.

Although it was a mere fifteen minutes in duration, the ensuing fight was characterised by intense action and vicious violence. Indeed, so fast-paced and thrilling was the encounter that it completely over-shadowed Cribb's disappointing display. 'This battle lasted only about a quarter of an hour,' the *Morning Chronicle* exclaimed excitedly. 'But the blows were by far more numerous, and of more serious consequence, than the former [contest between Cribb and Pig]'. Youssop was a doughty customer, already 'well-known as a fighting man among the Jews' and, emboldened by the crowd's enthusiastic support, he assumed early control, keeping Richmond off balance with neat boxing skills while also expertly blocking his attempted counter-attacks. The *Chronicle* report captured the intensity of the fierce and meaty exchanges, noting the preponderance of genuine knockdowns as opposed to slips, shoves or deliberate falls: 'neither fell without being fairly knocked down, except once that the Black's foot slipped'.

The third round was particularly torrid for Richmond as, looking to build on his early ascendancy, Youssop increased the tempo and frequency of his attacks. Such was the ferocity of the ensuing assault that Richmond was nearly beaten out of the ring. As the start of the fourth round neared, Richmond looked on his way to a second successive defeat, and the likely end of his pugilistic career. But then something both significant and strange occurred ... The *Chronicle* noted, with an air of mystery, that: 'between that [the third round] and the fourth, he [Richmond] received some instructions from one of the most experienced and lively pugilists of the present day. He made good use of the advice he got.' Frustratingly, the identity of this mysterious pugilist is not specified in any accounts of the fight, although it is probable that it was one of three men who were in attendance: Tom 'Paddington' Jones, who had earlier seconded Cribb; former champion Jem Belcher, who Richmond would have known from his association with Camelford; or John Jackson. All three men's elevated standing within the sport fulfils the criteria of the *Chronicle*'s description, however the likeliest candidate of the three is probably Jones, who would second Richmond on several occasions in the future, including his very next contest. Having said that, if the mystery advisor was Jackson then it would add credence to the theory that Richmond had already begun sparring at the Fives prior to this date, in which case his boxing skills, sophisticated deportment and enterprising spirit had perhaps already caught Jackson's discerning eye.

Regardless of who the mystery tactician was, of more importance was what his intervention represented. Significant moments in the history of sport that also stand as landmarks in human progress often consist of grand gestures, mighty victories or rhetorical flourishes; for example, Jack Johnson's victory against Tommy Burns to lift the World Heavyweight Championship, the Brooklyn Dodgers' decision to break the segregation of Major League Baseball by fielding Jackie Robinson, and Muhammad Ali's principled refusal to be drafted by the US Army during the Vietnam War. However, history can also be made with small gestures, or simple acts of kindness whose symbolism can only later be fully appreciated, and this was such an example, for the advice that Richmond received that afternoon was not only a crucial moment in his career but also a landmark moment in the history of black participation within pugilism and, by extension, English sport and society as a whole.

Previous to this day, Richmond had taken an interest in boxing, but the Fancy had shown little reciprocal interest in him. Now, though, for the first time, the pugilistic establishment had taken serious notice of a black boxer; by intervening with a few encouraging words, this mystery advisor had ignored the colour of Richmond's skin, and instead judged him on his sporting potential. In doing so, pugilism had taken a tentative step towards the far distant goal of equality – the sort of step that English society as a whole was also making as the abolitionist movement continued to gain momentum and public support. For the first time, a black boxer was being drawn into the protective bosom of the Fancy, rather than being made the object of its scorn or mockery.

Re-energised by such encouragement, Richmond strode out for the fourth round with renewed purpose. Freed from the shackles of nervousness and over-eagerness that had inhibited him versus Maddox and for the first four rounds against Youssop, Richmond was now light and confident on his feet, and ruthless in the execution of his skills. Allowing Youssop no space to manoeuvre, he launched a series of vicious attacks against his surprised and soon outgunned opponent. Within a few minutes, and after just two more rounds of combat, Youssop had been beaten nearly senseless by Richmond's 'repeated desperate blows'. At the end of the sixth round, the slaughter finally ceased; the Jewish boxer was 'totally disfigured' and 'compelled to yield, after very brave resistance'.

Although the winning purse was a mere 10 guineas, a jubilant Richmond was entitled to feel a great degree of satisfaction with his afternoon's endeavours; not only did he have a handsome victory to his name, but some of the most respected figures within pugilism had been present to observe it.

To add to the sense of poetic perfection, he had totally upstaged Cribb with a performance of ring-craft and controlled violence far superior to that of his much-vaunted rival. Most important of all, though, Richmond's physical feats had won him acceptance within the Fancy.

Confirmation of Richmond's newfound recognition arrived soon after. Among the impressed spectators at Blackheath had been influential patron Fletcher Reid. The Dundee-born Reid was typical of the sort of upper-class gentleman who frequented the sport. Effortlessly wealthy, thanks to his landed family who owned a string of estates in Scotland, Reid was described by William Oxberry, a prominent actor and boxing writer of the period, as 'one of the greatest patrons of gymnastic genius'. Reid had previously backed and supported a wide range of top fighters including Mendoza and Belcher, and was renowned as a compulsive gambler. After witnessing the impressive demolition of Youssop, he decided to add the name of Richmond to this illustrious roll call, throwing his financial weight behind the black boxer by brokering a contest for 50 guineas against Jack Holmes at Cricklewood Green on 8 July.

It was an unprecedented achievement for a black boxer to be backed by a patron as significant as Reid, and to be fighting for such a handsome reward, albeit still some way short of the purses habitually earned by the top white fighters.[3] Furthermore, unlike his impromptu and haphazardly arranged bouts against Maddox and Youssop, Richmond's bout with Holmes was not a supporting contest but the sole attraction which would draw spectators and gamblers to Cricklewood. In a further demonstration of the fact that Richmond was now being taken more seriously, *The Sporting Magazine*, whose descriptions of his previous fights had been littered with unflattering racist epithets and snide jokes, now treated him as a legitimate pugilist, rather than as an easy target for strained puns. They set the scene for the fight thus:

> Holmes first entered the list of pugilists in a very hard battle with Blake, about a twelvemonth since, and he was considered a slow, but a bottom man. Richmond first had a taste with George Maddox, at Wimbledon, which gave him but small hopes of pre-eminence in the art of boxing: he however since fought a good battle with a little Jew on Blackheath, when he manifested improvement in the art ... He is a quick, hard hitter, but his bottom has always been doubted.

Despite his victory against Youssop, Richmond was regarded as the underdog. The *Morning Post* shared *The Sporting Magazine*'s doubts about Richmond's 'bottom' and reported that the contest began with Holmes a six-to-four favourite. It seemed that Richmond's decision to withdraw from the fray against Maddox, despite the severity of the blow that had forced his surrender, had engendered doubts about his capacity to endure a long contest. In contrast, Holmes was renowned for his durability; he had displayed huge courage in an epic defeat to Tom Blake in January 1804 and was reckoned by Egan to be a '*bit of stuff* that might be depended upon'. Holmes was therefore fancied to successfully weather Richmond's early assaults and outlast him. The common and offensive stereotype that black fighters often quit when the going got tough also, no doubt, had something to do with the favouritism extended towards Holmes.

There was certainly a lot riding on the outcome of the fight; whichever of the two men triumphed would be among those jostling for position as potential contenders for champion Pearce's crown. A second eye-catching win in a row for Richmond would put him in a similar position to Cribb, who was also hopeful of a title shot, while there were putative whispers about the appeal of a Richmond versus Cribb match-up. No wonder that Cribb was among the fascinated spectators who eagerly surrounded the 20-foot ring as Richmond and Holmes prepared to square off.[4]

The contest began at 11 a.m. and lasted, depending on which source you consult, anywhere between thirty-five and fifty minutes – approximately three times the length of Richmond's victory against Youssop.[5] However, where that contest had been an oscillating battle in which Richmond had eventually wrested the initiative from his fast-starting opponent, the Holmes bout was a one-sided slaughter from first punch to last. As many had speculated, Richmond did indeed start fast, the precise and hurtful nature of his punches opening a severe cut over Holmes' eye in the very first round.[6] It was a precursor of what was to come, as a ruthless Richmond dominated his increasingly demoralised foe. Tellingly, *The Sporting Magazine* noted of the seventh and eighth rounds that Richmond was 'gay and full of fight', in contrast to Holmes who was 'inclined to puff'. Laughably, despite Richmond's evident superiority, the odds-makers stubbornly persisted in favouring Holmes – surely, they reasoned, 'the black' would begin to tire, and then Holmes would assume control? Only after ten successive rounds of Richmond dominance did the ringside odds shift and become even, before moving inexorably in Richmond's favour.

The eleventh round was a thriller as Holmes, realising he needed to do something to halt his slide towards humiliation, attempted to rally. For a while, the two men stood toe-to-toe and flailed savagely at each other. However, any notion that Holmes was dragging himself back into the contest was soon shown to be illusory; Richmond was by now confident that his opponent was neither quick nor powerful enough to hurt him, while his own punches were beginning to exact an appalling toll. The eleventh ended with Holmes toppling wearily to the floor after a maelstrom of rapid Richmond punches. As Holmes fell, Richmond instinctively leapt over his stricken opponent in order to avoid stepping on him, an impressive display of athleticism and sportsmanship that underlined his utter superiority.

Richmond boxed cautiously for the next few rounds, continuing to wear down his opponent's resistance. *The Sporting Magazine* observed that rounds seventeen to twenty-four were 'bad, hugging rounds' but, far from being bogged down in attrition as this comment suggests, Richmond was merely conserving his energy for a final assault. The cumulative effect of his punches had already wreaked savage punishment on Holmes' face which was now 'dreadfully punished ... both his eyes being laid open'. Having eased up for a few rounds, Richmond had replenished his reserves of stamina and decided it was time for a final flourish; in the twenty-fifth round he looked sharp and full of vigour before placing a dramatic full stop on a performance of utter dominance by knocking Holmes down to end the twenty-sixth round. With blood dripping from his face, his eyes stinging and his body a mass of painful welts and bruises, Holmes could see no rational reason to get up again and 'after lying a few minutes, he with great reluctance gave in'.

Richmond's dazzling performance, a perfect cocktail of sound tactics and controlled violence, had fully justified Reid's faith in his fast developing talents. From first round to last, it had been an utterly dominant performance; Richmond had not only demonstrated physical superiority, but acute tactical and technical skill too. The *Morning Post*, in its dissection of the contest, could not help but be impressed: 'Holmes ... had not a shadow of chance from the time of setting to; *Richman* always rallied, and at other times shifted from him. Whenever Holmes hit, he generally hit short, and received a handsome return; and at other times, when he put in a blow, it was often with an open hand.' *The Sporting Magazine* was somewhat blunter in its appraisal of the victor's superiority and the defeated man's flaws: 'The Black won from his superior length of arm, wind, and activity; Holmes being short in the reach, and by far too fat.'

Impressively, Richmond's fighting style had, in the space of just three contests, evolved into a coherent pugilistic philosophy. With his comparatively slender build, Richmond knew that he could not contend on an equal footing with the sturdiest physical specimens of the day. Instead, he realised (with unusual prescience, given the similar tactics employed over a hundred years later by Jack Johnson and Muhammad Ali) that speed, athleticism and defensive ring craft were crucial to his pugilistic success. Rather than stand in front of an opponent and trade blows in a macho display of power, as he had fatefully done against Maddox and as many of his contemporaries assumed was the only route to fistic glory, Richmond realised that his interests, and self-preservation, were best served by boxing on the retreat. To do this, he utilised his footwork to evade the lunges of his almost invariably clumsier opponents, and then relied on his considerable speed of hand and thought to score with damaging counter-punches.

Egan later acknowledged that Richmond's mastery of defensive boxing, or 'milling on the retreat', helped to transform the perception of what constituted effective pugilistic tactics. Writing in 1818 he declared that Richmond's success 'decided the advantages of *milling on the retreat* towards victory.' Defending such a style of boxing against charges that it was 'unmanly', Egan cited an apt analogy, namely that of a fencing match, declaring: 'Would it not be absurd to say to a man, whose only care is the preservation of his life – "You must not avoid your enemy's sword by changing your ground; you must not make use of that activity of which you are capable, because it is unmanly"'.

His fistic philosophy thus established, Richmond would pursue the noble ambition of 'hitting and not being hit' – the aesthetic peak of the pugilistic arts – for the rest of his career. It was a style that he would perfect to a level that most of his contemporaries could only dream of, as Egan would later rhapsodise: '[Richmond] stands nearly unrivalled, and is considered to excel every other pugilist in hitting and getting away.' Even more impressive, Egan emphasised, was the fact that Richmond's 'theoretical and practical' knowledge of pugilism and his pursuit of aesthetic perfection was 'completely intuitive, having never received any lessons from any of the professors'.

However, for all its acuity, Richmond's counter-punching philosophy possessed a potential flaw: yes, such tactics had proven effective against a fighter such as Holmes, who marched relentlessly forward and was unable to adapt his style to any other circumstance, but how would Richmond cope if he came up against *another* counter-puncher, rather than an honest workhorse who merely stood in front of him, like a human punch-bag? Before the year was out, he would discover the painful answer.

9

Bitter Tears for Bill

While Richmond waited for a new opponent to emerge from boxing's assembled ranks of toughs and strongmen, the Fancy were aflame with excitement about an approaching pugilistic spectacle. Having returned to the ring with two easy wins against unchallenging opposition, champion Henry Pearce was keen for a more lucrative assignment; his desire was rewarded when Fletcher Reid hatched an ambitious master plan for a fistic extravaganza the likes of which England had never previously witnessed – namely, a multi-bout event featuring three eagerly-awaited match-ups involving six of the era's top fighters.

The planned date for this 'rich treat for the admirers' of pugilism was Saturday 20 July, less than two weeks after Richmond's victory against Holmes. The star attraction, naturally, was Pearce, while his opponent was to be one John Gully, a twenty-one-year-old Gloucestershire butcher's son whose youthful obsession with boxing had seen him neglect the family business and subsequently be imprisoned for debt. While in jail Gully had been visited by Pearce and the two men had shared a lively sparring session. On the basis of this, as well as his formidable reputation in his native county, Gully was reckoned to be a sound match for the champion. Emboldened by his performance in sparring, Gully was confident that he could become the first man to defeat the Game Chicken. Reid was similarly convinced; when he heard how well Gully fared against Pearce, he had settled Gully's debts, secured his release from prison and set him up in a training camp. Thus was launched one of the more remarkable careers in English sporting and political history, a career which would ultimately see Gully accede to the status of English boxing champion, own a string of top racehorses (which would win the Derby, St Leger and the 2,000 guineas among others), as well as serve as a member of parliament for Pontefract between 1832 and 1837.

To supplement Pearce versus Gully, further contests were also arranged involving two more of Reid's stable of fighters: Tom Belcher, younger brother of former champion Jem, was paired with Samuel 'Dutch Sam' Elias, a Jewish fighter reckoned to be the hardest puncher in the business, while Bill Ryan, a hard-drinking young Irishman with a swagger in his manner, was matched against wily veteran Caleb Baldwin. In order to maximise the performances of his charges, Reid left nothing to chance, spiriting the trio into intensive training camps for several weeks in Virginia Water and Epsom Downs.

Unfortunately, no sooner had 20 July dawned, than the planned day of 'grand and classical' combat descended into farce and confusion. Fearing local magistrates might disapprove of the intended festival of pugilism, the plan had been for the fighters and spectators to gather early in Virginia Water, and then find an appropriate site where they might fight in peace, with the first contest due to begin at 8 a.m. The Fancy, as well as many current and former pugilists – Jem Belcher, Mendoza, Cribb and Richmond among them – duly assembled at first light, having travelled down from London the evening before. An unseemly scramble then ensued to hire horses from local farm hands to aid with transportation to Bagshot Heath, which it had been determined was a safe site for the fights. Soon the roads around Virginia Water were characterised by disorder, the hoards of spectators on horses and in carriages creating a cloud of dust so huge that it was, according to *The Times*, 'impossible at times to see a yard before the horses heads'. Unsurprisingly, a rash of accidents occurred, and the roads were soon 'strewed with the wreck of broken gigs, buggies and carts'. In one such incident, the carriage Dutch Sam was travelling in overturned, and he suffered a leg injury that was sufficiently serious for him to withdraw from his contest against Belcher.

Amid the chaos, the masses made for Bagshot Heath in the fervent hope of finally getting the day's events under way, only for magistrates to send them packing. To try and salvage the event, a twelve-mile trek over the Surrey Hills was now necessary, ending just beyond Blackwater in Hampshire, now 32 miles from London. Throughout the morning's wanderings, various disputes had arisen and rumours of corruption and double-crosses were rife; some contended that a certain Mr Chertsey had suspiciously placed large bets on both Pearce *and* Gully to win, while others were convinced that a betting scam had preordained the outcome of the big fight, or even that it had been secretly decreed that all three favourites were going to lose. Faced with such rumours and suspicions, nervous bookmakers announced all bets were void, prompting an exasperated Reid to declare that, in that case, Pearce versus Gully was cancelled. It was left to Baldwin and Ryan to save the day but, by the time he was called to scratch, Baldwin – due to some mysterious 'accident' – was also nowhere to be found.

A day that had aimed to celebrate fistic endeavour and skill had, instead, encapsulated the sport's worst flaws, from the ever present threat of magisterial intervention to the petty squabbling over money that often characterised pugilism's patrons and fans. Desperate to salvage something from the wreckage, a compensatory contest was rapidly arranged between Cribb and a fellow Bristolian by the name of George Nichols. The latter's ring experience was limited but he was well built, muscular and, most important of all, willing to fight. Nevertheless, the still undefeated Cribb was installed as a heavy favourite to win the 40-guinea purse (assembled via a ringside collection of spectators and patrons) and cement his position as one of the leading contenders for the championship.

As the bout unfolded, though, Cribb's ambitions of manoeuvring himself into a challenge for the highest pugilistic honours gradually unravelled. From the outset, he was perplexed by Nichols' awkward style, particularly his habit of 'breaking', a tactic whereby he pushed his arms forward suddenly into Cribb's face whenever his opponent shaped to swing a large blow. To add to his woes, Cribb was severely cut under his right eye early on. By the twentieth round, the eye was completely closed and Cribb was tired and frustrated. In contrast, Nichols was confident and dominant enough to engage in showboating – the *Chronicle* noting that he was 'frequently pointing his finger and lolling out his tongue at Cribb'. Despite several gallant attempts to force his way back into the fight, Cribb was felled by a mighty Nichols blow in the fifty-second round; exhausted after an hour and ten minutes of Nichols' relentless aggression, he promptly conceded.

Although Cribb had looked unimpressive in his previous contest against Ikey Pig, it was still a shocking and unexpected reverse. In mitigation, his cause wasn't helped by the fact that he had apparently been up drinking the night before and had walked several miles before the contest began (although the latter presumably applied to Nichols too). In later years, Cribb's supporters, seeking to embolden his case to be recognised as the greatest of all champions, would either overlook the Nichols reverse, seek to airbrush it from history or explain it away with myriad excuses. Easier to do that, perhaps, than admit that their man had lost fair and square.[1]

Richmond, having observed Cribb's defeat from ringside, was as shocked as anyone at what had unfolded, as well as ever alert to an opportunity to upstage Cribb and reinforce his own reputation. Therefore, as a further contest began between two unknowns, Richmond entered into feverish negotiations to attempt to broker a match-up involving himself and an unidentified white man. It had been less than two weeks since he had vanquished Holmes, but Richmond was keen to maintain the momentum his career had suddenly acquired. Ultimately he was to be disappointed though, as the proposed fight fell through: 'either sufficient money could not be made up,' the *Chronicle* claimed, 'or the terms could not be agreed.'

Despite Richmond's failure to arrange a further fight, the day's tumultuous events had left both him and Cribb with plenty to ponder as they, and the rest of the Fancy, embarked on the arduous journey back to London. Gradually the notion seemed to crystallise in both men's minds that a contest between the two of them made perfect commercial and pugilistic sense. A significant and rousing victory for either man against the other would undoubtedly propel the victor into title contention, although this enticement had to be measured against the prospect that defeat would, in all probability, be fatal to their chances of ever becoming champion.

Ultimately, having assessed the ratio of risk to reward, both Cribb and Richmond, to their credit, elected to favour ambition over caution. Terms were duly agreed for a 25-guinea contest and Cribb versus Richmond was announced as the supporting bout for the rearranged Pearce versus Gully contest, due to take place in Hailsham, Sussex on 8 October. The news was announced in several newspapers, including the *Morning Chronicle*, who noted that the early betting favoured Cribb: 'Young Cribb is backed by a military Gentleman to fight Richman, the noted black. Three to two on Cribb.'

It was a measure of Richmond's progress that he was described as 'the noted black' rather than 'Mungo' or some other racially dubious soubriquet. Although his chances of defeating Cribb were being assessed as slight, Richmond was well accustomed to being in the position of underdog. No one had fancied him to succeed against Maddox, or even to make as much of a fight of it as he did; he had braved a hail of spectator abuse against Youssop, and Holmes had been favoured to make mincemeat of him. On each occasion Richmond had, to varying extents, proved his critics wrong. Perhaps this installed in him a surfeit of confidence, for accepting the Cribb fight was to prove a rare miscalculation.

The fight was scheduled to begin straight after the Pearce versus Gully contest and, in the event, the direct comparison between the bouts was not to Cribb and Richmond's benefit. For sixty-four thrilling rounds, Pearce and Gully knocked each other as close to unconsciousness as is humanly possible; in contrast, for an hour-and-a-half Cribb and Richmond bored the fast dwindling number of spectators who had stayed to see them do battle into a state of somnolence. Gully proved as fierce a competitor as his backers hoped, succeeding, through an arresting combination of bravery and savage hitting, to convince the awestruck spectators 'of his manhood'. After twenty rounds, with Pearce unable to see and bleeding heavily, it even looked like he might succeed in wresting the title from the Game Chicken's grasp.

However, over the next few rounds, Pearce showed considerable courage to regain the initiative. After thirty-seven rounds, blood was flowing freely from Gully's ear, and his head had begun to swell hideously. Somehow, Gully survived until the sixty-fourth round when finally, and reluctantly, he conceded. By this stage Pearce himself could scarcely see out of either eye, although, remarkably, he still 'appeared quite fresh'. The Game Chicken, with the consummate sportsmanship for which he was renowned, shook Gully's hand and told him 'You're a damned good fellow, I'm hard put it to stand; you are the only man that ever stood up to me.' Even *The Times*, usually sniffy and condescending in its attitude to pugilism, seemed excited about the contest, as well as the calibre of fans in attendance, noting, 'The company was of the better order, and not molested by the rabble who frequent the fights nearer to town. Amongst the company present were some of the first characters of the kingdom. The Duke of CLARENCE was a spectator on horseback.' It was somehow appropriate that Royalty, in the form of the aforementioned Duke, later to become King William IV, was in attendance, for the Pearce-Gully contest was one of the defining moments of English pugilism – it was a fight that contained everything the Fancy admired: action, honour and sportsmanship.

As a patriotic celebration of the sturdy and virile virtues of English manhood, the fight could not have been better timed. As it was unfolding, Lord Horatio Nelson and his fleet were lying in wait for the French and Spanish in Cádiz; two weeks later he would stun them with his innovative tactics in gloriously leading the British fleet to triumph in the Battle of Trafalgar, albeit at the cost of his own life. Egan, among many others, would later draw a connection between the spirit demonstrated in memorable pugilistic contests such as Pearce versus Gully and great British military victories like Trafalgar and Waterloo, arguing that 'athletic sports ... inspire additional confidence and courage in the breast of a soldier'.

Before Cribb and Richmond emerged with the impossible task of trying to top the drama of Pearce and Gully, there was still one final act of magnificent pugilistic theatre to enjoy; with the spectators still ablaze with excitement, and large wagers and wads of cash still being exchanged, the great Jem Belcher swaggered forward in a determined fashion. Apparently envious of the attention being lavished on his former protégé Pearce, and despite the fact he only had the sight of one eye, Belcher challenged Pearce to meet him in the ring within two months for 500 guineas in order to settle who the true 'Champion of England' was. Pearce accepted, and the contest was declared on. The enthusiasm and excitement for this match-up of undefeated fighters was unparalleled, mainly because both men had a valid claim for the championship – Belcher had never lost his title in the ring, while Pearce had secured impressive victories against leading contenders Berks and Gully.

While excited speculation concerning Pearce versus Belcher swept through the crowd, Cribb and Richmond entered the ring, their presence barely causing a ripple of interest. Their contest, which had appeared so tantalising on paper, would prove to be the very definition of anti-climax. 'At any other time,' remarked Oxberry. 'A contest between these heroes would have demanded the greatest attention, but so highly were the minds of the amateurs engrossed by the merits of the first contenders, that little notice seemed to be paid to the present battle.' Part of the problem was that, in terms of their pugilistic styles, Cribb and Richmond were a horrible fit. Both men were predominantly counter-punchers, and, with so much at stake, they appeared nervous and inhibited. As round after stultifying round unfolded with barely a significant exchange of action or a clean punch being landed, neither man proved willing to take the fight by the scruff of the neck and abandon their usual style in favour of a more attacking approach. As a consequence, the crowd soon lost interest, and many drifted away before the fight had concluded with a Cribb victory.

Unsurprisingly, the newspaper reports were universally damning in their tone. 'It would be insipid for us to enter into particulars respecting this fight, which, if it may be so called, lasted nearly an hour and a half,' claimed *The Times*. 'It was altogether tiresome; the Black danced about the ring, fell down, &c. while Crib through fear or some other motive, declined *going in* and beating him off hand. It was altogether an unequal match; and an interval of twenty minutes together elapsed without a blow of any consequence being struck.' Despite his inherent caution, it is clear that Cribb's advantages in strength and youth were decisive to the outcome of the contest. The sketchy newspaper reports offer little detailed explanation of how the fight unfolded or ended, or even how many rounds it lasted, however, it appears that either Richmond was gradually worn down by Cribb and gave up, or that he was persuaded to yield the fight once it became clear he simply could not defeat his opponent. 'Crib beat him without a hurt,' *The Times* concluded in a report as light on detail as all the regional press, including the *Hampshire Chronicle* which dismissed the contest as 'altogether tiresome'. The *Oxford Journal*, after an excited and exhaustive account of the Pearce-

Gully contest, didn't even see fit to give Cribb and Richmond a mention. Perhaps the most illuminating comment was in the *York Herald* which noted, interestingly, that Richmond was 'obliged' to 'yield to the superior strength and science of his antagonist', implying perhaps that members of the Fancy simply lost patience with the fight and persuaded Richmond to concede.

However the fight ended, it would remain a stain on Richmond's career, and a stick which his more virulent and bigoted critics would use to beat him with in future, for example, Oxberry in 1812 and John Badcock in 1826 would use their accounts of the fight to belittle Richmond in terms that unequivocally drew a connection between his counter-punching, light on his feet style and his ethnicity. 'Richmond hopped and danced about the ring, sometimes falling down, at others jiggling round somewhat in the style of an Otaheitan dance,' Oxberry declared. Badcock would trump even this lazily offensive invective by condemning Richmond's 'frolic of blackey' as 'mere burlesque ... [which] ought not to have been tolerated one minute'.

Cribb came in for plenty of criticism too, but at least he had a win to celebrate, albeit a tarnished one. For the forty-two-year-old Richmond though, defeat was a devastating blow. His victories against Youssop and Holmes had won him the sort of widespread fame and recognition rarely extended to 'men of colour' in Georgian England, with the details of his thrilling pugilistic exploits having featured in the pages of newspapers up and down the land, from London to York and Bath to Ipswich. However, on the biggest pugilistic stage he had yet inhabited, in close proximity to one of the most celebrated prizefights of all time, and against a rival with whom he shared a prickly rivalry, Richmond had, quite simply, failed to perform.

As this uncomfortable reality, and the probable ruination of his prize-fighting career sunk in, Richmond began to cry. 'Poor Richmond,' the *York Herald* lamented. '[he] was so affected by his defeat that he wept bitterly.' So upset was Richmond as he shed those bitter tears, that he would not throw another competitive punch for almost three years.

Unbelievably, almost inconceivably, Richmond's comeback, when it finally arrived, would see him embark on one of the most remarkable runs of fistic excellence the prize ring had ever seen.

10

'The Dexterity of His *Coup de Main*'

If there was one consolation for Richmond in the wake of his defeat at the hands of Cribb it was that his peers within the prize ring did not abandon him. Pugilists, beneath their macho bluster and posturing, understood better than anyone else the considerable reserves of bravery that were required to engage in combat within the hallowed and unforgiving confines of the roped square and, as such, the tiresome nature of Richmond's contest with Cribb was easily forgiven, if not forgotten. Petty rivalries and jealousies might often divide boxers, but the community of pugilists, of which Richmond was now an accepted member, maintained a consistent and discernible, if unspoken, sense of brotherhood. Once you were a member of that brotherhood, as Richmond now was, you remained so for life.

As a consequence, although he had thus far failed to advance to the highest level as a boxer, Richmond's standing within pugilistic circles, forged by his victories against Youssop and Holmes and his appearances in exhibitions, remained considerable. The loss against Cribb had certainly not damaged his reputation as an excellent second or tarnished his charisma. Therefore, although Richmond did not engage in any prizefights in 1806 or 1807, he remained a regular participant in the benefits that continued to draw large crowds to the Fives Court. April 1806 saw him exhibiting his skills against Tom Belcher at a benefit for William Ward and Daniel Mendoza in front of around 700 spectators, while in June, Richmond sparred with Bill Ryan at a benefit for Elias Spray and John Gully. When it became clear that Ryan was drunk and disruptive, Richmond even assisted in throwing him out of the event.

A further illustration of the fraternal but also combustible nature of the pugilistic community was in evidence later that month, when former title challenger Joe Berks was indicted for snatching a five-pound note from a man named Thomas Ruddy and giving him a counterfeit note in return. Richmond was among the group of pugilists, which also included Jem Belcher and Cribb, who attended the Old Bailey in a show of solidarity with the hot-headed Berks. Such support did not prevent Berks from being found guilty of larceny, though, and he was imprisoned and sentenced to be transported to Botany Bay.[1]

In October 1806, Richmond and Cribb also found a strange way to supplement their income when they became briefly entangled with the political scene after being hired as enforcers for politician and playwright Richard Brinsley Sheridan. The Irish-born Sheridan, famed for plays such as *The School for Scandal*, was competing against Sir Samuel Hood and James Paull in the Westminster parliamentary election. The poll lasted several days, with the candidates appearing at several hustings. Such events, with their fervent political manoeuvring, were always on the verge of descending into chaos, and so it proved with this election. By the eighth day of polling, Sheridan was trailing in third and last place and in danger of not being elected. Out of desperation, he employed some dubiously undemocratic tactics by enlisting a group of bruisers, nicknamed 'Mr Sheridan's *Forty Thieves*' to help intimidate his rivals' supporters; this group of 'thieves' included both Cribb and Richmond. On 11 November, when Sheridan was challenged at a hustings by a '*narrow-faced* Orator, from Coventry', Cribb duly removed the dissenter from the hall 'and took him in triumph to the watch-house, where he was immured in the same apartment with one of Citizen Cribb's valiant friends, *Richmond, the black pugilist*'. Richmond encountered some resistance, with *The Times* noting that he was 'taken into custody ... for splitting the nose of one young man, and nearly chopping off the tongue of another, by the dexterity of his *coup de main*.' Presumably, he was released without charge, as the matter doesn't seem to have ended up in court, a somewhat typical conclusion for an assault case during a period of history in which theft of property was considered a far more serious offence than violence between individuals. Such strong-arm political tactics were clearly considered fair game in Georgian England, and didn't harm Sherdian's cause, as he ultimately succeeded in being re-elected.

The timing of Richmond's association with Sheridan is fascinating, for the 1806 general election was the last national poll before the landmark Slave Trade Act received parliamentary assent in 1807, an act which abolished the slave trade within the British Empire, even though it did not abolish slavery itself. As a former slave, it certainly made sense for Richmond to support the election of Sheridan who, although more widely renowned as a playwright, drunk and superlative parliamentary wit, was also an ardent abolitionist.[2] The growth of abolitionism, which had accelerated after the formation in 1787 of the Committee for the

Abolition of the Slave Trade, had coincided with Richmond's time living, working and rising to pugilistic prominence in England and had undoubtedly aided him and other black citizens in their battle for societal acceptance. Besides his support of Sheridan there is no other explicit evidence linking Richmond with the campaign, but the success and increasingly high profile of his career undoubtedly provided a potent symbol and example of a well-educated, articulate and successful role model for other black citizens to look up to. Furthermore, Richmond's impressive deportment and smooth social skills (his personality was invariably described in flattering terms such as 'lively' and 'entertaining' by Egan) also succeeded in sending a message to white society that black men were not the unrefined, uneducated brutes of common stereotype.

Richmond's growing popularity among the general public was nowhere better illustrated than before the second John Gully versus Bob Gregson fight in May 1808. As the crowd gathered, Richmond was given the responsibility of being the 'public face' of pugilism, by standing at the Magpye Inn and directing spectators to the planned site of the battle at Ashley Common, on the border of Bedfordshire and Buckinghamshire.[3] Richmond, always a natty dresser, was the perfect choice to attract the attention of the crowd and he made quite an impression as he stood proudly and decisively directing and marshalling spectators while attired extravagantly in 'a blue coat, white waistcoat and pantaloons and a white hat lined with green'. Before the day's contests began, a parade of prominent pugilists took to the centre of the ring to milk the audience's applause and adulation – Richmond was right there among them in the centre of that ring, Oxberry noting that it was 'impossible to describe the pleasure that beamed in the eyes of every spectator at this moment, and the welkin re-echoed their repeated plaudits'. To complete a busy day's work, Richmond worked in Gregson's corner for the fight.

By this stage, the ownership of the English Championship had become a somewhat complex and tangled web. Henry Pearce had duly subdued the comeback of the envy-ridden and one-eyed Jem Belcher with an eighteen-round victory in December 1805. However, in the wake of winning universal acceptance as champion, the still undefeated Pearce had embarked on a drunken circuit of the country's fleshpots and alehouses, and was soon in no condition to participate in a prizefight. The title therefore lay dormant throughout 1806 and most of 1807 as constant talk of a rematch between Pearce and the gallant Gully came to nothing, despite apparent agreement of terms on several occasions. Pearce eventually resigned the title in September 1807 when he withdrew from yet another planned date to face Gully. By now the Game Chicken was but a shadow of his former formidable self and suffering from the early effects of tuberculosis. Recognition of the title of champion therefore passed, by general assent, to Gully, whose claims were reinforced when, in October 1807 and May 1808 (in the contest aforementioned) he twice defeated the giant Lancastrian Gregson in convincing fashion. After the latter contest, Gully publicly confirmed that he too was resigning the title.

A month earlier Richmond himself had returned to the prize ring, the uncertainty surrounding the championship having doubtless encouraged him that there were myriad opportunities for pugilistic honours, and maybe even the chance to engineer a shot at the title. His comeback began with a bout on 14 April 1808 on Epsom Downs. Amusingly the *Morning Post* declared of the day's fights: 'We regret to find, that another of these disgraceful exhibitions was yesterday permitted to take place so near the Metropolis,' before somewhat undermining the validity of their disapproval of the 'disgusting scene' with an exhaustive account of the contests in question. After Jem Belcher's brother Tom had defeated Dan Dogherty in a one-sided contest for 50 guineas, Richmond took on a man only identified in contemporary reports as a 'West countryman' for a subscription purse, namely a collection of small contributions from assorted patrons. Egan, in *Boxiana*, would later describe what is probably the same contest, although he claimed erroneously that it took place in 1809, identifying Richmond's opponent as being from Nuneaton and named Carter.[4]

As was often the case, Richmond, due to his slender frame, began the fight at a considerable disadvantage, with 'his adversary being a man of size and strength much superior to him'. Early on, Richmond struggled; indeed, Egan claimed that after four rounds, he was on the verge of losing:

> In the fourth round the odds ran so high against RICHMOND that twenty to one was sported that Carter won the battle, and ten to one that BILL did not come again. This great odds was occasioned by a severe blow that RICHMOND received on the side of his head, that rendered him nearly senseless.

By using his movement and defensive skill, Richmond gradually turned the fight around, succeeding in making his opponent frequently miss and gradually lose heart and energy. Newspapers also commented that his opponent was so full of 'gaiety' and 'bravado' that he wasted precious energy showboating to the crowd; in the latter stages of the fight, he proved more successful in this endeavour than in actually hitting Richmond. Once Carter was worn out by continually swinging and missing, Richmond assumed control and began to connect at will with a succession of hard and chopping punches.

The *Kentish Gazette* also described an interesting passage of what seemed to be a bad-tempered contest: 'The countryman, who appeared rather tired, stood and sparred with his adversary, when he met Richman's science by some severe left-handed facers, which ultimately so much displeased him, that he took Richman by the legs and hit him over his head.' Once Richmond gained the advantage, his opponent's bravado and energy evaporated and he quickly gave up. Such a rapid concession persuaded the *Morning Post* that the West Countryman had a 'little of the white feather' about him, a slang term for cowardice. Ironically, Egan claimed that Richmond himself was abused throughout the fight with accusations of possessing a 'white feather', and that when the fight ended, he took it upon himself to confront his heckler:

> Immediately upon [the fight ending] ... RICHMOND jumped over the ropes, and caught hold of a man, denominated *china-eyed Brown*, threatening to *serve him out*, (if he had not been prevented,) as it appeared that *Brown* had loudly vociferated, during the time RICHMOND was suffering from the effects of the above blow, that BILL *had got a white feather in his tail*!

As well as proving this particular spectator wrong, Richmond had, at nearly forty-five years of age, begun his comeback in winning style, and the restoration of his pugilistic reputation was under way. In the wake of this victory, Egan describes two other Richmond triumphs, which probably also took place in 1808, although accounts of these bouts do not seem to have appeared in any of the local and national press at the time, so they should perhaps be treated with caution:

> In seconding a baker a few months after the above circumstance, near Willesden Green, a man of the same trade, weighing close upon seventeen stone, challenged RICHMOND on the spot, when a *turn-up* commenced, and in about two minutes the baker's *dough* was so well *kneaded*, that he would have no more of it at that time; offering to fight RICHMOND for £50 in a month, which was agreed to by BILL, and two guineas put down to make the bets good before that period - but the baker, it appeared, preferred losing his two *quid* than submitting his overgrown carcass to the *punishment* of RICHMOND.
>
> BILL fought a man of the name of *Atkinson*, from Banbury, at Golder's Green, near Hendon, a barge-man, for a subscription-purse: it was a good fight, but in the course of twenty minutes *Atkinson* was perfectly satisfied the chance was against him, and acknowledged that he was beaten.[6]

While Richmond was relaunching his prizefighting career with this trio of triumphs, albeit against low-level opposition, another familiar face had also returned to active pugilistic duty. Tom Cribb, Richmond's old friend and antagonist (it was never quite clear which description was more fitting), was also keen to fill the void left by Pearce and Gully. However, after his defeat against Nichols and unsatisfactory showing against Richmond, his career had stalled somewhat, and the early hopes the Fancy had harboured that he would prove worthy of the mantle of Mendoza, Jackson and Belcher was looking somewhat far-fetched.

Slowly but deliberately, though, the determined Cribb had set his mind to pugilistic and physical improvement. In this cause he had been aided immeasurably by the fact he had attracted the attention of an influential and beneficent patron in the form of Capt. Robert Barclay Allardice, one of the legendary figures of the Georgian sporting world. Of wealthy and aristocratic stock, Barclay was the Laird of Ury in Aberdeenshire, and was renowned for his love of walking, boxing and betting. His remarkable feats of 'pedestrianism' would win him much fame and a considerable fortune too, such as in July 1809 when he walked a mile every hour for an astonishing 1,000 hours in a row, winning 1,000 guineas in the process. He would eventually secure even greater riches through his association with Cribb.

Barclay had been a close friend and associate of pugilistic patron and fellow Scot Fletcher Reid, who had maintained a stranglehold on the majority of English title fights since the days when Mendoza was champion. However, on 24 January 1807, Reid, aged just thirty-two, had been found dead in his apartment in Shepperton after a night drinking to celebrate the inheritance of several estates from his recently deceased mother. Barclay, with a typical lack of sentimentality and surfeit of business sense, put his grief to one side and manoeuvred himself into position to assume Reid's mantle. In a conversation with Barclay, John Jackson had apparently commended Cribb's potential to him and Barclay acted promptly on Gentleman John's advice, putting up 200 guineas to match Cribb against the great Jem Belcher in April 1807. Alongside Bill Ward, Barclay personally supervised Cribb's training for several weeks. Many thought that Barclay had taken leave of his senses in throwing Cribb in with Belcher, albeit a diminished and one-eyed Belcher who had suffered a hiding against Pearce. 'It has been a matter of surprise to many that Capt. B. should have ventured to have backed Crib against so celebrated a professor as *Belcher*,' declared the *Morning Post*. 'When Belcher's prowess was at its zenith, it would have been farcical to have matched Crib against him.'

In fact it was a canny piece of promotional wizardry: the art of a boxing promoter is in making the ideal fight at the ideal time and Cribb-Belcher fit the bill perfectly in terms of re-establishing Cribb's reputation without undue risk; Cribb's intensive training and extraordinary ability to absorb punishment, coupled with Belcher's decline and disablement, meant the fight was eminently winnable. The fact Belcher was still seen as a giant of the sport also meant that defeating him would earn Cribb plenty of plaudits. Interestingly, Richmond was enlisted alongside Ward as one of Cribb's seconds, the first time he had been in the latter's corner since the Blake contest in February 1805, although personal relations between the two men remained frosty.

As the fight unfolded its vicious drama in front of a huge crowd at Moulsey Hurst, Surrey it initially looked as though Barclay might have erred in his judgment. Belcher, in a performance redolent of his pomp, summoned the memory of past glories and utilised all his considerable skills to outbox the less experienced Cribb. When the latter was heavily knocked down in the eighteenth round a sensational Belcher victory looked likely. However, unbeknownst to the majority of the spectators, Belcher had injured his right arm[7] and was fast running out of energy. Thereafter Cribb, showing improved science and skill and his customary heart, inexorably wore Belcher down and triumphed after forty-one tough rounds. The victory was not without controversy, however. Egan, for one, later claimed that some sneaky gamesmanship by Ward had effectively rescued Cribb from defeat after a knockdown, probably a reference to the end of the eighteenth round:

> Before the strength of *Jem's* right hand had left him, the battle was saved to CRIBB by the following manoeuvre of *Bill Warr* - the odds were five to one on *Belcher*, and while *Gulley*, who seconded *Jem*, was offering the above odds to *Warr*, at the conclusion of a round, when CRIBB had received so severe a blow that he could not come to time, *Warr*, on accepting the bet, insisted that the money should be posted, and by this stratagem gained more than a minute, sufficient time for such a *glutton* as CRIBB perfectly to recover in.

If Egan's account is accurate, and Ward wangled more than a minute for Cribb to return to scratch rather than the regulation thirty seconds then Belcher was cheated, plain and simple, despite Egan's diplomatic deployment of the euphemisms 'stratagem' and 'manoeuvre'. It was not the first or last time that allegations of foul play would be levelled at Cribb and his connections, although it should be emphasised that contemporary reports make no mention of the incident. Nevertheless, the suspicion lingered that Cribb's association with the wealthy and influential Barclay, who often wagered heavily on Cribb winning, was to his benefit whenever he found himself in a tight spot. Instead of any controversy surrounding the eighteenth round, most newspapers focused on analysing the reasons for Cribb's incredible improvement. The consensus was that his rapid development was a consequence of the 'lessons he has received from Bill Ward and the amateur who backed him [Barclay],' as well as the high quality sparring he had been engaged in.

Despite his victory, it was obvious Cribb still needed some seasoning, so Barclay ensured that he was enlisted as a sparring partner for Gully as he prepared in Eastdean for his October bout with Gregson for the vacant title. Meanwhile, Richmond was holed up in Brighton assisting with Gregson's training. After Gully's thrilling thirty-six-round victory – which was so savage that the two men were reduced in the latter stages to slugging each other 'like two helpless men inebriated' – Richmond travelled to Cambridge with Tom Belcher, one of his closest friends among the pugilistic corps, for one of the stranger interludes in his career. The intention was to make some money out of teaching undergraduates at Cambridge University how to box. However, the university authorities soon intervened and Richmond and Belcher were forced to return to London, as the *Hampshire Chronicle* recounted:

> Several persons having lately taken up their residence in the town of Cambridge, for the purpose of teaching the young members of the University the art of boxing, the Vice Chancellor and Heads of Houses, issued a notice, in which they, in strong terms, declare their disapprobation of the same, and that any of the members found offending, will be proceeded against with the utmost severity. Since the above resolution, Tom Belcher and Richmond the Black, have left the place.

Four months after his ill-fated spell in Cambridge Richmond returned to the prize ring against the 'West Countryman', in the bout described earlier in this chapter. Cribb was also soon back in action, a month after Richmond's comeback victory, with a confidence-building bout against an overmatched George Horton, a curtain-raiser to Gully's second victory against Gregson. Cribb vanquished Horton with ease and, no sooner had Gully's retirement been announced, than Capt. Barclay made an aggressive move on the championship, putting up a 500-guinea stake for a Cribb versus Gregson battle with the title at stake. Barclay's coup was far from unanimously welcomed by Cribb's rivals, Richmond chief among them, but in the absence of any formalised governing body to determine exactly what was, or wasn't, an English Championship contest, there was little anyone could do.

The bout was duly scheduled for October 1808. To add a soupçon of extra spice to the occasion, Richmond seconded Gregson, and the two men spent several weeks in the Isle of Wight sparring and training, while Barclay prepared Cribb in Croydon. Still smarting at his defeat by Cribb three years previously, Richmond was, by all accounts, desperate for his rival to be defeated. He was also keen to continue his own comeback by fighting on the undercard of the main event and, throughout the autumn, attempted to find a suitable and willing opponent. Promisingly, a butcher from Kent named Barnes emerged as a possible foe and a group of patrons in London signalled their willingness to back him for 100 guineas, which would have been the largest purse Richmond had ever fought for. However, in early October the contest collapsed, as the *Kentish Gazette* explained:

> *Jem Belcher*, the pugilist, is lately returned to London from Margate, where he has been training a butcher from Canterbury, of the name of *Barnes*, preparatory to a battle for which he was matched with *Richman* the Black, and which was to have taken place after the *set-to* with *Crib* and *Gregson*. *Barnes* had been backed for 100 guineas by some London amateurs, the deposit of 20 to be made before fighting. *Belcher* was sent down to *try* as well as to *train* him; but he proved so inferior, that *Belcher* could beat him easily with gloves on, and consequently the deposit has been forfeited, and the match is off.

Presumably, Richmond collected the 20-guinea forfeit, but it was scant compensation for losing the opportunity to impress on the undercard of a championship fight. Attempts to broker a rematch with his old foe George Maddox also failed to bear fruit, and Richmond was therefore in a dark mood when the Gregson-Cribb contest began. His spirits didn't improve over the next thirty-six minutes as he was forced to watch his greatest rival accede to the status of English champion, at the expense of the luckless Gregson, who in his third title fight in succession yet again failed to win. Cribb signalled his willingness to go to war from the very start, adopting a fighting pose the instant the two men had shaken hands. Gregson battled with alacrity, but Cribb, who was often forced to box on the retreat or cover up against the ropes, maintained a narrow edge throughout. Both men shipped significant punishment, and at the end of the twenty-second round Cribb was knocked down heavily and looked vulnerable. However, in the following round it was Gregson whose resistance finally dissolved when he was wrestled heavily to the floor and was severely stunned after landing on his head. Lying on Richmond's knee between rounds, as was the custom, Gregson's head slumped worryingly on to his shoulders and he failed to make it back to scratch.

Cribb was now the champion of all England; 'it was probably the happiest moment of Crib's life,' argued *The Times*, while noting he was so exhausted that he only 'had just animation enough to hear the news'. Richmond, for one, found it hard to believe that Cribb – the man whose clumsy lunges he had evaded with relative ease in Hailsham, and the man who had lost to the unheralded Nichols – had scaled the summit of pugilism's greatest peak. As Cribb celebrated, Richmond failed to control his frustration and offered some choice observations about Cribb, possibly focusing on Ward's alleged shenanigans during the Belcher contest. Cribb, muscles and veins bulging aggressively, didn't take kindly to Richmond's sentiments, as *The Times* noted: 'Crib offered to fight Richman the black, who had offended him, for 50 guineas, without putting his shirt on, in the same ring where he had conquered Gregson.'

Richmond declined the offer. His rivalry with Cribb was brewing promisingly, but he reasoned revenge could wait for another day. When such a day did arrive, as he was firmly convinced it would, Richmond also believed it should come with a far higher price tag attached.

II

'Native Valour'

The life of a Georgian pugilist was a strange and somewhat uncertain existence. As we have established, boxers were simultaneously feted and reviled and, whether for the purpose of approval or condemnation, the public's voracious hunger for details of the fistic exploits of Belcher, Cribb, Richmond et al was fuelled by the press, whose pages regularly reverberated with accounts of their heroics or misdeeds, as well as excited speculation surrounding potential future match-ups and even, on occasion, gossip concerning their lives and activities outside of the ring. As a result, pugilists found themselves in the somewhat disconcerting position of being household names, yet few, if any, among their number could rely solely on their exploits in the ring for their livelihood. When big fights came around, the financial rewards could be lucrative, but such occasions were not frequent. Certainly, the riches any fighter won in the ring, even if they succeeded in gaining the hallowed laurels of the championship, paled into insignificance compared to the vast sums wagered by the fabulously wealthy patrons and members of the nobility who brokered the fights in the first place.

During the years 1803–15, with the Napoleonic Wars raging, earning as much money as possible was a particular imperative for pugilists as they, like their fellow citizens outside of the moneyed classes and aristocracy, had to cope with a harsh economic climate, which had led to rapid rises in the costs of essential items such as bread and other foodstuffs. In order to supplement their prizefight income, many boxers would tour towns and cities and charge spectators a fee to view an exhibition of their pugilistic skills; such events might take place in gymnasiums, local theatres or even in the streets or on local commons. Other pugilists offered boxing tuition to members of the upper classes, John Jackson and Richmond being particularly successful and renowned examples of what Egan termed 'professors of the gymnastic arts' – both men, it was said, tutored the renowned Romantic poet Lord Byron, as well as a wide variety of nobles and prominent gentlemen. Other boxers turned their hands to writing self-defence manuals or autobiographies, such as Daniel Mendoza, whose book *The Art of Boxing* was published to widespread interest, or pursued business interests or occupations outside of the sport. Cribb, for example, was a coal heaver and then a coal merchant, while Jem Belcher, during his short-lived retirement, opened a public house, an occupation many of his peers, including both Cribb and Richmond, would also later adopt. Be they butchers, bakers or bargemen, there were many pugilists who maintained their original trades throughout their fighting careers, while others branched out in unusual directions, such as Tom Tring who was an average pugilist but frequently in demand as a life model for artists, including Sir Joshua Reynolds.

In economic and educational terms, Richmond possessed distinct advantages compared to many pugilists: not only was he a trained cabinet maker, but he was also able to read and write, meaning he was far better qualified, and more literate, than many of his peers (Maddox and Pearce, for example, were both illiterate). To what extent Richmond continued to work as a cabinet maker during his boxing career is unclear, but it is certainly the case that he was frequently on the lookout for creative ways to earn extra income, hence, for example, his unsuccessful sojourn with Tom Belcher to Cambridge University at the end of 1807.

A further example of Richmond's entrepreneurial spirit occurred in January 1809, when he hatched a quite bizarre and highly dangerous moneymaking scheme, as detailed in the *Kentish Gazette* of Friday 20 January 1809:

> A rencontre of a curious nature is about to take place between Richman the Black, and a Bear; the former is to be armed with a quarter-staff, and the latter, who has been for some time in training, to make him as savage as possible, is to meet his antagonist unmuzzled, and quite at liberty. Three keepers are to be at hand, in case Bruin should hug too closely. The match is for 500 guineas; and considerable bets are already laid. The brown brute is the favourite of the two!

Aside from the cringeworthy racial pun at the end, the most notable aspect of this report is the fact that Richmond was willing to entertain the notion of such an absurd and potentially fatal contest, even taking into account the substantial inducement of 500 guineas, which was ten times higher than any purse he had yet earned in the ring. The scheme, one could argue, provides ample demonstration of Richmond's bravery, as well as his eye for publicity; a less charitable interpretation would be that it indicates a dangerous excess of bravado. Thankfully, commonsense appears to have prevailed and there is no evidence that the 'Richmond versus Bruin' contest ever went ahead. The reports of the plans for the contest did appear in several newspapers though, helping spread Richmond's fame and renown as a fearless member of the pugilistic corps.

In retrospect, it was a blessing that Richmond did not tempt the pugilistic gods by engaging in battle with the Bruin, for the forbiddingly dark shadow of death seemed to be hanging over the Fancy in early 1809. Former champion Pearce, suffering from the advanced effects of tuberculosis, was granted a benefit at the Fives in February and it is likely that Richmond was among those who exhibited their skills in the Game Chicken's honour. It was a grim experience for all present to see a man whose physical prowess had once elicited awe reduced to a pathetic object of pity; shockingly, Pearce was hardly able to even walk. Within two months he would be dead, a few days shy of his thirty-second birthday, having returned to his native Bristol to see out his last days, before passing away on 30 April. On his deathbed, *The Times* movingly reported that he 'hoped forgiveness from all those whom he might have ill treated in the way of his profession'. Another member of the Fancy to be claimed by tuberculosis in the early months of 1809 was Bill Ward, whose passing was much mourned, in particular by Cribb whose career he had helped resurrect. Pearce and Ward's untimely deaths made Richmond's sound health and resurgent career, at the advanced age of nearly forty-six, appear all the more miraculous.

A month before Ward's death, Cribb had turned to Joe Ward (most likely Bill's brother, although some sources disagree) to lead his corner for a lucrative rematch with Jem Belcher. It proved a mismatch, with Belcher succumbing far more tamely than in the first contest and, thankfully, without even a whisper of foul play this time. Belcher's discernible decay made for uncomfortable viewing for his many supporters and the predominant mood at the conclusion of the contest was downbeat as opposed to exultant; *The Times* captured this sense of *ennui* perfectly, declaring that 'this battle was of a nature which excited more commiseration for Belcher than triumph for Cribb'.

As for the victor, Cribb gave the Fancy 'an assurance of his never intending (for his own reasons) to fight again', a pronouncement that undoubtedly piqued the interest of Richmond, who was in attendance to second a boxer named Farnborough against Tom Belcher on the undercard. With Cribb apparently retiring, the championship was once again within Richmond's orbit of ambition, although he realised it would require some high-profile wins, and a generous patron, if he was to be able to engineer a title shot. To these ends, Richmond initially attempted, once again, to secure a rematch with his old antagonist Maddox, in the hope of avenging one of the two stains on his fistic record. The *Morning Chronicle* of 2 March 1809 went as far as to announce that a Richmond versus Maddox rematch was a done deal and that a 'great stake' had been gathered for the duo to contend for. However, for reasons unknown, the fight fell through, and instead Richmond was matched against Isaac Wood, a waterman,[1] in a bout scheduled to take place near Coombe Wood, Kingston in Surrey on 11 April with a handsome purse of 100 guineas at stake.[2] Wood was not considered a top-rank pugilist, although he could boast of an impressive victory against awkward former Cribb opponent Ikey Pig in September 1806, a fight which had ended with him savagely knocking Pig into a 'sleeping fit'.

Sensationally, Richmond versus Wood was nearly scrapped before the men even stripped; having arrived at Coombe Wood at 1 p.m. in a *post-chaise*, Richmond examined the site of combat and 'at first refused to exhibit in it', expressing his concern that the 'materials' used to assemble the 25-foot ring were 'such as risked their safety'. We can assume that Cribb, who was seconding Wood, let Richmond know exactly what he thought of such complaints. In fairness, Richmond's caution was probably accentuated by the fact that the rain was falling 'in torrents', conditions that were sure to impair his nimble footwork and penchant for using his speed to move in and out of his opponent's reach. If the conditions were too wet to allow him to box and move, then Richmond would be at a discernible disadvantage against an opponent compared to whom, typically, he was inferior in size. Nevertheless, after an intense half-hour of negotiations, Richmond finally agreed that the fight could go ahead.

If the delay, the rain or the potentially disconcerting presence at ringside of Cribb had unnerved Richmond he didn't let it show. He did decide to adapt his regular tactics though; the slippery conditions underfoot mean that his usual retreating style, for which his feet would ordinarily have been moving in a largely backwards motion, would have left him susceptible to frequent slips, creating the danger of sustaining a serious sprain or muscle pull. Hence Richmond decided to adopt a more front-footed approach, seeking to keep his feet more still than usual and firmly anchor them when throwing his punches. It was a risky strategic decision and one which was far from guaranteed to succeed; like the majority of Richmond's opponents, Wood was a larger man with a considerable punch – therefore to stand in front of him and trade was to run the risk of one such blow dangerously detonating on a vulnerable portion of Richmond's smaller frame and knocking him out.

In the event, Richmond succeeded in utilising a successful mixture of a more attacking and offensive style with his usual defensive wizardry, with Wood duly baffled at various moments by his knack of 'hitting and getting away'.

In the very first round, Richmond established his steely intent by landing a crushing left hand 'on his adversary's jawbone, the report of which resounded to all parts of the ring'. Wood showed great courage to stay on his feet, though, and forced Richmond back on to the ropes, before Richmond threw him to the floor. Wood attempted to retaliate at the beginning of the second round, but Richmond blocked his attack, replying with a solid right-left combination. This time the round ended when both men fell, but it was already clear that Richmond's skill and ring-craft were superior to Wood's. 'The science of Richman was manifest to every beholder,' purred the *Morning Post* in their description of round three, in which Wood once again attempted to start fast, prompting several blows to be 'dexterously exchanged' between the two men, before Richmond connected with a series of stiff punches and once again tossed his foe to the floor.

The fourth round was confirmation of Richmond's willingness to adopt a more attacking approach than usual; throughout he pursued Wood to 'every part of the ring', landing a succession of solid shots before hurling Wood over the ropes. Again, the gutsy Wood tried to fight back at the beginning of the fifth, and again Richmond remained firm and resolute; the two men stood toe-to-toe for half a minute and exchanged heavy blows, with Richmond proving 'decidedly the best hitter'. Wood was yet again thrown to the floor, and the *Post* observed that his head was already 'much disfigured'.

Richmond also floored Wood in each of the next two rounds, firstly with a flurry of punches and then with a throw. In the eighth round, though, just as a Richmond victory was beginning to look inevitable, Wood edged his way back into contention, striking Richmond with two clean and heavy shots before throwing him. A Richmond slip ended the ninth round, evidence that conditions remained slippery, while the tenth was utterly thrilling, the two men exchanging fierce blows before 'each were fatigued, and both fell'. The eleventh was another tight round and, for a while, as Richmond and Wood attempted to punch each other to a standstill, it looked as though the latter was contending on an even footing. However, as the rain continued to fall and both men continued to swing their weary arms, it soon became obvious that Richmond's snappier and quicker punches were the more hurtful and his physical conditioning far superior. Wood suddenly flagged, while Richmond was able to keep swinging, ensuring his opponent was viciously 'fibbed ... until the blood flew in torrents'. Both men fell to the ground soon after, drained by their immense exertions, but Wood's challenge was close to expiring.

What had been a keenly fought contest was now acquiring the grim visage of an execution; Richmond threw Wood over the ropes in both the twelfth, thirteenth and fourteenth rounds, and landed three huge punches to his opponent's head in the fifteenth. The 'waterman' was nothing if not gutsy though, and he determinedly plodded on for another eight rounds, despite frightful punishment and disfigurement to his face. As the signal was made for the twenty-fourth round to begin, Wood 'was unable to get off Cribb's knee', the fight was signalled over and Richmond's comeback had extended to a fourth successive victory. The *Hampshire Chronicle*'s report was a model of concision and analytical accuracy: 'This was a trial of skill against strength and bottom. Richman, was considerably behind his adversary in size, weight and length, but was much his superior in the grand requisite, skill.' John Wilson, who was present at the fight, later declared of the contest that 'Bill was slightly pinked on the left side of his nob, but his beauty was not at all spoiled – and he kept laughing during the whole fight'. In contrast, Wilson noted that Wood received such 'cruel punishment' that 'his wife could not have known him'.

As Cribb surveyed Wood's wounds it would have doubtless occurred to him that Richmond was now a far more imposing and accomplished pugilist than the man he had fought more than three years before. However the champion, whose retirement seemed far from assured given rumours linking him with a fight against Gully, would also have been confident that there would be scant calls for a rematch between himself and Richmond; the stench caused by their first set-to had not been forgotten and there would be little appetite for a return unless his perennial rival could defeat a higher class of contender than Wood.

As for Richmond, duly emboldened by his latest triumph, he decided it was time to avenge his 1804 humiliation at the hands of Maddox by finally securing a rematch. Maddox, something of a fistic phenomenon, was now, incredibly, in his mid-fifties, but he was still willing to respond to the siren song of the prize ring. Eventually, the rematch was made, but only after tortuous and long-winded negotiations as alluded to by the *Oxford Journal*:

> The long depending match between the veteran boxers George Maddox and Richman the black, has at length been settled, and the parties will fight for a stake of 100 guineas. The amateurs look to the day as one of considerable amusement, the veteran being a tough veteran of the old school, not easy to be conquered, and Richman is a scientific fighter of the day, and a better giver than a taker.

When assessing the relative merits of the two men, who were due to square off on 11 August, the Fancy found it fiendishly hard to pick a winner, which only added to the contest's enticing nature. Recent form, without doubt, favoured Richmond, who had clocked up four wins in just over a year, compared to Maddox, who had only fought twice in major contests since his victory against Richmond in 1804 (one of which was his gallant losing effort against Cribb). However, Maddox's considerable powers of punch resistance and stamina, as well as his vast experience,[3] meant many believed he retained the edge. Add to that the psychological advantage of having already defeated Richmond, and it is easy to see why Maddox began the fight as a narrow favourite, with odds of five and six-to-four being offered at ringside.

The intriguing rematch certainly piqued the interest of the public, with around 3,000 spectators lured to the remote Kent coast in between Margate and Reculver, within sight of the crashing waves and ebbing and flowing tides of the North Sea, to bear witness to a contest between two men with a remarkable combined age of nearly 100. With a larger than average 27-foot ring assembled, Richmond had a bit more space than usual to maximise his hit-and-run tactics and, from the first exchange of the contest, adopted the role of fleet-footed matador to Maddox's enraged bull. No sooner had the bout begun than Maddox charged directly at Richmond with his 'characteristic rush of gaiety', however Richmond coolly stood his ground, and delivered two perfectly timed counter-punches with his right before retreating to safety. Maddox took both punches on the neck and the effect of the second was particularly startling and unexpected – it floored him heavily. As Maddox hauled himself off the springy turf, the pre-fight odds had already narrowed, both men now evenly favoured.

In the second round Maddox responded to the embarrassment of the rapid knockdown with roaring defiance, as to be expected from a man who Egan praised for his 'peculiar *forte* [of] manliness'. He once again immediately attacked, punishing Richmond with a flurry of blows before summarily flinging him over the ropes. It was the last significant success Maddox would enjoy in a bout that soon became a one-sided slaughter. Richmond's actions in the third round showed just what an accomplished pugilist he had now become. To 'the astonishment of the spectators', who were all too aware of Maddox's vast strength, Richmond boxed patiently, before decisively, almost derisively, hurling his much sturdier opponent to the floor. Nobody had expected Richmond to display such 'superiority of strength', yet here he was flinging Maddox around the ring like a rag doll.

Richmond pressed his advantage ruthlessly. For the next half an hour,

Maddox fought with his usual commitment, as he was peppered with accurate and hurtful blows, but such was the sustained and fearful nature of the punishment meted out by Richmond's spiteful fists that, by the tenth round, Maddox's head was 'hideously disfigured'. It was now clear that Richmond's 'mind, strength and science' were so overwhelmingly superior that Maddox had no chance of winning. Yet, despite the hopelessness of his cause, the veteran manfully fought on for a further twenty-two minutes.

The closing rites were administered in the wake of one final act of magnificent Maddox defiance after fifty-two minutes of combat; falling to his knees, and now effectively blind due to the horrific swelling and bleeding in both his eyes, Maddox somehow found the energy to leap to his feet, and 'by a sudden effort of nature' grabbed a startled Richmond around the neck with one hand and began to beat him over the head with the other. Too shocked to free himself from Maddox's grasp, Richmond took the blows with equanimity, seemingly content for his opponent to enjoy one last hurrah. At which point Maddox, thoroughly exhausted, 'fell motionless' to the floor, where he lay for a while as his seconds attempted to rouse him, before he was led away looking 'a frightful spectacle'.

Maddox's long and meritorious career was over and Richmond's pugilistic rebirth was complete. It had been a mighty contest; Richmond had demonstrated strength, skill and mental fortitude in abundance, while Maddox, despite his ageing body having finally failed him, had fought with every ounce of his being in an ultimately vain attempt to rage against the dying of the light. One particularly fascinated spectator who had watched keenly as the contest had unfolded its terrible but compulsive drama was William Windham MP. Awestruck at Richmond's skill and Maddox's heart, as well as the spectacle of 3,000 spectators roaring their encouragement and approval, Windham discerned a connection between the valour demonstrated by Richmond and Maddox and the spirit that British troops had demonstrated in battle, most notably in the Battle of Talavera, a hard-earned and bloody triumph for British and Spanish troops against France's Grand Armée which had taken place at the end of July. So enamoured was Windham with the contest that six days later he penned a letter in which, using magnificently persuasive rhetoric, he offered an impassioned patriotic and moral justification for the art of boxing:

A smart contest this between Maddox and Richman! Why are we to boast so much of the native valour of our troops, as shewn at Talavera, at Vimeira, and at Maida; yet to discourage all the practices and habits which tend to keep alive the same sentiments and feelings? The sentiments that filled the minds of the three thousand spectators who attended the two pugilists, were just the same in kind as those which inspired the higher combatants on the occasions before enumerated. It is the circumstance only in which they are displayed, that makes the difference.

He that the world subdued, had been
But the best wrestler on the green.[4]

There is no sense in the answer always made to this; "Are no men brave but boxers?" Bravery is found in all habits, classes, circumstances, and conditions. But have habits and institutions of one sort no tendency to form it, more than of another? Longevity is found in persons of habits the most opposite; but are not certain habits more favourable to it than others? The courage does not arise from mere boxing, from the mere beating or being beat; but from the sentiments excited by the contemplation and cultivation of such practices. Will it make no difference in the mass of a people, whether their amusements are all of a pacific, pleasurable, and effeminate nature, or whether they are of a sort that calls forth a continued admiration of prowess and hardihood?

For a British politician to be interpreting a fight won by an American-born former black slave against a native-born Englishman as a symbol of the country's military strength might strike some as ironic, or even hypocritical. Yet it is significant that Windham neglected to refer to Richmond's ethnicity to differentiate him from Maddox, thus suggesting that he viewed Richmond as a fully assimilated Englishman. Furthermore, Windham's reference to bravery being 'found in all habits, classes, circumstances, and conditions,' also seems particularly pertinent, indicating a progressive awareness of the fact that admirable qualities such as valour were not the exclusive preserve of any one section of society or people of merely one ethnic background. Windham's letter, written just two years after parliament abolished the slave trade, can therefore be seen as a further symbolic stride towards racial equality. With his performance against Maddox, Richmond had proved that the qualities of bravery, and even patriotism, which were so valued and treasured by Georgian England, could apply to black men as well as white. To Windham, as well as to many members of the Fancy, Richmond was no longer a stereotype, or mocked as a comical 'Mungo' figure or exotic 'Blacky'; instead, he was a man who was increasingly accepted and lauded on his own merits. Viewed through this prism, Windham's letter represents an extraordinary moment in the social history of England.

Yet a crucial question remained unanswered. Outwardly, it appeared that Richmond was now a feted pugilistic hero, and seen as an admirable exemplar of English virtues, but how deeply accepted or integrated into British society was he *really*? Yes, Windham had lauded his courage, while the Fancy had accepted him as one of their own. However Richmond's cherished status as a respected pugilist arguably owed much to the fact that although he was regarded as an accomplished boxer, he was not considered a threat to the established order. He was yet to fight for the English title and his level of achievement as a pugilist placed him within the sport's massed ranks of contenders, rather than as the 'champion' at the sport's summit, a position that was still occupied by Cribb. As long as Richmond knew 'the situation in which he is placed in society', as Egan put it, or was considered to have 'borne his sable colours meekly', as William Hazlitt later suggested, then everyone was content.

Everyone, that is, apart from Richmond himself who, in his quest to conquer sporting territory never before conquered by a black man, would soon join forces with another black pugilist in Tom Molineaux, a former slave who possessed none of Richmond's social graces or English affectations, but was blessed with the physical attributes Richmond lacked – namely, tremendous power, intimidating bulk and youth.

Molineaux, with Richmond as his mentor, would challenge the English sporting and social order with a ferocity that would split the Fancy and shake John Bull to the very bottom of his boots.

12

The Molineaux Myth

In the wake of his thrilling victory against Maddox, Richmond's desire for a contest that might nudge him closer to a shot at the English Championship was palpable. However, no sooner had his career acquired seemingly irresistible momentum, than a series of fraught occurrences checked his progress. It was a harbinger of things to come, for the next three years would be the most turbulent period thus far in the history of prizefighting, as well as in Richmond's own professional life.

Overshadowing every other event throughout 1809 was the fall from grace of Richmond's pugilistic comrade Jem Belcher, which was proving as swift as it was cruel. After his second defeat against Cribb in February, Belcher had been arrested for 'breach of the peace', and the threat of possible imprisonment subsequently hung over him for several months. Belcher's travails particularly impacted on Richmond, who by this stage had become a firm friend of both Jem and his brother Tom. Private correspondence by William Gell, a well-known illustrator and topographer who was close to the Belchers, indicates that Richmond supported both men throughout a desperately difficult time. Gell's letters also reveal the anger among Belcher's circle that Jem was facing costly legal action while Cribb had escaped without censure or punishment. For example, in July 1809, Gell wrote that he had 'been fagging myself to death to settle the business of my ally Jim Belcher,' while also expressing his fury with 'That Brute Tom' [Cribb], who 'ought to have gone with him'. Gell was particularly incensed with Cribb's decision to leave London with fellow pugilist Tom Shelton to visit Capt. Barclay in Newmarket, rather than stay and support Belcher or offer him 'bail or security'. Reflecting on this, he wrote to his brother in a fit of fury, declaring, 'I will blow them both well up when they return, d--- them.'

In November, after months of legal wrangling, Belcher was sentenced to a month in prison in Horsemonger Lane – a verdict which provoked further anger on Gell's part and an emotive declaration that the magistrates who had sent Belcher to jail were 'damned sons of b-----s'. Anxious to support his friend, but realising Jem was too proud to accept charity, Gell enlisted Richmond to visit Belcher and secretly ascertain how he could be helped, commenting, 'I don't think he wants anything, but he is so modest I cannot found out except by a trap so I have sent Richmond to find out.' Richmond's admiration for Jem was deeply felt and his concern for his welfare sincere; Richmond would later admit to John Wilson that he had been willing in his career to fight 'any twelve-stone man in England, except Jem'.

Given Belcher's travails it is unsurprising that there was a sense of palpable nervousness among the Fancy throughout the autumn and winter about arranging any high-profile pugilistic matches lest they be disrupted by any further magisterial interference or arrests. Perhaps this explains why, in the immediate months coinciding with Belcher's prosecution and imprisonment, no less than three proposed fights involving Richmond were agreed but then cancelled; in October he came close to fighting Tom Belcher, most likely in an attempt to raise money for Jem, while in November Bill Cropley forfeited rather than go ahead with a planned fight. To add to Richmond's frustration, later that month he accepted a challenge from George Nichols, conqueror of Cribb back in 1805, only for that fight to also collapse. The failure of the latter contest to take place was a particular blow, as an eye-catching victory for Richmond against the only man to have beaten Cribb would have put him in a persuasive position to challenge the champion to a rematch.

The sense of unease among the pugilistic community was not helped by a series of controversial events in London which saw many boxers ill advisedly drawn into a period of unrest at the Covent Garden Theatre known as the 'Old Price Riots'. In September 1808, the famous theatre had burnt down, killing twenty-three firemen in the process, before being rebuilt at great expense after a huge subscription effort as well as a typical act of munificence – to the tune of £10,000 – from Richmond's old mentor Earl Percy, who had succeeded his father as the Duke of Northumberland in 1786.[1] However, when manager John Kemble introduced 'new prices' for the theatre's reopening on 18 September 1809, as well as a smaller gallery of cheaper seats and larger expensive private boxes than before, there was widespread public anger. On opening night shouts echoed around the auditorium demanding the reinstatement of 'old prices', a call that intensified over the following weeks. The shouts and catcalls of the protestors regularly drowned out the onstage performers, and the whole affair received considerable press attention. With the threat of violence hanging potently in the air, a desperate Kemble turned to a group of pugilists, led by Mendoza and Dutch Sam, and also including Richmond, for some reassuring muscle to deter the 'old pricers'. The move merely inflamed an already volatile situation, as one letter writer to *The Times* described:

> Sir – I went to Covent-Garden Theatre yesterday evening ... To my great astonishment, I observed the seats of the Pit near the stage occupied by 50 or 60 persons of the very lowest of society, headed by Dutch Sam, the prizefighter, and other characters of a similar description.
>
> It was very evident, from the appearance and conduct of this formidable party, that they were sent there for the purpose of intimidating the audience; for upon the first expression of public voice, these miscreants rushed from their seats, and attacked in the most violent manner every person who was disposed to resist their authority. The most disgraceful proceedings took place, and in the different conflicts which were produced by the interference of these wretches, many innocent people were knocked down, and otherwise ill treated.
>
> I shall make no comment on this outrage on a British audience, further than remarking the absurdity of an attempt to restore the tranquillity of the Theatre, by confiding the preservation of it not to the established Police, but a class of persons who notoriously subsist by violation of the laws of their country.

Mendoza and Dutch Sam's status as the ringleaders of the physical backlash against the 'Old Pricers' led to widespread anti-Semitic comment in the press. By co-opting other pugilists into the sorry episode, the duo occasioned severe damage to the sport's reputation, particularly among the working classes, many of whom felt the pugilists had betrayed them by sticking up for the established order, rather than everyday folk. Eventually, after a sixty-two-day stand-off, Kemble was forced to back down, returning prices to their previous levels after delivering a public apology for the whole fiasco. In the meantime, a parody playbill had circulated the streets of Central London, mocking the involvement of Mendoza, Richmond et al:

NEW THEATRE ROYAL, COVENT GARDEN
This present Wednesday, October 11, 1809, will be presented, by an entire New Company of Performers, and not noted these sixty years, a Tragic Comedy, called:
HOCKLEY IN THE HOLE.[2]
Principal characters by Messrs. Mendoza, Belcher, Gregson, Cribb, Will Perry, Harry Lee, Dutch Sam, Solly, Richmond, and Pittone. - To conclude with a Grand Chorus of hired Ruffians, fighting Israelites, and Bow-Street Officers. - Preceding the Play, Mr. K____e will recite the

celebrated popular Address, called 'Set a Beggar on Horseback and he will ride to the Devil;' and at the end of the third act he will sing a new comic Song, written and composed expressly for the occasion, entitled:
'I cringed and bowed 'till a fortune I made,
'Then I bullied my Masters, and knocked up the trade.'
To which will be added, for the third time, a new Melo-Drama, called THE BEAR GARDEN; OR JOHN BULL BULLIED.
Performers as before. - The above Pieces having been received with the most unbounded and reiterated applause, will be repeated every evening until further notice. - For the better accommodation of the Public, and to give greater spirit to the Performance, the stage will in future be removed from the centre of the Pit.

Richmond's next endeavour was of a more constructive nature as, sometime in 1810, he assumed proprietorship of the Horse and Dolphin public house at No. 25 St Martin's Street.[3] Richmond's victories against Wood and Maddox had earned him a handsome sum, which most likely helped him fund this enterprise. The Horse and Dolphin was a well-established pub, having been in operation since at least 1791,[4] and becoming its landlord was a further illustration of how firmly established Richmond now was economically and socially, as well as within the pugilistic community. *Bell's Life in London* provided a vivid description of the status Richmond enjoyed during the height of his stewardship of the Horse and Dolphin:

> Bill carried on a roaring trade; indeed, a fortune appeared to be within his grasp. Scarcely anything else sluiced the pearls of the Magnificents but Champagne in the bar and the snuggery above the stairs, where commoners dare not intrude; black strap and brandy and water in the parlour from morning till night, and oceans of heavy wet were continually on the move in the tap-room. 'Milling, glorious Milling,' was the theme throughout Bill's lush crib ... The patronage, in fact, that Richmond received, was of the highest order.

Ideally situated close to the Fives Court, where Richmond leased rooms for the purpose of giving pugilistic instruction, the 'Prad and Swimmer', as Egan nicknamed it, became a valued location for sporting gossip and deal brokering. Many 'men of the first rank of the country' frequented the pub, even using it, on occasion, to settle their differences with pugilistic set-tos in the snuggery, such as the contest between George Kent and G. H. Cowlam in 1811.

However, it was at Gregson's pub, not the Horse and Dolphin, that Richmond's next pugilistic outing came about. On 1 May 1810, the

Lancastrian, who had retired in the aftermath of his defeat to Cribb, was granted a dinner in honour of his services to boxing, which attracted a healthy crowd of around eighty. Richmond, Gully, Jackson, Cribb, Dan Dogherty and Tom Belcher were among those in attendance, having bought tickets for a guinea apiece. After a sumptuous dinner, the gathering assumed a more raucous demeanour; several songs were sung, the 'bottle circled freely' and it was soon decided, somewhat drunkenly, that the ideal post-dinner entertainment might consist of a couple of boxing matches. Firstly, a £20 purse was cobbled together for a set-to between Cribb's younger brother George, a famously inept pugilist who was not at the dinner but was drinking downstairs, and the determined but limited Dogherty. The party 'adjourned to a convenient room in the neighbourhood' and, with Cribb seconding for his brother, it was little surprise that Richmond rapidly volunteered to assist Dogherty, who was so confident of victory that he 'backed himself for an extra ten guineas'. His faith was rewarded when he gave Cribb a solid beating for nearly an hour.

By now, with the drink still flowing, the communal sense of blood lust had been piqued and a second contest was swiftly arranged between Richmond and Jack Powers, a hot head of Irish descent. The contemporary accounts of the evening offer few clues as to how the contest came about, although Oxberry and Egan each provide some background colour. According to the latter, Powers had not been at the dinner but 'accidentally' called into Gregson's on the way home for an extra drink or two while 'totally inebriated'. Powers later claimed he was reluctant to fight and had instead requested that he face Richmond when sober. However, after a couple more drinks, he apparently relented and accepted the challenge.

Both men were aided in their corners by prominent society figures, with 'an Honourable Baronet' seconding Richmond and 'an amateur Colonel' supporting Powers. The fight itself was brief, lasting just fifteen minutes and Powers was well beaten. According to Oxberry,

> for the first round [Richmond] had the worst of it, but as every amateur might have expected, his science gave him the best of the remainder … Powers, who is a resolute fighter, was continually boring in upon his opponent, and this sort of GAME always gets a man the worst of the battle and with such an opponent as the black, and by this system Powers was completely beat.

Interestingly, Oxberry's report also drew attention to Richmond's exceptional hand-speed ('he [Powers] was frequently hit twice in the face in a second'), as well as the destructive nature of his 'favourite left-handed hit'. In contrast to the punishment absorbed by Powers, Oxberry remarked that Richmond 'received no other injury throughout the whole battle than a slight blow in the face'. At the end of the contest, Powers was consoled with forty shillings, while Richmond, with a grin of satisfaction, was able to sit down and continue socialising until 3.00 a.m. with an extra twenty guineas in his pocket and a glass of his favoured tipple Noyau in his hand.

According to Egan, the defeat rankled with Powers, who a few days later publicly announced at the Fives Court the reasons for his defeat. He claimed that the day before the fight with Richmond he had been mixing paint and had drunk castor oil to lessen its toxic effects. He maintained that this – combined with the alcohol he had drunk – had 'rendered him unprepared' to fight. Powers' excuses further antagonised Richmond, who in turn claimed Powers had been 'very far' from drunk and that it was actually he – Richmond – who had been at a disadvantage, having seconded Dogherty for fifty-six tiring minutes before his battle with Powers.

In time, the 'considerable acrimony' between Richmond and Powers would be reignited. For now, though, more pressing matters intruded which led Richmond away from active participation in the prize ring and instead into the arena of management; Richmond's next pugilistic contest would not be for another four years, by which time he had passed his fiftieth birthday. The main reason for his withdrawal from the front-line of boxing was the fact that, sometime in mid-1810, his life fatefully intersected with that of one of the most colourful figures to ever grace the prize ring, the former American slave Tom Molineaux, to whom Richmond soon became a friend and mentor, as well as manager, promoter and trainer.

Even more so than Richmond's, Molineaux's early life is resolutely mysterious, with existing accounts offering few, if any, solid facts and sources. Instead, when attempting to ascertain who Molineaux was and where he came from, we are forced to predominantly rely on unsubstantiated and highly fanciful anecdotes, the verification of which remain elusive and probably impossible. One of the most influential accounts of Molineaux's early life, certainly in terms of the way it has been recycled and recited without question by later writers, is offered by Fred Henning in his 1902 book *Fights for the Championship* which appears to have been the primary source used,[5] in turn, by American boxing journalist Nat Fleischer in his 1938 book *Black Dynamite*.[6] Details and common threads from these accounts seem to have gradually seeped into other sources, with occasional variations and contradictions, to the extent that tracing the genesis of the myths surrounding Molineaux's life is somewhat akin to participating in a giant game of Chinese whispers.

Despite the fact that, as pieces of historical research, Henning and Fleischer's accounts of Molineaux's life are highly problematic, they nevertheless advance a fascinating and compelling narrative, which has formed the basis for what might be best termed the 'Molineaux myth'. Through force of repetition and, perhaps, an understandably romantic desire for some of the myth's more delicious and dramatic twists to be true, the 'Molineaux myth' has become accepted by many writers and historians as fact, rather than speculation or anecdote. Like many myths, it probably contains kernels of truth, but separating them from instances of invention, embroidery and exaggerated fact is an impossible task.

Henning claims that Molineaux's surname originated from the family under whose aegis the young Tom was born into slavery in 1784 in Virginia, writing that the family were descended 'from one of the aristocratic houses to which King Charles had wisely granted lands'. Having stated, in breathtakingly objectionable terms, that Molineaux was born 'a piccaninny as black as a lump of coal', Henning neglects any mention of his immediate family, although Fleischer insists his father was named Zachary and was a 'tremendously powerful person'. It is Zachary who Fleischer credits with being the founder of pugilism in America, along with his brothers Elizah, Ebenezar, Franklin and Moses. Of these formidable sounding siblings, Fleischer writes that they 'were men of muscle' who 'outclassed all rivals in Virginia'.

Henning focuses on the role of Algernon Molineaux, son of the head of the Molineaux family, in Tom's fistic development, writing that he took 'a great fancy to the nigger lad ... for he had found him very useful as a body guard, and he had twice backed him to beat others older and more experienced with his fists'. The next stage in Fleischer's narrative is similar, recounting how, when Tom was fourteen, his father died and, as a result, the youngster became 'chief handy man around his master's estate'. Both Henning and Fleischer then describe in almost identical terms how Tom's first foray into boxing came about, with Henning writing,

Algernon Molyneux, whilst with a gay set in Richmond, where his father had a town house, and a number of these gay young sparks met, and the conversation turned upon fighting, when one named Peyton,[7] a young planter, whose father had recently died and left him a considerable amount of money, offered to back one of his slaves named Abe, against any black in Virginia. Molyneux, who was more than half intoxicated at the time, immediately accepted the challenge, and nominated Tom. Stakes were posted and bets were made, and in the morning, master Algernon, when he came to his senses, was rather shocked to find that he stood to lose no less a sum than a hundred thousand dollars.[8]

Fleischer's variation on the same tale includes the dramatic flourish of

Tom volunteering to try and save his master's fortune. In return, Tom was promised his freedom if he won 'and with that as an inducement, a merry contest was assured'. At this point both writers introduce a sailor named Davis into their narratives, who they claim had fought in England and then trained Molineaux. The problem was, apparently, that Tom was too 'docile' in training so, Fleischer claims, 'Squire Molineaux made an added inducement' by promising him $100 if he won, as well as his freedom. Diverging from Fleischer, Henning maintains that Molineaux was only offered his freedom once it became clear he was not training properly. According to his account, Algernon was set to flog Tom for his lack of effort in training, whereupon Davis suggested, 'Promise him his freedom and a hundred dollars if he wins, and I'll stake my existence that young Tom will thrash any nigger in the country.' Motivation duly provided, Molineaux trained with formidable alacrity and, on beating Abe, Henning claims that Algernon upped Tom's reward to $500.

Henning and Fleischer's accounts then diverge; Fleischer claims that, with his freedom won and money in his pocket, Molineaux was told by Davis about the riches pugilists could earn in England, and resolved to cross the Atlantic, succeeding in getting a job on a vessel in Baltimore, before arriving in Liverpool sometime in 'the Winter of 1809' and making his way to London. Henning's version is that Molineaux ended up in New York, where he styled himself 'Champion of America' and stayed for five years, fighting several contests before heading to England.

The majority of accounts of Molineaux's early life stick closely to Henning and Fleischer's basic structure, although some are adorned with further details which have fed the 'Molineaux myth', for example, Bill Calogero claimed that Molineaux's father fought in the American War of Independence and that Molineaux began boxing in New York's Catherine Market area around 1804. He even recounts an outlandish claim that George Washington introduced Molineaux to bare-knuckle boxing. Meanwhile, Thormanby claimed that Molineaux was associated with the American diplomat and statesman Thomas Pinckney, declaring he was 'for several years in the service of Mr Pinckney, the then Ambassador of the United States in London. I have no doubt that it was the fact that his old master held this important appointment in London that induced Molineaux to come over here ... Pinckney was a very good friend to him'.[9]

The details may vary, but the truth of Molineaux's life story remains elusive. It is probable that aspects of the 'Molineaux myth' may even have been invented by Molineaux himself, or by Richmond, as a way of adding to the mystique that surrounded his introduction to English pugilism. Having entered oral and anecdotal tradition during his lifetime, these details then worked their way into newspapers and books, until it was no longer possible to distinguish between fact and fiction. In fairness to Henning, Fleischer et al, there is reason to believe that at least some of the basics of the 'Molineaux myth' may coalesce with the truth; Henning and Fleischer's birth date for Molineaux of 1784 tallies with newspaper reports of 1810 which give his age as twenty-six,[10] although it is a mystery how Fleischer alighted on the peculiarly precise date of 23 March. However, other details and assertions, for example that Molineaux was of Virginian birth, are contradicted by sources that were actually written in Molineaux's lifetime, for example, *The Sporting Magazine*, described him as 'a Baltimore man of colour', while Oxberry in *Pancratia* referred to him as 'a native of the State of New York'.

Interestingly, sources during Molineaux's lifetime are also very vague concerning whether he was ever actually a slave, often referring to slavery only by implication, rather than explicitly. In his first biographical essay of Molineaux, published in 1812, Egan makes no reference to Molineaux having been a slave, although he does imply that Molineaux's antecedents included a fighter of some sort, which might be the original source of the story of Zachary Molineaux, claiming that 'the brave MOLINEAUX arrived in England: descended from a warlike hero, who had been the conquering pugilist of *America*'.

The ambiguity of Egan's account and other sources means it remains a possibility that Molineaux was a free citizen from a northern state in America, which would tally with the contemporary references to New York and Baltimore, as opposed to a former slave from the south. A further alternative is that he was indeed a slave, but from the north and not from the south. The first explicit reference to Molineaux being a slave seems to be the poem written by Bob Gregson entitled 'British Lads And Black Millers', published in *Boxiana* in 1812. In the second verse, Gregson writes in the form of a dramatic dialogue between Molineaux and Cribb:

> Brave Molineaux replied, I've never been denied,
> To fight the foes of Britons on such planks as those;
> If relationship you claim, bye and bye, you'll know my name,
> I'm the Moorish milling blade that can drub my foes.
> Then CRIBB replied with haste,
> You slave, I will you baste,
> As your master us'd to cane you, 'twill bring things to your mind:
> If from bondage you've got clear,
> To impose on Britons here,
> You'd better stopp'd with Christophe, you'll quickly find.

The references to 'bondage', 'slave' and 'master' are far from definitive evidence that Molineaux was a former slave or even claimed he was one; they may instead represent poetic licence or a stereotypical assumption on Gregson's part that *all* black Americans must have been former slaves.

Despite its flaws, the 'Molineaux myth' and its widespread adoption and acceptance within historical discourse teaches us something vital about human nature, as well as the turbulent history of black experience in America and England. The conventional interpretation of the 'Molineaux myth' is aptly summarised by Calogero, who links the myth's seductive appeal to its relationship to the American Dream:

> Molineaux's is a quintessential American story, an up-from-the-bootstraps tale in which an individual could rise from abject poverty and, through skill and perseverance, challenge the world's best. Molineaux was perhaps the first black man to exemplify the American ideal that your place in life is not situated in birthright but created by your acts.

As Calogero's interpretation demonstrates, there is a widespread desire for the story of Molineaux's romantic journey from slave to pugilist to be true, despite the absence of any solid historical documents or verification concerning his early life. However, we should be wary of any attempt to adopt the 'Molineaux myth' for ideological purposes; by asserting or appropriating Molineaux as an exemplar of the American Dream, who was later abused and cheated by the English, the 'Molineaux myth', for Calogero as well as other American boxing historians, not only attempts to verify the validity of the American Dream, but also, albeit at an unconscious level, offers comfort to white Americans by shielding them from the true horrors of slavery. The unwritten but clear implication of glorifying Molineaux as a 'great American' and an exemplar of the American Dream is the insidious implication that if, through strength of will and character, Molineaux could win his freedom, then slavery must have possessed some form of meritocratic dimension. In other words, if Molineaux could escape slavery through endeavour and determination, then so too could other slaves, had they been motivated or talented enough to do so. A corollary of such sentiments is the revisionist accounts of slavery which declare that it 'wasn't that bad'. Such interpretations are not as rare as you might think: as recently as March 2013, the Republican politician Jim Brown declared, 'Basically slave owners took pretty good care of their slaves.' Along similar lines, Walter Block has written that 'slavery wasn't so bad. You could pick cotton, sing songs, be fed nice gruel ... The only real problem was that this relationship was compulsory.'

Such interpretations must be avoided at all costs, for they obscure several essential truths – predominantly the all-pervading evil of the institution of slavery in the first place. The 'Molineaux myth' also obscures an uncomfortable truth for many Americans, namely that when Richmond and Molineaux arrived in England in 1777 and

1810 respectively, the prospects for advancement, wealth and societal acceptance for a black man were far superior in Britain than they were in America. The War of Independence might have been won and founded on the laudable principles of 'life, liberty and the pursuit of happiness', but the English, whose rulers the American patriots had condemned for their tyranny, were far less tyrannical in their approach to black people than the United States, where slavery still flourished, particularly in the south, and was not finally abolished until 1865.

In the final analysis, though, it is vital to remember that the lives of Richmond and Molineaux should not be defined by the respective merits, or otherwise, of American or English society in the late eighteenth and early nineteenth centuries. Although both men were born in America and won fame in England, their legacy is not to authenticate the notion of England as a 'cradle of civilisation' and 'inclusivity', or to validate the concept of the 'American Dream'. Rather, their experiences teach us a more personal lesson; a lesson about the awesome powers of determination which exist within all human beings, and how these powers, when marshalled wholeheartedly, can overcome the disadvantage of capricious historical happenstance in order for an individual to make their mark on the world. Only when we recognise this, are we able to see that the achievements of Richmond and Molineaux are theirs and theirs alone, and that to appropriate either man for a nationalistic or ideological cause is a fallacy indeed.

A STRIKING VIEW of RICHMOND.

Robert Dighton's hand-coloured etching *A Striking View of Richmond*, published in March 1810. Its heroic rendering of Richmond and the print's commercial popularity indicates the high esteem in which the pugilist was held. (Author's collection.)

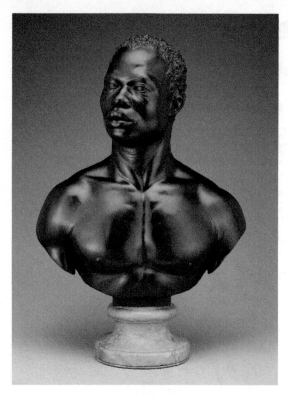

The black stone sculpture *Bust of a Man*, frequently credited as being by Francis Harwood in 1758. It has been theorised by Jerry Leibowitz that this is a later work and that the sitter was actually Richmond. (Digital image courtesy of the Getty's Open Content Program.)

Percy Roberts' engraving of Richmond's rival Tom Cribb, based on an original painting by Sharples. By the 1820s, Cribb and Richmond had buried their enmity and become friends. (Author's collection.)

T. BELCHER.

Above: Tom Belcher's portrait from *Boxiana*. Brother of the legendary champion Jem, Belcher was a close friend of Richmond. The two men even attempted to teach students at Cambridge University the art of boxing. (Author's collection.)

Right: *Molineaux* by Dighton. A hand-coloured etching of Richmond's former protégé turned bitter enemy. Published in January 1812, just as Molineaux was beginning the descent into dissolution that would lead to a tragically early death in 1818. (Author's collection.)

BILL RICHMOND,
From a Portrait by HILLMAN, 1812.

To face page 289.

A portrait of Richmond published in Henry Downes Miles' *Pugilistica* and based on Hillman's 1812 portrait. Richmond's extravagant and colourful clothing reflects his reputation for style and high fashion. (Author's collection.)

The Interior of the Fives Court, based on T. Blake's famous aquatint. The Fives on Little St Martin's Street was the most famous site for pugilistic exhibitions during the early nineteenth century. Richmond can be seen to the right of centre, dressed in the height of fashion and eliciting admiring glances, making clear his prominent position within the sport's hierarchy. (Author's collection.)

Famous Fights magazine, published in the early twentieth century, recreates the climax of the Cribb versus Molineaux fight at Copthall Common in 1810. Richmond and Tom 'Paddington' Jones tend to Molineaux while Cribb is congratulated in the background. This artist was no historian – the fight took place on sodden turf, not a raised wooden stage.
(Author's collection.)

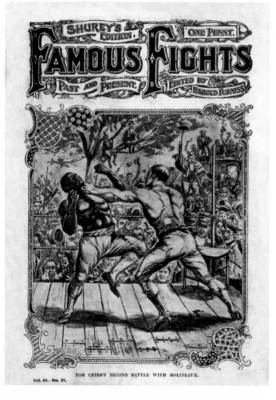

The second Cribb versus Molineaux fight at Thistleton Gap in 1811, as re-imagined by *Famous Fights*. Note the grotesquely exaggerated rendering of Molineaux's facial features. (Author's collection.)

RURAL SPORTS. A MILLING MATCH *Took Place at Thistelton Gap, in the County of Rutland Sept.r 28 1811. between* CRIBB AND MOLINEAUX *in a 25 feet Stage and was the second Public contest between these two Pugilists. It lasted 19 Minutes and 10 Seconds and was decided in favour of Cribb.*

Rural Sports, A Milling Match by Thomas Rowlandson. A vivid hand-coloured etching of the second Cribb versus Molineaux contest. Richmond can be seen to the left of Molineaux watching the contest intently. Rowlandson was one of the leading caricaturists of the age. (Reproduced with permission of Derby Local Studies and Family History Library; Original illustration held by Derbyshire Record Office, D5459/4/32/2.)

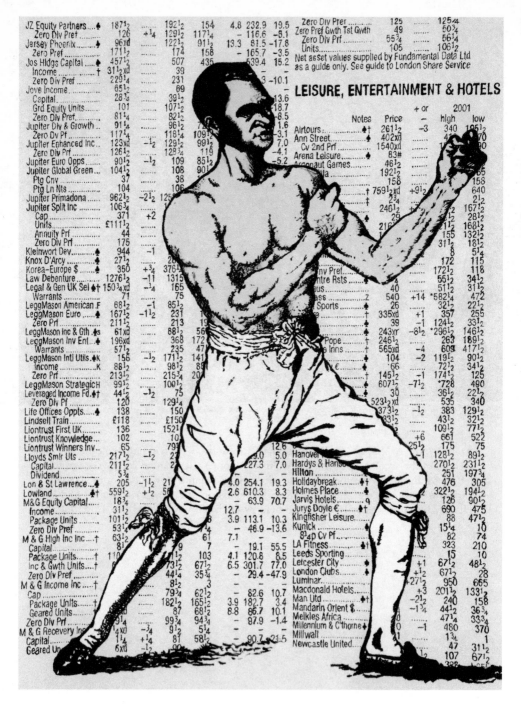

The Olympians IV by Godfried Donkor. The London-based Ghanaian artist has produced many works of art inspired by Bill Richmond. This piece utilises Donkor's version of Dighton's original etching against the background of pages from the *Financial Times* newspaper, a comment on the economic motives behind slavery and commodification in sport. (Courtesy of Godfried Donkor.)

13
Molineaux 'Threatens to Mill the Whole Race of Fighters'

Exactly how the 'unknown, unnoticed, unprotected, and uninformed' Molineaux made the acquaintance of Richmond is unclear. Some accounts claim he was directed to Richmond's training rooms having first visited Gregson's public house. Others maintain that Molineaux deliberately sought out his 'coloured brother' at the Horse and Dolphin, where he was given a 'hearty welcome'. A third possibility is hinted at by the *Morning Chronicle*, who described Molineaux as a 'black, who was found by Richmond', implying Richmond somehow discovered Molineaux in an obscure corner of London and persuaded him he had the attributes to pursue a pugilistic career.

However it occurred, it is easy to see why the men struck up a bond; in terms of their backgrounds, they had much in common, namely their ethnicity, their American birth and their (probable) shared status as former slaves. In personality and temperament, though, they were polar opposites; Richmond was educated and refined, whereas Molineaux was illiterate and lacked social graces. Furthermore, Richmond's modest nature formed a stark contrast with Molineaux's loud boastfulness. It is probably fair to say that both men saw in each other attributes they wished that they possessed themselves; Molineaux desired the social acceptance and status Richmond had achieved, while Richmond, having come to boxing too late to fulfil his significant potential, doubtless craved Molineaux's exuberant youthfulness and imposing physique.

The two men's somewhat enigmatic relationship raises the question as to what extent the bond between them was a friendship, or a pseudo father-son relationship, as opposed to merely a sporting and business relationship. The fact Molineaux was invited to live at the Horse and Dolphin certainly hints at the former; Richmond was twenty-one years Molineaux's senior and perhaps detected, as Earl Percy had once discerned in him, a promising young man in need of guidance. We must also remember, though, that Richmond was a man who possessed a streak of cold commercialism, which had enabled him to survive and thrive as a black man in Georgian England, and therefore his motives in befriending Molineaux cannot be solely attributed to altruism; he was also intrigued and excited by Molineaux's earning potential.

Molineaux's arrival came at an opportune time for Richmond; he had earned a decent income from boxing and was one of the leading pugilists in a country positively obsessed with the sport, but the frustrations of having seen three fights recently fall through had also forced him to confront some harsh realities. Chief among them was the fact that he was now forty-seven – a highly advanced age for a boxer in any era. Additionally, Richmond was no longer the 'novelty' which his status as a foreign-born but refined former slave had once ensured he was; on the contrary, as the laudatory reaction to his victory against Maddox had proved, Richmond was effectively now regarded as an honorary Englishman. Furthermore, although his boxing skills were a match for any man alive, his elusive boxing style made him, for many of his contemporaries, a foe best avoided.

As if to reinforce this point, in July 1810, for the second time, a potential fight between Richmond and his friend Tom Belcher was scuppered when William Gell advised Belcher that it was too risky a proposition for the minor financial reward on offer: 'They have matched T Belcher against Lilly White,' Gell wrote on 16 July 1810. 'But as I was told the black would prove the best man[1] I have given Tom a lecture about his brother losing his fame by over fighting & convinced him that unless he is sure of winning he ought not to try ... He is convinced by my arguments & as £50 is wanting in the purse Hi doant think it wull be a fite.'[2]

Hence, by the summer of 1810, Richmond had few options to advance his own career and the prospect of instead becoming a full-time trainer of other fighters looked increasingly attractive. Molineaux's arrival was therefore a piece of fortuitous timing. Richmond saw in Molineaux a delicious business opportunity, namely the chance to introduce, promote and parade a new black sensation in front of the Fancy. He cannily realised that Molineaux had the potential to become an exotic curiosity; his status, real or invented, as a former slave, coupled with his unrefined habits and loud-mouthed nature, would, Richmond reasoned, attract many spectators, particularly those unaccustomed to brash displays of American braggadocio.

Most important of all, though, was the fact that Richmond sensed in Molineaux, 'the instrument of vengeance' with which he could finally gain the upper hand against Cribb. From the moment he first met Molineaux, the notion seems to have crystallised in Richmond's forensic brain that the young American was ideally suited for the purpose of ultimately defeating the champion. Aged just twenty-six, Molineaux possessed all the enviable advantages of youth that would be required to stretch Cribb to the limits of his considerable powers; physically he was as sturdy and muscular as Cribb, as well as being of a similar weight (between 13 and 14 stone) and height (5 foot 8 or 9 inches to Cribb's estimated 5 foot 10 inches). True, the American's boxing skills were, initially at least, distinctly unimpressive, but any deficiency in skill was compensated for by the fact he could punch like the proverbial mule and absorb punishment without blinking that would fell many lesser mortals.

Rumours of Molineaux's prowess soon spread. According to a possibly apocryphal tale, Capt. Barclay, Cribb's patron, was sufficiently curious that he arranged to spar against Molineaux one morning at Jackson's rooms in Bond Street. Thormanby recounted the incident as follows:

> Capt. Barclay was a fine, powerful man, and was reckoned the best amateur boxer of his day ... whenever any fresh man came forward in the London Ring, the captain put on the gloves with him to try him ... But it was among the "things not generally known" that Barclay had a pair of gloves stuffed especially for the trials - in reality, not half stuffed - whilst the other man, of course, had regulation mufflers. When Bill Richmond brought Molineaux out he took him round to Jackson's rooms, and it was agreed that the Black was to have a set-to with the Capt. ... Barclay was late turning up, and when he arrived found that Molineaux had got on his *special gloves*. Being either too proud or too much ashamed to ask for his own mittens, the Capt. was "hoist with his own petard," for the Black landed him a blow on the body which broke one of his ribs. Barclay never forgave the nigger.

Given Barclay's later obsession with training Cribb for his second contest with Molineaux, Thormanby's story may even be true. Of more certain providence is the fact that Molineaux's pugilistic debut took place on 24 July 1810. How long he had been training with Richmond for by this point is unclear, but it is unlikely to have been long given the untidy performance he produced, which hinted at little intensive instruction. Interestingly, exactly two weeks earlier, on 10 July, Richmond had appeared at a benefit for Dutch Sam at the Fives; if he had already made Molineaux's acquaintance by this point then this would have seemed a logical event at which to introduce him to the Fancy. We can therefore draw two conclusions from the fact that reports of this event make no mention of Molineaux; either Richmond had not met him yet, or he was keen to keep his new discovery under wraps until his debut contest.

The benefit was a grand occasion with 'a more numerous assemblage of persons than ever was witnessed in the court', demonstrating that, despite the controversies of the 'Old Price Riots', pugilism's popularity was untarnished. Although he had been suffering with illness since being released from prison, Jem Belcher was even in attendance and sparred with Cribb, to the crowd's delight. The relaxed Cribb, who had not fought since dismantling Belcher the previous year, looked considerably more corpulent than in that contest. Most observers were under the impression that he had fought his last battle and was settling into retirement. Little did they, or he, realise that the two fiercest battles of his career were still to come.

Molineaux's formal introduction to the Fancy, in a piece of deliberate and canny provocation by Richmond, came on 24 July at Tothill Fields in a contest against a protégé of Cribb's, who also hailed from the environs of Bristol. Later identified as being named Burrows, he was described by one newspaper simply as 'a navigator from the Bristol nursery'. Molineaux was granted similar anonymity, with most reports of the fight merely referring to him as 'the Black'. Although his name was not yet widely known, news of Richmond's 'new black' had obviously spread rapidly and there was sufficient interest and intrigue concerning how he might fare to attract 'some thousands of persons' to observe his debut.

The contest proved an unscientific brawl, rather than a high-class pugilistic encounter, mainly because the 6-foot Burrows was severely limited, with the *Morning Chronicle* dismissing him as a 'bad ... specimen of the Bristol school' who possessed 'no requisite but bottom'. As for Molineaux, his physique may have rippled with well-defined musculature, but technically he was under-seasoned, as the *Chronicle* made clear:

> The Black, who is far from a good fighter, kept himself close, but when he hit he never gave the strength of his body with it, but kept the first joint of his arm close to his body, and what is technically termed kept flipping his adversary over the face, and by so many repetitions of this kind of flipping, he disfigured the head of the Navigator, so as to prevent his features being discernible.

Although Molineaux's style of punching was unconventional, it was surprisingly effective and 'from loss of strength and blood', Burrows conceded defeat after an hour. At this point the long-brewing tension between an exultant Richmond and a surly Cribb exploded. The champion swung a heavy punch at Richmond, who had made some kind of provocative remark; Richmond promptly 'returned a hit' but 'declined a combat', leaving Cribb to stew and curse grumpily. From Richmond's point of view there was no need for any further physical confrontation: public curiosity had already been piqued by the day's display of pugilistic theatre and the seeds for a future Cribb versus Molineaux title showdown had been sown.

Richmond realised, though, that before Molineaux could be matched with Cribb, he would need to dramatically improve his technique. The flipping punches that accounted for Burrows would serve little effective purpose against a bear of a man such as Cribb, so Richmond immediately got to work tutoring Molineaux in the art of putting his full weight behind his punches. For an intense month, Richmond and Molineaux worked together to improve every element of the novice's technique, from his stance to his punching style, from his defence to his wrestling skills. And all the while, Molineaux, prompted and supported by Richmond, began to grow in confidence and volubility. The two men were soon talking openly and provocatively about their desire to wrest the championship from Cribb. The Fancy's reaction to such talk was mixed; Egan thought such rhetoric was 'manly, fair, and honorable', but others found such impertinence hard to stomach, particularly when the source was foreigners, and *black* ones at that. 'It was ... objected to MOLINEAUX, that he was too ambitious,' Egan wrote, 'by threatening to wrest the laurels from the English brow, and planting them upon the head of a foreigner.'

As Molineaux and Richmond's verbal taunting of Cribb accelerated, so too did the eager anticipation for Molineaux's next bout, which had been arranged for 21 August near Margate (where Richmond had fought Maddox in their rematch). The opponent was to be the teak-tough Tom Blake, who held a win over former Richmond victim Holmes and had engaged Cribb in a fierce battle in 1805. Although Blake was in his forties, his 'bottom' was much admired. The *Morning Post* went as far as to label Blake the best fighter 'next to Cribb' within boxing, which was a wild overstatement, but he nevertheless entered the 100-guinea fight as a firm six-to-four favourite, although the *Post* also warned that Molineaux possessed 'considerable promise'. As for Cribb, he was, at this stage, remaining determinedly aloof from any overtures to defend his title, but he made it clear where his loyalties lay; for the second fight in succession, he decided to oppose Richmond by seconding Molineaux's opponent.

The Fancy's excitement intensified as fight day approached. Two days before the fight, the roads to Margate were already packed with fight fans, while in the final hours before the first punch was thrown 'every vehicle from Margate, Ramsgate, Broadstairs, &c was put in motion for the field of action'. At 1 p.m., Blake arrived in a 'Baronet's *barouche*', with Cribb and his other second Bill Gibbons. It was a show of intimidating strength that made it obvious which combatant the majority of the pugilistic establishment favoured. Molineaux's introduction was more low-key, Richmond introducing him to the crowd to a mixture of applause and jeers.

At half-past one Blake and Molineaux shook hands and set to, circling each other cautiously for about a minute before the contest exploded into savage action. Blake connected first, with a hard right and then a rapid left to Molineaux's body, which made the crowd, if not Molineaux, wince, before the two men began wrestling furiously. Then something extraordinary and unexpected happened – as Blake 'slipped from the arms of the Black', Molineaux suddenly struck, connecting with a 'violent chopping blow' to the back of Blake's neck and then a clubbing right-handed blow to his head. Blake slumped to the floor, the crowd gasping at the severity of the American's power. With those two smites of Molineaux's mighty fists, the odds shifted to even.

Despite his grogginess, Blake made it back to scratch and began the second round positively, landing two or three 'well-placed hits', but they had little discernible effect on Molineaux's balance or momentum; he simply shrugged them off with 'great coolness'. Then, after patiently measuring his opponent with his left, Molineaux smashed Blake to the ground again with a devastating right-hand blow. It was, all agreed, the very model of timing and precision; *The Times* declared admiringly that such a punch 'would have done honor to the science of Dutch Sam or Young Belcher'. As Cribb desperately attempted to rouse Blake and Richmond dispensed technical advice to Molineaux, all the excited chatter ringside was of the newcomer's astonishing improvement since his debut. Not only did Molineaux look in phenomenal physical condition, but he was also picking his punches with perfectly controlled aggression.

The Fancy took a collective breath and prepared for round three. In the event, it was a round that proved a rare exception to Molineaux's early dominance. Betraying his lack of experience, the American was overeager throughout, pursuing Blake around the ring, and receiving a 'chattering facer' to his jaw as punishment for his carelessness. Once again the men engaged up close and, after a flurry of punches, both fell. The pattern of the first two rounds was re-established in the fourth, though, with Molineaux blasting heavy punches through Blake's guard. Blake gamely persevered and landed some punches himself, but the difference in power between the two men was striking; Blake's punches simply 'had not the same effect, as [his] head hideously exemplified'. The round ended with Blake once again knocked down.

Molineaux's control was now total and unyielding. As the fifth round began, Blake was bleeding heavily and Molineaux was in no mood for mercy. He seized Blake's head under his left arm and clubbed away at his skull with his right, a succession of blows that saw a helpless Blake again slump to the floor. By now, *The Times* informed its readers grimly: 'The ground resembled the floor of a slaughter-house.' To an observer of modern boxing it will seem inconceivable that such a one-sided contest would be allowed to continue, but continue the fight did. Blake could not win, of course, but it was an unwritten rule of pugilism that a man should return to scratch again and again until he was so exhausted or immobilised that he simply could not move. So it was that Blake duly staggered back to scratch for the sixth round, which saw Molineaux land his most destructive punch yet. Rushing towards Blake, apparently as full of energy as when the fight began, Molineaux blasted his way through his opponent's guard before landing a 'tremendous quick and heavy hit' with his right. The effect of the punch was awe-inspiring; it lifted Blake off his feet before depositing him back on the blood-soaked turf.

And so the slaughter continued. Throughout the seventh, Blake stumbled forward, attempting to rally, but all strength had drained from him, and he soon fell from exhaustion. In an act of futile but admirable bravery he made it back to scratch for the eighth, before desperately retreating from Molineaux's inexorable advance. Somehow, Blake landed a glancing punch to Molineaux's cheek, but the American shrugged it off, countering with a fearsome punch of his own. Blake tumbled, drifted out of consciousness and lay motionless on the floor. Thirty seconds elapsed and, although he had begun to regain his senses, Blake was unable to make it back to the centre of the ring.

As the crowd reacted with a mixture of amazement and fury, Richmond charged forward to congratulate his pupil, who had won in just seventeen brutal minutes. It was, all observers agreed, an astonishing performance, as well as a vindication of Richmond's skill as a tutor of pugilistic science. '[Molineaux] has improved greatly since his first battle,' *The Times* raved. 'He hit at half-arm at that time, but in this battle he dealt out his blows from the shoulder, and gave the effect and strength of his body with his hits, which are sufficient to stun a bullock ... He has taken lessons from Richmond frequently since his battle with the Bristol man, and he has acquired the art of giving, whilst nature had endowed him with the grit of taking.'

The Times may have been awestruck, but many within the Fancy were unsettled by the brash, black challenge to English pugilistic hegemony; as Molineaux and Richmond celebrated, 'very bad fighting' broke out among the crowd who were, the *Kentish Gazette* observed, 'much dissatisfied'. One sentence in particular from *The Times* report summed up the uneasy mood sweeping the nation, a sentence which resonated sufficiently that it found its way verbatim into countless newspapers up and down the length and breadth of England: 'The Black, who is 26 years of age, threatens to mill the whole race of fighters of the day.'[3]

It was, at once, a warning, a threat and a challenge; Cribb, as he roused Blake back to consciousness, knew that better than anybody. Later it was claimed that after the fight Blake turned to Cribb and said, bitterly, 'Tom, I don't mind being licked by you, but to think I should have been beaten by that black thief!' Cribb, his eyes narrowing menacingly, replied, 'Never mind, old fellow, I'll thrash him for you before you're much older.'[4] From that moment, Cribb versus Molineaux was an inevitability.

14

England's Anxiety

No sooner had Molineaux flattened Blake, than Cribb gave verbal assent to defend his title against the American pretender; the news was included as a mouth-watering postscript in most newspapers' accounts of Molineaux's stunning victory. Meanwhile, the dominant nature of the American's performance and the incredible improvements in ring science produced by Richmond's training regimen, were sending shock waves across the country. *The Times* reported gravely that Blake had returned to London with 'hideous marks of the Black's skill and strength' over his face, head and body. 'Blake once fought Crib an hour and ten minutes;' the newspaper exclaimed. 'Such was the violence of the Black's hits, that he could only receive them seventeen minutes.'

Molineaux and Richmond arrived back in London at 5 a.m. the next morning in a mood of jubilation, expressing confidence that final agreement of terms with Cribb was a formality. The Fancy knew Molineaux was the only logical challenger and if Cribb failed to commit to a defence, or remained in retirement, then the title would either pass unchallenged to Molineaux, or Richmond would be in a position to arrange a championship match between his protégé and another contender. Nevertheless, arranging a Cribb-Molineaux bout did not prove as simple as it first seemed; as August drew to a close crucial questions such as where and when the fight was to take place, as well as how much money would be at stake, were still to be agreed. Optimistically, several newspapers speculated the contest would take place in October, with the *Morning Chronicle* stating on 1 September that 'the battle betwixt [Molineaux] and Crib will take place in about six weeks.' By mid-September, though, confirmation of venue or date remained elusive, while rumours the contest was set for Pegwell Bay, near Ramsgate had come to naught.

The main obstacle to finalising terms rested with Richmond and his lack of financial resources compared to the riches at the disposal of Cribb's backers – Capt. Barclay, Paul Methuen and Lord Stradbrooke. Raising the 200-guinea stake that Cribb insisted was the minimum requirement for the fight to be held was a grind and, despite Richmond's tireless endeavours, it seemed no one from within the higher echelons of the Fancy was willing to back 'the Black', perhaps for fear that such an act might be seen as treacherous or unpatriotic, after all, for the English champion to be deposed by a black foreigner would be a potentially devastating blow to national morale, particularly at a time when the Napoleonic Wars were in the balance.

Indeed, England was in a state of almost permanent nervous anxiety, having seen France's power and territory extend across the continent, with the Swiss Confederation, the Duchy of Warsaw, the Confederation of the Rhine, and the Kingdom of Italy all now under Napoleon's control, and Westphalia, Spain, Naples, Prussia and Austria also allied to his cause. The finely balanced state of the Peninsular War coupled with the prospect that the English Championship (which had always been the preserve of white Englishmen, and had never previously passed into foreign or black hands) might end up in Molineaux's grasp made for a toxic brew. The uneasy atmosphere engendered by this twin challenge to English supremacy was vividly articulated in an extraordinary article that appeared in the *Chester Chronicle* on 14 September. This article laid bare the widespread public anxieties about the possibility of Cribb being vanquished, and the devastating effect of such a defeat on the perception of England's 'fighting character' during a time of war:

Many of the *noble* patronizers of this accomplished art, begin to be alarmed, lest, to the eternal dishonour of our country, a negro should become the *Champion of England*! Those who have seen *Blacky* fight, are very shy with the odds in favor of Crib. Unless *Blacky* shows a *white feather*, it is said he will *mill* Crib in half an hour. An alarm for the championship has gone so far, that a young nobleman is said to have addressed a letter to *John Gully, Esq.* requesting him to get in training at all events. – In case of Crib being *milled*, and Gully obstinately declining a contest with *Mungo*, it is reported that the *gentlemen* boxers will take up the affair, for the honour of the country; and that a dozen of these heroes are now taking their *sparring* lessons *without muffs*. Among many of our noble families, the approaching contest between Crib and the Black, has excluded all other topics - not omitting Lord Wellington and the fate of the Peninsula – Our *fighting* character is more at stake in Crib than in a dozen of our generals. – We shall continue to notice the odds, as they vary; – a subject now infinitely more interesting than the rise or fall of the funds.

Writing in 1812, Oxberry would also reflect on the alarm with which England greeted the prospect of a black champion, declaring that 'the NATIVES felt somewhat alarmed that a man of colour should dare to look forward to the championship of England, and threaten to decorate his sable brow with the hard-earned laurels of Crib.' Some writers have since disputed the extent to which anti-Molineaux feeling was motivated by racism, with several arguing that a more dominant factor in the violent opposition many people displayed towards him was his status as an American, particularly given the tensions between the two countries since the War of Independence, which would lead to America declaring war on Britain in 1812. In actuality, close examination of the rhetoric within the public discourse surrounding the Cribb-Molineaux fights seems to indicate that the latter's ethnicity and nationality were both factors in arousing suspicion and dislike against him.

The widespread nervousness surrounding a possible Molineaux victory abated somewhat in mid-October though when, dramatically, it appeared the fight had collapsed. A summit had been arranged between the two camps on 17 October at which agreement on rules, regulations and monetary terms would be finalised. Richmond was said to have found an array of backers to satisfy the 200-guinea stipulation, as well as having collected an additional 'subscription' purse. However, although the Cribb faction appeared as planned, Molineaux was left hanging when Richmond and his mystery backers failed to show, for unknown reasons. A sense of relief seemed to permeate reports of this latest twist in the tortuous Cribb-Molineaux saga. 'Poor Mungo's patrons were not forthcoming,' mocked the *Kentish Gazette*, while the *Derby Mercury* claimed 'the match will never take place'.

However, Richmond refused to accept that the fight was off. Within days of its apparent collapse, the contest was resurrected after he persuaded a group of 'American Capt.s' and 'Masters of ships' to stake the final sum needed to reach the 200-guinea mark. 'The battle will be for 200 guineas a side,' The *Kentish Gazette* announced, 'and it is to take place on the 5th January.' The terms were binding and severe, with both parties agreeing to 'pay or play' terms – a settlement which made it impossible for either man to pull out without penalty, as to withdraw would mean sacrificing their original stake. Such a clause made Cribb-Molineaux the closest thing to a certainty you could get in pugilism.

It soon emerged that the January date was merely provisional, with the *Oxford Journal* of 3 November issuing a correction and clarification: 'the battle between Molyneux and Cribb is fixed for the 18th December. They are to fight within 24 miles of London.' The report added that one of the terms for the contest was that the time each fighter would be allowed to return to scratch after a knockdown was 'fixed at thirty seconds', a vital point bearing in mind the controversy that would later plague the fight's outcome.

With the fight confirmed, the Fancy entered a fever of speculation and anticipation; their hunger for fight gossip was sated by frequent newspaper reports which appeared alongside and jostled for attention with the exhaustive accounts of the continuing progress of the Napoleonic Wars. Despite the earlier panic that Molineaux might win, the Fancy were now convinced that Cribb was the favourite because of 'his known science, strength and bottom'. However, the *Morning Chronicle* added the caveat that 'the cognoscenti ... are very cautious ... particularly those who have seen the Black exhibit'. The fight was attracting many significant wagers, with the *Morning Post* remarking that 'thousands' had been bet, with Cribb a six-to-four favourite. News of the contest and Molineaux's endeavours had even spread across the Atlantic. 'Boxing is become a great amusement in America since Molineaux has vanquished such sturdy opponents of the Mother Country,' *The Bury and Norwich Post* revealed. 'A correspondent, who has just left America, states, that there are regular sparring matches at New York amongst the lower order, and that patrician bands have nightly meetings for the same exhibitions.'

On 15 November, there was a delicious hors d'oeuvre before the main course of Cribb versus Molineaux as Cribb's younger brother, the hapless George, squared off against Tom Hall, a boxer from the Isle of Wight, at Old Oak Common, near Uxbridge. Richmond had been training Hall for several months and he apparently hailed from a 'family ... notorious as provincial boxers'. As usual 'young Cribb' fought with heart but was found wanting when it counted, eventually being bludgeoned to defeat after an hour and nine minutes. 'Crib did not disgrace the name,' reflected the *Morning Chronicle*, while admitting Hall had dominated throughout. More significantly, for the third time in five months a Richmond trained fighter had got one over on the Cribb family, although it does not seem that Tom was in attendance to witness his brother's latest defeat.

As 18 December drew closer, the frenzy of the Fancy intensified and so did the hype. As if the atmosphere across the country was not uncertain enough, at the same time as the fate of the English Championship lay in the balance, so too did the immediate fate of the monarchy, with Prime Minister Spencer Perceval preparing to introduce a Regency Bill into parliament, having concluded that George III's descent into mental illness left him unfit to continue ruling. The bill had brought Perceval into conflict with the Prince of Wales, who fiercely objected to the restrictions that the Prime Minister was seeking to place on his powers as Prince

Regent. Despite his frustrations and the constant political manoeuvrings in London, however, the Prince remained as absorbed as the rest of the nation in the outcome of Cribb versus Molineaux, despatching his 'favourite groom', Jack Radford, to Sussex to ensure he could be given a thorough, eyewitness account of the fight.

As Christmas approached, 'various reports' continued 'to be circulated relative to plans of Regency, new Government &c,' but Cribb versus Molineaux held its own in the pages of newspapers across the country. It was reported that Molineaux was 'very much elevated' in mood and had defiantly declared that he would 'conquer or die'. For his part, Cribb was said to be in 'fine condition and high spirits'. With the absence of Capt. Barclay from his training camp in Kent,[1] Cribb was being trained by Gully and had 'reduced a stone', with reports claiming his weight was down to 14 stone 8 pounds. Meanwhile Molineaux, who was training with Richmond in Hertfordshire, was apparently scaling 14 stone 6 pounds. Both training camps were the subject of fierce scrutiny with the *Hampshire Chronicle* reporting: 'So great is the attention paid to the object of this approaching contest, that they are daily visited by several noble amateurs.' It was widely reported that Richmond and Molineaux's camp had been both focused and productive, with Molineaux 'much improved'. An amusing anecdote also found its way out of the camp; one day, in a rare moment of leisure, the American had been invited by a local landowner to go shooting in a local park. While stalking through the undergrowth, he had encountered the gamekeeper who 'not being aware of the indulgence given to Molineaux' attempted to take his gun away from him. A shocked Molineaux responded by throwing the equally surprised gamekeeper over the 'park pailing'.

The news that both men had been preparing hard increased the sense of anticipation, while the betting odds nervously oscillated, with the price on Cribb shifting from six-to-four to two-to-one, before moving again to three-to-one on the morning of the fight. The Fancy were undoubtedly edgy about Cribb's prospects; *The Times* perfectly evoked the prevailing mood in its final preview article, declaring, 'No battle on record has ever excited more anxiety.'

It was as if this anxiety was transmitted to the heavens, for as the day of the fight finally dawned the sky assumed a dark and dreadful countenance. For hours before the contest, torrential rain poured down on the appointed site of Copthall Common, near East Grinstead in Sussex, and soon the green turf was a quagmire of dark mud. Despite the rain and the bitter cold, somewhere between 5,000 and 10,000 spectators still slogged their way through the sludge to eagerly cluster around the 24-foot ring, whose assembly Jackson had overseen. As the crowd excitedly awaited the appearance of the combatants, the rain continued its ceaseless torrent – it would, in fact, continue to rain throughout the contest and for hours afterwards, ensuring the 'Lords, Nobles, and Commoners' present got a 'complete soaking'.

Despite the terrible weather, the drama that unfolded in front of the hardy souls present was so acute that those members of the Fancy not in attendance would envy those who were for decades to come. It was not merely the fact the fight was so fierce, unyielding and action-packed which secured its pugilistic immortality; a huge factor in the prominent status it still occupies within sporting history is the fact that it was a contest beset by controversy, infamy even. Cribb versus Molineaux is a fight that has been hailed as one of the greatest of all time but also, conversely, has been referred to as 'one of the darkest chapters in the history of British sport'. Accounts and interpretations of what occurred on 18 December differ wildly and remain the subject of fierce speculation, conjecture and debate to this day.

All of which begs this question: is it even possible to accurately and fairly speculate about the contest, or has it entered the realms of the mythic (much like the events of Molineaux's early life) where it is no longer possible to discern what was reality, what was exaggeration and what was fiction? Can we ever truly grasp the truth of what really happened between Cribb and Molineaux, and what Richmond's role was in the drama on that grim December afternoon? Or has any hope of establishing a definitive record been somehow washed away by the ceaseless rain, obscured by the roar of the rabid crowd, and buried, forever, beneath the sodden earth of Copthall Common?

15

'Old England For Ever'

With the possible exception of the Jack Dempsey versus Gene Tunney 'Battle of the Long Count' in 1927, the fairness and propriety of no other pugilistic match-up has provoked such fierce controversy and debate as the first Cribb versus Molineaux bout. Yet while these two contests are comparable from a dramatic and sporting perspective, to weigh one against the other in socio-cultural terms is an absurdity: for while Tunney versus Dempsey was a significant and memorable sporting occasion, Cribb versus Molineaux was so much more than that. It was a contest that, like Jack Johnson's victory against Tommy Burns in 1908 or Joe Louis' demolition of Max Schmeling in 1938, transcended the facile boundaries of 'sport'. Indeed, had the fight's bitterly disputed outcome – a victory for Cribb after a desperately fought bout – edged in the opposite direction, as many thought it should have done, the course of English social, cultural and political history might well have looked very different.

What would the effect have been of a black man in Molineaux, managed and trained by another black man in Richmond, becoming English Boxing Champion in 1810? One can only speculate, but it would have been an achievement that resonated and resounded across the British Isles and beyond with a seismic force that can scarcely be imagined. Perhaps, we might optimistically ponder, a Molineaux victory would have served to promote and inspire greater racial harmony, equality and acceptance, by proving that in the athletic arts, as in every other endeavour, ethnic background need be no bar to achievement or excellence. On the other hand, a Molineaux triumph might have been so unpalatable to 'Old England' that it could have led to a violent backlash against the country's existing black citizens, in much the same manner as Johnson's victory against Burns led to rioting in towns and cities across the United States. Certainly it is easy to imagine that the country would have struggled to deal with the blow to its pride, self-image and self-belief engendered by a black American annexing the championship from a former member of the Royal Navy in the midst of the Napoleonic Wars.

However, such musings remain in the realm of the hypothetical, for Molineaux, officially at least, did not 'win' and the world would have to wait until the twentieth century to witness a trio of sporting feats which would symbolically and definitively debunk the tired and racist notion of inherent white physical supremacy – namely, Jack Johnson becoming Heavyweight Champion of the World in 1908, Jesse Owens winning four gold medals at the 1936 Olympic Games and Joe Louis vanquishing Max Schmeling in one stunning round in 1938.

Nevertheless, the tantalising historical 'what if' that attaches itself to the Cribb-Molineaux fight is one of many reasons why it has endured in the popular imagination. As well as its controversial outcome, the fact is that the fight also has a good case to be recognised as the first international sporting contest of significance.[1] As journalist Frank Keating wrote in 2010,

> the dramatic episode at Copthall Common a week before Christmas 1810 happened all of three-score years before England played Scotland in the first international matches at both football and rugby; it was 67 years before England would play Australia at cricket, or before Wimbledon began its 'international all-comers' lawn tennis championships. Dammit, 1810 was a whole 92 years before two football teams representing 'foreign' countries played one another ... So Cribb (GB) v Molineaux (USA) was a world première 'first' all right.

A further factor in establishing the fight's mystique is the doubt that still surrounds what actually happened at Copthall Common. Maddeningly, the vast majority of newspaper accounts of the epic contest originate from just one frustratingly vague source, a source which described barely a quarter of the fight in detail, with whole rounds and sections missing, not referred to or summarised in general rather than specific terms. Most accounts published in the days after 18 December appear to be only minor variations or rewrites of the almost identical reports which appeared in *The Times*, *Morning Post* and *Morning Chronicle* on 19 December. Although it was usual for the copy from these London-based newspapers to appear in recycled form in local journals, the extra or variant details often added by local correspondents or observers are suspiciously conspicuous by their absence in the accounts of the Cribb versus Molineaux contest which appeared in newspapers such as the *Kentish Gazette, Oxford Journal* and *Northampton Mercury*. Indeed, the only contemporary reports of the Cribb-Molineaux fight that do *not* seem to have originated from the same single source used by *The Times, Post, Chronicle et al*, are those in *The Sporting Magazine* of December 1810 and *Bell's Weekly Messenger* dated Monday 24 December. The account offered in *The Sporting Magazine* is by far the most detailed contemporary report of the contest, and was later recycled by Oxberry in *Pancratia* in 1812. Egan's *Boxiana* also featured a lengthy report of the fight, although it is unclear whether he actually attended the contest. There are several potential reasons for this puzzling paucity of detailed reports: the terrible weather on 18 December may have made record keeping difficult during the contest itself, or even have deterred or prevented some writers from attending in the first place. Perhaps, though, there is a more sinister explanation, namely, a sense of widespread embarrassment and unease about how the fight unfolded and, more to the point, concluded – an embarrassment that was so far reaching, that there was no appetite to give it the oxygen of publicity.

Given all the doubts that surround the fight, attempting to recount the events of Cribb versus Molineaux is, for any historian, a somewhat thankless task, but a task that must be attempted nevertheless. However, before we surrender to speculation, we should firstly consider the facts at our disposal, which are mainly concerned with the first twelve rounds of the forty-four-round contest[2] which were described by newspapers in a fair degree of detail, unlike the remainder of the thirty-two rounds which are merely mentioned in frustratingly sketchy terms.

One such fact is that the fight finally got under way a little after midday on 18 December. Molineaux, with Richmond and Tom 'Paddington' Jones flanking him, was the first to enter the roped area. As he stood amid the driving rain, within the maelstrom of the howling, cheering, jeering mass of the Fancy, no one would have blamed him for feeling nervous. Not only was he a black challenger in a land still largely foreign to him, but he was also surrounded by a crowd of white spectators most of whom had arrived nursing the fervent desire that he would be defeated. As *The Sporting Magazine* remarked, 'What alarmed natives most was the prospect that an African had threatened to decorate his sooty brow with Cribb's title'. Richmond, having finally secured the opportunity for which he had laboured so long – namely, a tilt at the hallowed laurels of the English Championship – was most likely also in a state of nervous agitation which verged on agony; he had invested so much in Molineaux, both in financial and emotional terms, and now, finally, he was about to discover if this investment had been worth it.

The deafening roars of the crowd would have indicated to Molineaux and Richmond before they sighted the champion that Cribb, seconded by former champion John Gully and the wily Joe Ward, was on his way to the ring. Given the horrendous weather and the fact that only an estimated half of the spectators had secured a bed the night before, the crowd's enthusiasm was remarkable. After Cribb had swaggered to the ring and the preliminaries had been dispensed with, the two men shook hands, under the watchful eye of the referee and umpires, including the experienced Sir Thomas Apreece.[3] Only then, with the pre-fight machinations finally over, could the contest, at last, begin.

The first round, as to be expected from such a momentous occasion, was relatively wary, the two men gradually easing their way into the fight with 'cautious sparring'. Molineaux landed a glancing blow to Cribb's chest, the champion responding with a combination to the challenger's head and body, before throwing him to the floor. Heartened by this success, Cribb lustily engaged with Molineaux toe-to-toe in the second round. The champion was made to suffer for this over-confident attack though when, after a 'determined and desperate rally', Molineaux landed a heavy shot to his mouth, drawing 'first blood'. Nevertheless, Cribb ended the round on top, knocking Molineaux to the ground.

To the pro-Cribb crowd's relief, the champion continued to dominate for the next few rounds; a heavy body blow of 'the most obstructive kind' in the third round doubled Molineaux up, although he 'immediately got on his legs'. However, he was also knocked down in the fourth, fifth, sixth and seventh rounds, as Cribb continued to dominate. And thus was established the early pattern of the contest; despite some ferocious exchanges, the champion appeared both stronger and sharper, while Molineaux struggled with his footing and the 'wetness of the ground'. The odds on a Cribb victory were narrowing with every minute and a sense of relief permeated the crowd. 'The black' was, at this stage, not proving as formidable a foe as they had feared – old England's honour and pugilistic reputation appeared safe. Indeed, the eighth round was so one-sided, with Molineaux beaten 'apparently senseless', that many observers felt the contest was virtually over.

Yet the determination and self-belief instilled in Molineaux by Richmond's brilliant tuition was not to be under-estimated. Showing 'true courage', Molineaux seized the initiative in the ninth by standing and trading blows with Cribb until, this time, it was the champion whose resistance broke first, as he slipped to the ground. Suddenly, the atmosphere in the crowd assumed a quieter demeanour, with *The Sporting Magazine* reporting that, 'the knowing ones exchanged looks ... as much to say, "things look a little queer, master"'. In the tenth round, Molineaux, his confidence soaring, began to punish Cribb with regularity. For two minutes the men stood bludgeoning each other, every punch being thrown with hurtful, malicious intent, and for the first time it was Molineaux who displayed 'superiority of strength', while Cribb 'manifested weakness'. Molineaux fell to end the round, but was not seriously hurt; Cribb, on the other hand, was breathless and tiring fast. The eleventh was also 'courageously maintained by the black', with Cribb knocked down again. In the twelfth, Cribb fought back and 'hit his adversary a dreadful body blow' but Molineaux replied in kind with an equally heavy blow to Cribb's head.

It is at this crucial point, with Molineaux having assumed control, that newspaper reports become extremely vague. The *Morning Post* and *The Times* both skirt over the next few rounds by stating: 'the fight continued until the 20th round in favour of Molineaux, inasmuch as he had shown himself superior in strength to his adversary, and had bored on him with that sort of courage which bent down science in hitting'. *The Sporting Magazine's* account also offers scant mention of these rounds, although it emphasises Molineaux's dominance, claiming 'if it could not be called a murder, it was something like manslaughter'.

Egan in *Boxiana* does offer an intriguing, albeit unverified, commentary on these missing rounds though. He somewhat downplays Molineaux's dominance, as referenced in *The Times* and *Morning Post*, suggesting these rounds were more of a see-saw war of attrition than a period of total Molineaux control. In the thirteenth round, Egan notes that Molineaux had become narrow favourite, 'to the no small chagrin of those who had sported their money that [he] would not become the favourite during the fight', while in his account of the fourteenth he describes a furious attack by the American which leaves a helpless Cribb '*levelled*' on the ground. However, in the following round, Egan describes Cribb fighting back and knocking Molineaux down with 'a severe hit' to the throat. By the seventeenth round Egan claims the fight was 'any body's battle' and in his remarks about the eighteenth he claims both men were 'in an exhausted state'.

Despite their slight divergences, both Egan and the newspaper accounts of the first half of the fight are in agreement that it was an uncommonly brutal and intense battle with both men, at various times, showing superiority. It is what happened next that remains unclear. According to *The Times* and the *Morning Post*, something odd happened in the twentieth round. 'The black again became weak, and he seized the ropes of the ring for support, and held Cribb there,' the reports state, before adding, somewhat cryptically that 'The outer ring for a short time was broken, but the fight was renewed.' It is clear from this comment that there was a delay in the fight at a stage when, although looking 'weak', Molineaux had enjoyed a period of dominance lasting several rounds. However, the reports leave unanswered such questions as exactly how the ring came to be broken, as well as for how long the fight was delayed and what the effect of these events was on the combatants. Furthermore, we can only speculate as to the motives of the members of the crowd who broke the ring. Were they enraged by the sight of a black man apparently on the verge of beating the white champion? Were they nervous gamblers who had staked money on a Cribb victory? Or were they merely partisan Cribb fans attempting to tip the balance of the fight back in their man's favour?

Regardless of what motives were at play, it seems extremely strange that such a dramatic incident is so quickly glossed over by *The Times* and the *Morning Post*, while the *Morning Chronicle*, in their shorter report, which utilises almost exactly the same copy in edited-down form, omits mention of it entirely. *The Sporting Magazine* adds to the intrigue by claiming that sometime around the seventeenth round 'a little national prejudice against the black' occurred. Bizarrely, its writer claims that 'being of a passive nature' Molineaux could 'derive no injury from it' and that 'the strictest fair play' was shown throughout. Although it should be treated with caution given its later provenance, Egan's account is more detailed. He claims the incident occurred one round earlier, in the nineteenth, and clearly implies a measure of foul play on the part of the crowd. By this stage, Egan claimed that both men were in a horrific physical condition, stating, 'To distinguish the combatants by their features would have been utterly impossible, so dreadfully were both of their features beaten – but their difference of *colour* supplied this sort of defect.' He then offers his account of the 'ropes incident':

> Cribb acting upon the defensive, and retreating from the blows of his antagonist, though endeavouring to put in a hit, was got by Molineaux against the ropes, which were in height about five feet, and in three rows. Molineaux with both his hands caught hold of the ropes, and held Cribb in such a singular way, that he could neither make a hit or fall down: and while the seconds were discussing the propriety of separating the combatants, which the umpires thought could not be done till one of the men fell down, about two hundred persons rushed from the outer to the interior ring, and it is asserted, that if one of the Moor's fingers was not broken, it was much injured by some of them attempting to remove his hand from the ropes.

If this is an accurate explanation of why the ropes were broken and the fight delayed it is understandable why the partisan English press omitted mention of it, as such an incident could clearly be argued to have influenced the outcome of the fight; for Molineaux, having a large section of the pro-Cribb crowd storm the ring and forcibly remove his fingers from the ropes, and seek to remove Cribb from his grasp, would have been a terrifying and intimidating experience – to say nothing of the disadvantage he would have been placed at in the succeeding rounds if the crowd did indeed injure or break one of his fingers. Yet Egan's account is also extremely frustrating, as although it describes the alleged incident in detail, it offers no clue concerning for how long the fight was delayed. He does, however, describe how the round finally ended with Cribb on the floor:

> All this time [during the ropes incident] Molineaux was gaining his wind by laying his head on Cribb's breast, and refusing to release his victim; when the Champion, by a desperate effort to extricate himself from the rude grasp of the Moor, was at length run down to one corner of the ring, and Molineaux, having got his head under his arm, fibbed away most unmercifully, but his strength not being able to the intent, it otherwise must have proved fatal to Cribb, who fell from exhaustion, and the severe punishment he had received.

Egan's untidy and ambiguous prose leads to further confusion and possible misinterpretation of the chronology of events he is describing. Nevertheless, read as a whole, his account seems to suggest that the events of the nineteenth round were broadly as follows: Molineaux and Cribb became entangled on the ropes and were only removed from this position by a ring invasion of spectators. While the ropes were possibly being restored and repaired (something that may not have happened until the end of the round), Molineaux maintained his grip on Cribb, with the two men then careering into the corner of the ring while Molineaux continued to hold and hit his opponent, at which point an exhausted and battered Cribb finally fell to the ground to end the round.

Aside from the question of whether a pro-Cribb ring invasion occurred, causing the breaking of one of Molineaux's fingers and thus putting him at a disadvantage during a contest he seemed to be winning, there is also a further controversy to consider, namely the possibility that Cribb was given the benefit, at some point during the fight, of a 'long count' and that he took more than the regulation and contractually agreed thirty seconds to return to scratch. If this was indeed the case then, by the agreed terms of the fight, Cribb should have been counted out and Molineaux declared champion. This frequently cited theory is a hypothesis that Egan's first edition of *Boxiana* gave credence to in a series of comments that appeared in the same chapter as the above report of the Cribb-Molineaux fight, albeit in general remarks about Cribb's career rather than in Egan's account of the bout itself. In these comments Egan argues that Cribb, who he otherwise appears to admire unreservedly, was somewhat fortunate in his first contest against Belcher in 1807 [4], as well as against Molineaux at Copthall Common: 'Our love of impartiality compels us to state, that, notwithstanding the superlative excellence of the CHAMPION OF ENGLAND, he [Cribb] has, in more than one instance, been considered indebted to good fortune in being pronounced the victor,' Egan states, before going on to explain that

> in the nineteenth round with *Molineaux*, when the *Moor* had seized CRIBB so fast that he could not extricate himself from his grasp, and which was only effected by some persons breaking into the ring to separate the combatants during which one of the fingers of *Molineaux* either got broke or much injured, when soon afterwards CRIBB fell in so exhausted a state from the severe *fibbing* which he had received, that the limited time had expired before he was able to renew the contest, and Sir Thomas Appreece, one of the umpires, cried out: '*time! time!*' but his second, *Richmond*, not noticing the circumstance, CRIBB recovered.

The reference to the long count occurring 'soon after[wards]' the ropes incident has been interpreted by many as meaning that it occurred later in the fight, possibly at the end of the thirtieth round, when many sources are in agreement Molineaux was firmly favoured by the odds-makers. However, read alongside Egan's account of the fight in the same chapter, it seems clear that Egan is implying that the long count occurred at the end of the nineteenth round, in proximity to the ropes incident. This is certainly a more logical explanation than it occurring several rounds later, for example, it seems plausible that after such a dramatic round, with the ring ropes possibly still being restored, that there would have been a huge tumult amid the crowd which would have distracted Richmond and prevented him from hearing the umpire's call of 'time' and claiming victory on Molineaux's behalf. Similarly, amid such chaos it would have been understandable, albeit against any spirit whatsoever of fair play, if Apreece, fearful of a crowd who had already once invaded the ring on Cribb's behalf, had decided not to insist on the fight being halted and Molineaux acknowledged the rightful winner.

If accurate, Egan's account certainly suggests that Cribb should have been counted out after nineteen rounds and Molineaux declared the champion. However, adding to the obfuscation, other later sources maintain that the 'long count' incident occurred later in the fight, possibly at the end of the twenty-eighth or thirtieth round, at which time, according to *The Times* and the *Morning Post*, '2 to 1 was betted in favour of Molineaux'. *The Sporting Magazine*, while not mentioning a 'long count', could possibly be the original source for the assertion of a long count at the end of the thirtieth round, having suggested that Cribb almost lost at this stage by stating that he was knocked down and 'the best judges did not suppose he would appear again in time, but as stated by James Belcher, in the ring, Crib 'would beat a good man after a momentary recovery'.

The writers who cite a long count in the latter stages of the fight have also frequently asserted that it was not merely engendered by the inevitably heightened passions of the crowd, but was part of a deliberate attempt on the part of Cribb's team to cheat Molineaux and Richmond out of victory after the champion appeared to be slumping towards defeat. For example, Henning, who labels the fight as the 'disgraceful battle for the crown', describes how at the end of one round, possibly the twenty-seventh, Cribb fell and was apparently close to exhaustion, to the consternation of the crowd, and even Apreece, who feared he would not make it back to scratch:

Those who were on the ground stood on tip-toe and, with strained eyes and craned necks, tried with feverish anxiety to see what was going on in Cribb's corner. Then as soon as 'Time!' was called (and even old Sir Thomas' voice faltered as he gave the summons, so agitated was he at the prospect of England's disgrace) the excitement ran high. The moment Cribb was lifted to his feet burst forth a cry that was almost pathetic in its earnestness. '*Now*, Tom, *now*, for God's sake, don't let the nigger beat you. Go for him, Tom, go for him; Old England for ever.'

On this occasion, Henning states that Cribb *did* make it back to scratch, however he maintains that in the twenty-eighth round he did not, and as such Molineaux should have been declared the victor:

In the twenty-eighth round Thomas Molyneux *fairly won the fight*. Tom Cribb could not come to time, and Sir Thomas Apreece allowed the half-minute to elapse, and summoned the men three times. Still Cribb could not come, and the Black awaited the award of the victory, his just due, in the centre of the Ring. But during the excitement Joe Ward rushed across the ring to Bill Richmond, and accused him of having placed bullets in the Black's fist. This was, of course, indignantly denied, and Molyneux was requested to open his hands, proving that nothing was there. The ruse, however, succeeded, and gave Cribb the opportunity to come around.

Variations of the 'bullets in the fist' story have also appeared in many other sources. Although it is impossible to verify its veracity or otherwise, it seems a somewhat far-fetched story; for one, Richmond was a highly experienced second, and it seems inconceivable that he would fall for such a trick, particularly with victory apparently in sight and Cribb lying insensible among his seconds. The earlier interpretation, based on Egan's account, that a long count occurred at the end of the nineteenth or twentieth round, while the ropes and order among the crowd were still being restored, is far more plausible; for one, it would make far greater sense that in such circumstances Richmond and others would have been distracted and not noticed that Cribb had failed to return to scratch in time.

As well as the 'ropes' and 'long count' incident, several accounts of the fight also mention other possible factors as decisive to the outcome. According to *The Sporting Magazine*, in the thirty-first round Molineaux was thrown by Cribb and 'pitched upon his head', an unfortunate injury that left him stunned and disorientated. Oxberry, who makes no mention of any incident with the ropes or long count, also makes note of this occurrence, claiming that Molineaux was 'so severely afflicted' by the fall that 'he could hardly stand'. Henning alludes to a similar incident around the same time, claiming that in trying to throw Cribb, Molineaux fell and his head collided with a ring post, leaving him in a 'semi-stunned' state. Several reports also mention the dramatic effect the weather had on Molineaux in the closing stages with Henning recounting that the cold had 'a serious effect upon the nigger. He was seized with violent shivering, and all at once he seemed to collapse'.

Whatever actually happened between the nineteenth and forty-fourth rounds, the fact remains that, whether the fight was fairly contested or not, Cribb was still standing at the end, while Molineaux was forced to concede, and as a consequence the champion retained his crown. *The Times* and *Morning Post* accounts of the end of the fight were infuriatingly brief and generalised, with the *Post* stating,

> Crib finding he could not beat his man by body of fighting, resorted to his safe mode, that of milling on a retreat, and it was perhaps by that Molineaux, who is good a man as ever entered a ring, lost his battle. His hitting on retreating is Crib's best forte, if the expression best may be allowed, and it is by this alone that he won this battle. If Crib had superior science, Molineaux had courage equal … The battle

lasted fifty-five minutes, in which 44 rounds took place, and it was all hard fighting. The two men were so dreadfully beaten that their sight was altogether lost, and their bodies were in the most emaciated state, from the rapid repetition of heavy blows. When the battle was decided nature had left Molineaux, and Crib could not have staid much longer, but his *gameness* bore him out.'

The Sporting Magazine's account of the fight's conclusion differs considerably, claiming the contest ended after thirty-three rounds when Molineaux fell 'by an effort to keep his legs, which being termed by Crib's party falling without a blow, a victory was claimed in favour of Crib'. For such an epic contest to be decided by a foul, the writer admitted, would have 'originated a dispute', however Molineaux then apparently declared, 'I can fight no more', therefore conceding the fight.

When considering whether or not Molineaux was cheated of victory, it is interesting that the accounts of the fight that appeared in December 1810 contained surprisingly little pro-Cribb triumphalism. Indeed, the extent to which the writer above was at pains to praise Molineaux's 'courage', and the fact he is referred to in this and other reports as 'without exception, the best fighter of courage in this country' and 'as good a man as ever entered a ring', could be interpreted as compensatory praise motivated by residual guilt about the fact there were doubts about the legitimacy of Cribb's victory.

In the following months and years, doubts about the outcome of the fight were expressed widely and frequently. For example, ten months after the contest during the build-up to the 1811 rematch between the two men, *Bell's Weekly Messenger* reprinted an item from the *Stamford News* which alluded to the rumours of foul play that still hung, like an acrid stench, over the first fight:

The odds are still in favour of Cribb ... But the Black and his friends nod their heads and look knowingly when this is mentioned. There were more than whispers abroad after the last battle, that the American did not receive all that fair play which Englishmen are noted for, and which surely a foreigner has a great claim on as a native. The ring, it is said, was broken in a most outrageous manner, and undue favour shown to *Cribb* by allowing him more than his time, while a failure in this respect on the part of his antagonist was instantly taken advantage of. We hope there will be no recurrence of such unhandsome behaviour.

Many other writers connected with the Fancy, who had the benefit of hearing various first-hand accounts from those directly involved with the fight, later expressed the firm conviction that Molineaux had not been treated fairly. For example, *Blackwoods Magazine* famously declared, 'What Briton will dare to say that Molyneux did not win the first battle with the Champion?' *Blackwoods* also summed up the symbolic nature of Molineaux's mighty performance by stating,

> We never felt so grateful to Mr Clarkson and Mr Wilberforce, for their humane exertions to procure the abolition of the slave trade, as when we first saw Molineaux knock down Crib. At once all distinction of colour was lost. We saw before us two human beings – and our hearts beat for the cause of liberty all over the world.

Daniel Mendoza was another spectator who maintained Cribb's victory was a hollow one. The former champion was in attendance at Copthall Common and clearly implied in 1824 that the motivation for the crowd's invasion of the ring and the 'long count' was to protect the huge wagers placed on Cribb by many members of the pugilistic establishment. 'In the battle between Cribb and Molineux,' he wrote, 'it is well known the latter had won three times. Some who had backed Cribb for hundreds, would have taken five pounds, before the battle was decided, for their money; but favouritism prevailed.' Egan, in the third volume of *Boxiana*, was also firm in his insistence that Molineaux was prevented from claiming the title, blaming racial prejudice as opposed to financial inducement, although he failed to state whether it was the prejudice of the crowd, umpire or Cribb's team that he held responsible. 'His [Molineaux's] first contest with Cribb will long be remembered by the Sporting World,' he wrote. 'It will also not be forgotten, if justice hold the scales, that his *colour* alone prevented him from becoming the hero of that fight.'

Despite a lack of first-hand evidence, the sheer weight of anecdotal evidence makes it likely that Molineaux did not receive the fair play he was entitled to against Cribb, although to what extent and in what form this 'unfairness' manifested itself it is impossible to definitively prove. At the very least, it seems fair to conclude that Molineaux suffered from significant intimidation and possible injury when the ropes were broken. On its own, this may have been enough to tip a delicately balanced contest in Cribb's favour, in which case Molineaux was extremely unfortunate, although Cribb himself cannot be held responsible for the actions of his supporters in the crowd who invaded the ring. However, if a long count also occurred, as Egan suggests and Mendoza implies, then Molineaux was clearly cheated of victory, albeit possibly via confusion and the weak reluctance of the officials to stand up to an intimidating crowd, rather than due to blatant skulduggery.

Meanwhile, if there is any truth to the Joe Ward story, then Molineaux was not only cheated, but the victim of one of the greatest frauds in sporting history.

The most fitting conclusion is that, in 1810, England simply wasn't ready for a foreign boxing champion, let alone one who was also black, and that Molineaux and Richmond faced an unequal playing field which made it well-nigh impossible they would leave Copthall Common bearing the laurels of the English Championship. The forces of the established order ultimately prevailed, and, whether she harboured a guilty conscience or not, 'Old England' was mightily relieved. As one writer for the *Royal Cornwall Gazette* made clear: 'It was a desperately contested affair, and victory, long doubtful, decided in favour of Crib, *for the honor of the whites.*'

Richmond wasn't going to take defeat lying down though. The injustice of Molineaux's loss festered for a couple of days while he weighed up his next move and then, just before Christmas, Richmond's brilliantly written riposte, challenging Cribb to an immediate return, exploded into the pages of the English press, igniting the passion, anxiety and anticipation of the Fancy to hitherto unprecedented levels.

16

'The Antipathy Against a Man of Colour'

The movements and actions of Richmond in the immediate aftermath of the contest between Molineaux and Cribb add to the evidence that the outcome of the fight was highly controversial and the American was, in all probability, cheated out of a rightful victory. It is clear that after the fight, when he returned to the Horse and Dolphin, Richmond was furious with what had happened; so furious, in fact, that he became embroiled in a bitter and violent altercation with a man named John Hart, who presumably had been a spectator at the fight. Richmond and Hart came to blows 'in consequence of a dispute between them, arising from the determination of the battle,' and the matter was sufficiently serious to come to court in the New Year, with Richmond being charged with assault. The case came before Bow Street magistrates in January 1811, when Richmond was bailed, although he ultimately escaped serious punishment or censure.[1]

Once Richmond's ire had abated, he got to work marshalling public support for a rematch. The first salvo in his campaign was an open letter from challenger to champion, which duly appeared in many journals just before Christmas. Although ostensibly by Molineaux (who could actually neither read nor write), it carried the imprimatur of Richmond's keen intellect, as well as the street address of the Horse and Dolphin. In its use of understatement and innuendo it was a masterpiece of the art of public rhetoric:

To Mr. THOMAS CRIB,
St Martin's Street, Leicester Square, Dec. 21.
SIR - My friends think, that had the weather on last Tuesday, the day upon which I contended with you, not been so unfavourable, I should have won the battle; I therefore challenge you to a second meeting, at

any time within two months, for such sum as those gentlemen who place confidence in me may be pleased to arrange.

As it is possible this letter may meet the public eye, I cannot omit the opportunity of expressing a confident hope, that the circumstance of my being a different colour to that of a people amongst whom I have sought protection will not in any way operate to my prejudice. - I am, Sir,

Your most obedient, humble servant,

Witness: J. Scholfield.

T. MOLINEUX.

The missive was perfectly judged, demonstrating that Richmond's knowledge of the English character and temperament were razor sharp; he correctly discerned that any direct references to foul play, whether by the crowd, umpire or Cribb's team, would make himself and Molineaux look graceless, and would have been considered by most readers to be somewhat distasteful and 'un-English'. Nevertheless, the reference to 'unfavourable' weather carries a clear double meaning: taken literally, the phrase might be interpreted as a feeble excuse for Molineaux's defeat – the weather having been as unfavourable for one man as the other, of course. However, the Fancy knew what was being insinuated through Richmond's cunning use of pathetic fallacy, namely, the poisonous atmosphere surrounding the fight, the crowd's inexcusable intervention and, most probably, the 'unfavourable' judgment of the officials in granting Cribb a 'long count'.

The insinuation that racial prejudice had been a motivating force in the public's actions at Copthall Common was also made clear by the irony of the letter's conclusion; in noting that the letter would be scrutinised by the 'public eye', Richmond's wording makes it clear that his appeal for a lack of 'prejudice' is directed at the public and the potential spectators at a rematch, rather than Cribb himself. The champion had, after all, now twice demonstrated (by fighting first Richmond and then Molineaux) the truth of Egan's judgment that '*colour* or *persuasion* made no odds to Tom', and Richmond knew all too well that finances, and not Molineaux's ethnicity, would be the decisive factor for Cribb when deciding whether to grant a rematch. The final touch to the letter, in the form of the polite, almost servile sign-off ('Your most obedient, humble servant') was also a clever touch, and seems to be Richmond's attempt to recast Molineaux in his own image as a courteous English-style gentleman, thus counteracting the widespread perception of him as a loudmouth braggadocio.

Initially, Molineaux seemed to have won the public's sympathy. On Saturday 22 December, just four days after the fight, Richmond took him to the London Stock Exchange in Capel Court. Out of appreciation for

Molineaux's showing against Cribb, or perhaps out of shame at how he had been treated, the traders collected a 40-guinea gift, which they presented to the delighted American. The following day, in a display of bravado intended to show he was fit and ready to take on Cribb once again, Molineaux appeared at the Fives Court to try his hand at the game, which for years had been a traditional public school past-time at institutions such as Eton, Winchester and Rugby.

Cribb initially maintained an obstructive stance to Richmond and Molineaux's challenge, neglecting to send a formal reply but letting it be known he would 'not fight again unless for double the stakes he last contended for'. Within days of this rumour appearing, though, the *Morning Post* appeared to suggest Cribb had relented:

> Crib has accepted the challenge from Molyneux. The match was made up last night at the house of MR. GULLEY, in Rupert-street, for 250 guineas a side, and a subscription purse of 100 guineas for the winner. The battle is to be fought on the 21st May. Fifty guineas of the stake are the actual property of Molyneux, whose friends came forward with the remainder.

This report was contradicted elsewhere though; the *Morning Chronicle*, for one, was somewhat more vague, stating that Cribb had agreed to a return, while admitting the financial details had not been worked out. As the New Year arrived it was clear no agreement had been brokered, and the fight was far from certain to proceed, so Richmond and Molineaux switched their tactics by instead attempting to exert subtle pressure on Cribb through good grace and manners; the black pugilists sparred against each other at a benefit for the champion on 28 January at the Fives, with *The Times* noting admiringly that Molineaux 'manifested considerable improvement'.

However, the courtesy the two men had shown in their reaction to the controversial outcome of December's bout was not always reciprocated. In March, Richmond's feud with Jack Powers was reignited in ugly circumstances, an affair which demonstrated there were plenty of members of the public who harboured hostility towards the 'black challenge' to white England's pugilistic pre-eminence. Since Richmond had beaten Powers after Gregson's dinner in 1810, persistent rumours had linked the men with a more formal contest – a 100-guinea set-to on 5 January 1811 had even, at one stage, been mooted, but the hullaballoo surrounding the outcome of the Cribb-Molineaux fight had put paid to those plans. In the meantime, the truculent Powers had broadened his grudge against Richmond to include all black boxers; it was a cause of particular consternation to him that the Horse and Dolphin had become the unofficial headquarters of black pugilism, Richmond's reputation now being so elevated that his public house was the first port of call for any black man who fancied trying their hand in the prize ring. At the end of January, for example, Richmond had trained and seconded a new black pugilist, referred to as a 'ten stone black of reported courage' in a contest against Caleb Baldwin-backed Spicer. To Powers, the vision of inclusivity represented by Richmond's lofty position within the pugilistic firmament was anathema and he was soon making a voluble nuisance of himself at the Horse and Dolphin with a series of derogatory taunts about Richmond, Molineaux and other black patrons' 'tawny complexion[s]'. His verbal discrimination seems to have been relentless, with *The Times* referring to the fact he 'swore destruction to the fraternity of black millers'. Molineaux was a particular target for Powers' loose and foul tongue until, one night in March 1811, neither he nor Richmond could stand any more, as *The Times* explained:

> On pointed insults over and over again being given to Molineux, in the house of Richmond, whose forbearance entitled him to praise, Molineux and Powers stripped, and had a few rounds, not for hundreds but for *love* (technically terming it), and that love on rough stones.

Two or three of Powers' cronies had accompanied him that night and, as a makeshift ring was assembled in the street, an excitable crowd gathered. The mood was one of ugly prejudice with 'the wrath of the multitude present ... eminently displayed against the blacks'. Richmond bravely ensured he 'stood by his friend' Molineaux, while Tom Belcher also loyally 'lent protection'. Once Powers was in the makeshift ring with the powerful and furious Molineaux, his courage soon deserted him though, as *The Times* recounted:

> Powers was not able to move the Black, and after hitting he was pursued by Molineux into the crowd ... Towards the conclusion, Molineux got a hit at his antagonist's head, but it was at too great a length to effect much; but in the subsequent round he gave Powers a doubler in the body. Whether that had the effect of putting an end to the combat, a white-feather, or suffering from the blow, the vanquished best knows, but Powers would fight no more.

Another interesting detail, guaranteed to enrage those of an anti-Molineaux bent, was left hanging at the end of the report: 'The Black had an eye-lid swollen, and a cut in the lip, but he afterwards accompanied four ladies to the theatre.' It was the first public recognition of what the Fancy had known for months; namely that, in addition to being a splendid athlete, Molineaux was also a consummate womaniser. In this respect, his roving eye formed a vivid contrast with the quietly married and restrained Richmond, to whom no evidence or innuendo of a single extra-marital dalliance has ever been attached.

The Times' detailed account of Molineaux's street fight with Powers appeared underneath a high-profile denunciation of Napoleon by the French deserter Gen. Jean Sarazzin, demonstrating that his fame was now widespread. Ever aware of a commercial possibility, Richmond calculated that a benefit for Molineaux at the Fives would prove a lucrative proposition, as well as a useful way to increase the pressure on Cribb. The event, which took place at the beginning of April, was a wild success with the court 'crowded in a manner never before witnessed'. From Cribb and his supporters' perspective, Molineaux's form was ominous. Isaac Bitton, Tom Belcher and Ben Burn all sparred with him but none 'were able to make any impression' on the increasingly confident American; it seemed that Richmond's continual exhortations had ensured that Molineaux was reaching an intimidating peak of pugilistic science. 'He has so far improved as to become formidable,' noted the *Morning Post*. 'And as he has always had the gift of hitting and quickness, so he has nearly reached perfection in stopping.' Lest the Cribb contest not come off, Richmond lined up an alternative opponent in the form of Bob Gregson's Lancastrian protégé, Heskin Rimmer. An impressive 6-foot specimen, Rimmer also displayed his skills at the benefit and the *Morning Post* were impressed with his potential. 'He manifested considerable courage,' their reporter noted. 'His strength ... will render him very formidable to the *Black*.'

With the Rimmer contest tentatively scheduled for May, Richmond continued his campaign to build a formidable aura around his man by accepting invitations in mid-April to visit various towns in the Midlands with Molineaux. In order to further build anticipation, Richmond and Molineaux took to arriving at each stop on their travels in a 'postchaise and four', ordering their drivers to 'gallop as fast as possible to the best inn in the place, in order to *cut a swell*'. These theatrics had the desired effect and, on their arrival in Birmingham, huge crowds assembled to see the '*ebony* professors' display their skills. Buoyed by this response, and some handsome earnings, Richmond and Molineaux then headed to Nottingham, where the latter had a gloved set-to with a local by the name of String who had challenged 'either of the blacks'. It was meant to be an 'amicable set-to' but within seconds of the men beginning to spar a 'very sharp conflict' ensued in which 'the exchange of hits was awful'. Molineaux, continuing the improvements visible against Powers and in his benefit, swatted String aside after ten rounds, despite the Nottingham man's imposing 6 feet height.

Returning to London on 17 April 'laden with treasure', it was clear that Richmond and Molineaux's sojourn in the Midlands had been a runaway success. The *Oxford Journal*'s report of the events in Birmingham and Nottingham also contained an extraordinary coda, in which the journal claimed that a boisterous Molineaux had, on his return to London, rechallenged Cribb or indeed 'any man in the world' to a contest 'the next day, or in three months' for £500. According to this report, the 'challenge was not accepted' and therefore the title had passed to Molineaux who was now 'the offensive Champion of England'. In the absence of any official pugilistic governing body, recognition of the English Championship had always operated on a process of undefined public consent and recognition. Without the widespread assent of other members of the Fancy, or the backing of any other journals, the *Oxford Journal*'s recognition of Molineaux as champion was effectively a meaningless gesture. Nevertheless, the fact such sentiments were being expressed made it clear that the pressure on Cribb to either retire or come to an agreement with Richmond and Molineaux was now acute. If Cribb did quit, then general recognition of Molineaux as the champion looked inevitable.

The campaign to corral Cribb back into the ring continued at Tom Belcher's benefit on 25 April. In front of a large crowd of around 900 fans, Molineaux and Richmond sparred with one another (Richmond's science winning more plaudits than Molineaux's, funnily enough), while Belcher squared off against Rimmer. The Lancastrian looked so impressive against the highly regarded Belcher that it was decided to resurrect the idea of him fighting Molineaux. Richmond realised it was a risk to throw his man into action against someone other than Cribb, but he also calculated that an impressive victory against Rimmer would ratchet up the pressure on the champion to agree terms or cede his crown.

By the beginning of May, the talk emanating from Cribb's camp was definitive: he would not concede the crown, and a 300-guinea purse would secure a rematch. However, tired of the constant negotiations and his never-ending struggle to raise finances without the backing of a wealthy patron, Richmond decided a Cribb match could wait until after Rimmer versus Molineaux. It was a shrewd, albeit risky, piece of business; Richmond was gambling that an impressive Molineaux victory would persuade an extra financial backer or two to come forward and fund the rematch against Cribb. However, the possibility also existed that Molineaux might produce a poor performance, thus undermining his case for a rematch. The worst-case scenario, that Rimmer might beat him, didn't bear thinking about.

With the pressure therefore building on both the champion and his number one challenger, Richmond and Molineaux departed for a training camp in Middlesex to prepare for the 100-guinea match, due to take place at Moulsey Hurst on 21 May. Belcher, who had a fight scheduled for 6 June, also joined the camp and the trio got to work, with Richmond's innovative training regime comprising weight throwing and cricket, as well as traditional sparring. Rimmer, meantime, was in Kent, training with Gregson and sparring with a local farmer named Maskall; one session between the two men was so heated that the duo removed their gloves and settled matters with bare knuckles, Rimmer disposing of his opponent in seven violent minutes.

So quickly had Molineaux's reputation grown, and so fascinated were the Fancy with the prospect of seeing him in action again, that between 10,000 and 15,000 spectators swarmed to the appointed site of combat on the south bank of the Thames by 1 p.m. on the day of the fight. 'This inviting fight, on this *inviting* day, is likely to afford more *hard hitting interest* than any match in the annals of pugilism,' announced the *Morning Chronicle*, which was probably overstating it, but the fight had certainly captured the imagination of the public, as well as a group of city traders, who had agreed that the winner would be presented with 'as many quarters of lottery tickets as they may fight rounds'. Molineaux began the fight as a firm three-to-one favourite but, as the 25-foot ring was measured and staked out, Rimmer certainly appeared confident, hurling his hat into the ring as a 'token of defiance'.

Just after 1 p.m. the fight got under way, and it was soon apparent that Molineaux was vastly superior to his well-built but limited opponent. In the opening round, Molineaux drew first blood; in the second, Rimmer was sent sprawling by a succession of quick lefts and rights, and in the third, Molineaux grinned delightedly before unleashing a hail of unanswered punches. The American's dominance was total; by the beginning of the fourth round, Rimmer's head was 'covered in blood', while a Molineaux right and left combination led him to fall 'as from a pistol ball'. With Rimmer also falling 'from weakness' in the fifth and sixth rounds the outcome was already looking like a foregone conclusion.

Somewhat surprisingly, the persistent Rimmer had the better of the seventh, and even succeeded in throwing Molineaux in the ninth. The next few rounds were more evenly balanced than the early exchanges, with the Lancastrian displaying great heart, but Molineaux dramatically reasserted his authority in the fifteenth round, levelling his foe with a huge 'stomacher'. The force of the blow was so great that as Rimmer lay 'prostrate' on the ground, it looked likely that he would be counted out. At this point, for the second Molineaux fight in succession, the crowd intervened. Many spectators' ire had become engorged by the sight of a black pugilist maintaining dominance over a white foe and this anger now exploded into violent protest with spectators swarming into the ring, breaking the ropes and surrounding the two pugilists in a sea of human chaos.

Unlike at Copthall Common, there was no ambiguity in the reporting this time, with the *Cheltenham Chronicle* describing the disgraceful scene in detail. In the process, its reporter explicitly linked the crowd's conduct to racist sentiment:

> The antipathy against a man of colour being considered a pugilist of first rate, has caused a good many uncharitable declamations, and the ardour of these people so illiberally disposed, aided by the assistance of those who had taken the odds, broke the ring in a moment and surrounded the men in action. Rimmer at this time was technically speaking, dead beat, and in a state of childhood. The scene which here presented itself would baffle the skill of the first artist. Lords and Nobles hustled in with sweeps and ploughmen, fighting men and assistants, who chose, indiscriminately horse whipping. The assembly, amounting to at least 10,000 pedestrians, were inclosed in the spacious ring, and every one at is own game. In this state, which lasted 20 minutes, those disposed to make their exit were unable.

The *Kentish Gazette* also admitted that racism was the crowd's primary motive, pinpointing the crowd's 'aversion' to seeing 'a man of colour become the victor', as well as the 'vexation' of those who had bet against Molineaux. Not all newspapers were quite so honest; the *Morning Post and Morning Chronicle*'s accounts of the same incident, for example, based on the same source as the *Cheltenham Chronicle*, completely excised any reference to racism.

Eventually, due to the endeavours of Richmond and several other pugilists, chief among them Cribb, order was restored. By then, the twenty-minute break in the action had, unfairly and to the Fancy's eternal shame, allowed Rimmer more than sufficient time to recover from the huge body shot that had levelled him, with several newspapers noting the 'great pains' which had been taken during the break in the action to get him to stand again. Thankfully, as distasteful as it was, the crowd's chicanery, on this occasion, made no difference to the outcome; once combat resumed, Molineaux merely continued to beat Rimmer with alacrity for another six rounds until his opponent 'resigned ... when unable to stand'. As Rimmer lay helpless on the floor, Molineaux stood, in the words of one eyewitness, 'grinning over his fallen adversary in Homeric triumph'.

Despite the best efforts of the bigots among the crowd, Richmond's gamble had paid off, and handsomely so. The decisive nature of Molineaux's victory meant that Cribb would have to grant his American rival a rematch or risk ridicule, as well as the likelihood that the American would retrospectively be recognised as champion. No wonder that the next day, Richmond and Molineaux, were sighted 'very gaily' walking the streets of London, with crowds following them excitedly. Molineaux 'bore no external marks of the battle about him, except a *black*-er eye', quipped one writer, whose laboured pun failed to mask his obvious fears and discomfort about the black American's seemingly unstoppable route to the title: '[Molineaux] is a very *ugly customer*,' the reporter also noted. 'It will be a matter of troublesome speculation again to find his conqueror.'

17

'Here Goes the Champion of England'

The final settlement of terms between the Cribb and Molineaux camps was painstakingly negotiated in the wake of the Rimmer contest. It was ultimately a process which stretched into July. By this stage the public appetite for a rematch was so insatiable that there was scant doubt the fight would take place. Press reports dated 31 May claimed the rematch would go ahead 'within three months', with the handsome sum of 300 guineas at stake on either side. These terms were officially confirmed in a meeting at the Horse and Dolphin on Saturday 8 June, with 100 guineas duly lodged by each side with John Jackson as a down payment – this sum would be forfeited by either faction if the total purse was not forthcoming by 27 July. In an eloquent tribute to the importance of the impending rematch a veritable 'who's who' of the noblest members of the Fancy was in attendance at the meeting, including the Marquess of Queensbury, the Earl of Sefton, Lord Archibald Hamilton, the Earl of Yarmouth and many others.

Interestingly, several of the 'articles of agreement' concerning the fight which were thrashed out ceded to demands made by Richmond seeking to ensure impartiality of the sort that Molineaux had been denied in the first contest with Cribb, as well as against Rimmer. For starters, Richmond ensured agreement that the fight would not take place within 100 miles of London, where anti-Molineaux sentiment was at its most fervent. It was further specified that the bout would take place on a raised wooden stage, as opposed to a patch of open ground, a rare and unusual occurrence which was a consequence, according to the *Stamford Mercury*, of 'two rings having recently been broken, whilst men were fighting' – a coy reference to the first Molineaux-Cribb contest, as well as the Rimmer match. A final important detail was a proviso which tried to ensure the fight would pass off without any 'long count' controversy; at the end of a round each combatant would have a 'half-minute' to return to scratch, unless they had been knocked off the stage in which case this time would be extended to a full sixty seconds.

Although several other patrons were said to have come forward to back Molineaux, the man with the most invested in him was undoubtedly Richmond, who had thrown every spare penny he possessed behind his fighter and had even, it was said, been loaned some of the deposit by a local fishmonger. Richmond was risking his family's financial future on the contest, reasoning that gaining control of the championship could pave the way for the accumulation of vast riches from future Molineaux title defences.

First, though, Richmond had to ensure the fight went ahead, which meant that between 8 June, when the 100-guinea deposit was banked with Jackson, and 27 July, when the final payment was due, he had to raise a further 200 guineas for the stakes, as well as further funds to provide for training expenses, as well as the safekeeping and staffing of the Horse and Dolphin and his family while he was away training Molineaux. In order to do so, Richmond alighted upon a provocative but brilliant money-spinner – an exhibition tour of Cribb's home territory of the West Country, to involve not only himself and Molineaux, but Tom Belcher too.

Before the trio could depart, however, there was the vital matter of appearing at a benefit for Tom's ailing brother, Jem, whose health after his stint in prison had so deteriorated that he was now a 'decayed invalid'. The event took place at the Fives on 2 July, with the *Morning Chronicle* declaring that 'the best set-to' was between 'the two blacks, Molineux and Richman'. The event was well attended, although conspicuous by his absence was Cribb; there was, of course, no love lost between him and the Belchers and, at any rate, the champion was highly conscious of criticism that he had taken the challenge of Molineaux too lightly last time. For the rematch he was determinedly focused on his training like never before, and had departed London for Scotland on 21 June for an intensive camp engineered and supervised by Capt. Barclay.

Their duty to Jem fulfilled, Richmond, Molineaux and Belcher left London soon after the benefit and the 'tour of the black pugilists', as the press termed it, proved a wild success. Rooms throughout the west of England were, *The Times* noted, 'crowded by amateurs, eager to witness particularly the exhibition of Molineux, the opposer of Crib, the native champion'. Thankfully, a sense of decorum was maintained, despite the crowds' clear dislike of Molineaux. For example, in Bristol, the city which 'gave birth to *Crib*', *The Times* reported that 'the crowd assembled beggared all description, and the antipathy against *Molineux* was buzzed around the exhibition-room by the natives, but his manner and pugilistic powers sufficiently protected his person.'

On returning to London, Richmond and Molineaux were able to safely deposit the remaining 200-guinea stake money; by this stage betting on the fight was widespread and frenzied, with an estimated £50,000 already wagered on the outcome, with Cribb a narrow favourite. The champion was now ensconced at Barclay's estate in Ury where, for nine tortuous weeks, his patron oversaw Cribb's training with a single-minded determination that verged on mania; the champion walked between 12 and 30 miles a day, and Barclay regularly sweated him, while also maintaining strict control of his diet. Cribb had soon lost several stones and been bullied into formidable shape. Arguably, no pugilist had ever received such thorough and intensive training.

In contrast to Cribb's focused preparations, Richmond and Molineaux prepared for a further series of exhibitions, in order to cover themselves financially. On 30 July, though, tragedy intervened when Jem Belcher passed away at his public house, the Coach and Horses, on Frith Street. It was hardly an unexpected development; ever since his losses to Cribb and his imprisonment, Belcher had been drinking heavily and suffering from the effects, most probably, of liver failure. For his brother Tom, in particular, and for Richmond too, who had grown so close to him, Jem's death, aged just thirty, was a savage blow. Belcher had not only been a great champion, but was also much loved within the Fancy for being, as Egan described him, 'good-natured in the extreme, and modest and unassuming to a degree bordering upon bashfulness'. His colourful life, beset as it had been with exhilarating triumphs and painfully disappointing defeats, not only served as a painful reminder of the vicissitudes of the pugilistic lifestyle, but also of the capricious cruelty of fate. One could argue that had it not been for the rackets injury which had robbed him of one eye, an event which an increasingly embittered and morose Belcher had cursed every day since, he might still have been the champion. Certainly many ring historians agree that with his sight intact Belcher would not have lost twice to Cribb, whose courage was manifest but whose pugilistic science was far inferior.

With Jem's corpse now cold and lifeless, though, such conjecture was pointless. In the meantime, the Fancy's grief was boundless and heartfelt. Belcher's funeral took place on 4 August and was characterised by, in the estimation of one writer, 'more solemnity' than the funeral 'of a prince'. For hours before Belcher's coffin emerged, men and women from all social strata stood quietly in the streets of Soho waiting to pay their respects to the 'Napoleon of the Ring'. Eventually, Belcher's remains were removed from Frith Street and transported to his final resting place of St Marylebone cemetery. One newspaper described the scene in particularly vivid terms:

> Upwards of ten thousand persons of all ranks ... displayed themselves in Soho-square, Greek-street, Batesman-buildings, Queen-street, and every adjoining avenue leading to the spot. Even the lamp irons were not without their occupants. As to the windows and balconies, which could command a view of the deceased's house, they were filled with elegant females, some of them sporting a white handkerchief with a black border, mourning for the deceased. Hackney coaches filled with Ladies and Gentlemen, formed a line along Frith-street; and happy was the man who, by paying a shilling, could gain permission to stand on the roof ... At half past three, the hearse drove up to the door, and a black coffin, six feet four, was brought out; as it was put into the hearse, upwards of two hundred hats were perceived lifted up in the air, and the rebounding voice proceeding from the uncovered multitude was, "*Here goes the Champion of England!*"

Richmond's close connection to the Belchers was indicated by the fact he was seated in the second of the three mourning coaches, alongside John Gully and Bob Gregson, with Tom Belcher and Jem's wife in the first coach and John Jackson and Jack Powers in the third. A glass coach followed, containing Bill Wood and an assortment of other pugilists. Such was the multitude of mourners that the procession had to be temporarily halted when it reached Oxford Street as the road became blocked. By the time the cortège reached St Marylebone, many mourners had lost their shoes and hats in the crush. At Belcher's graveside, as the funeral rites were performed and his body was lowered to rest, Richmond and many others began weeping. Wood was so overcome with grief and distress that 'almost in a state of frenzy', he leapt on top of Belcher's coffin as it was lowered into the ground, 'like Hamlet on the coffin of Ophelia'.

Their solemn duty to Jem concluded, Richmond, Molineaux and Tom Belcher left London on 12 August, having accepted invitations from 'several towns in the north of England, to instruct the untaught in the polite and fashionable art of boxing'. William Fuller, a young pupil of Richmond's who hailed from Norfolk, also accompanied the trio. The demand to see these exhibitions was immense: according to the *Hereford Journal*, 'cards innumerable' were received by Richmond 'from towns where the Mayors and Magistrates are in the *fancy*, soliciting their company'. Among the locations the pugilists visited was Richmond's former hometown of York, where a week was spent sparring, including at the racecourse where, all those years earlier, he had engaged in some of his earliest set-tos.

In later years, some would question how appropriate these tours were in terms of a training strategy for Molineaux. Miles in *Pugilistica*, for example, claimed that Belcher and Richmond made Molineaux 'an instrument of getting money', and that Cribb had been 'better supported by his many surrounding friends'. Such an interpretation seems unduly harsh; it should not be forgotten that Richmond did not possess the vast wealth of Capt. Barclay. As such, Molineaux's training could not be as focused or secluded from the general public as Cribb's. Far from being gratuitous money-spinners, the sparring tours were an essential way of securing Richmond and Molineaux's financial equilibrium and ensuring their training and living expenses in the months leading up to the fight were covered.

A legend has also built up that Molineaux under-trained and over-drunk in the build-up to the fight, but it seems likely that these stories, although containing elements of truth, have been exaggerated. Miles claimed that Richmond and Belcher kept Molineaux 'pliable' by 'allowing him to drink stout and ale by gallons'. However, this assertion does not square with the description in the *Morning Post* a few weeks before the fight which noted that Molineaux 'trained well ... and has gained much by practice'. Besides, with such a large proportion of his finances tied up in the fight, Richmond faced potential ruin if his charge lost, and it was therefore in his interests that Molineaux was well prepared. Given Richmond's restrained personality, his likely reaction to any needless indulgence on Molineaux's part would undoubtedly have been firm disapproval, rather than encouragement.

Having said that, it was undoubtedly the case that Molineaux was somewhat giddy on the fruits, both female and financial, of his new-found fame and did not focus on his training as wholeheartedly as he might have done. Instead, he seems to have spent much of the build-up loudly denouncing Cribb and talking up his prospects of victory; the *Stamford Mercury* remarked, for example, that 'the sable challenger is full of high vaunting'. When Richmond's back was turned it is also likely that Molineaux indulged in more alcohol and female company than was advisable for a man about to face the toughest pugilistic engagement of his life.

The theory that Molineaux's attitude in training was less diligent than Richmond desired certainly gains credence when we consider the disputes that later drove the men apart. Having generously accommodated Molineaux at the Horse and Dolphin and overseen his transformation from novice to formidable pugilist, Richmond undoubtedly felt his protégé was in a measure of debt to him, both literally and figuratively, and as the fight approached the friction between them increased. Molineaux, buoyed by the ease of his victory against Rimmer and bolstered by the whispers of those who maintained he was the true victor of the first fight against Cribb, certainly seemed to be less inclined to listen to Richmond's advice than when he had first arrived in London. It did not help, of course, that Richmond had so many other matters jostling for his attention, including negotiations surrounding where the fight would take place – Richmond initially pushed for Doncaster, a town he knew well from his days as an apprentice and an area that also conveniently fell outside the aegis of influence of Cribb and his patron Capt. Barclay. However, the publicity surrounding the fight was not to the liking of local magistrates, who made it clear they would not allow the match within their jurisdiction. The idea of having the fight in a field just outside Doncaster was also floated and rejected. In order to catch magistrates off guard, a plan was then hatched to hold the contest on the 'skirts of several counties', although exactly where remained a source of debate.

When Richmond and Molineaux returned to London from their northern tour in early September, there was still no agreement on the final location. As the appointed date of 28 September loomed alarmingly near, Richmond argued in favour of Cheltenham, while Cribb's team preferred Lincolnshire, which was less of a distance for the champion to travel from Scotland. *The Times* reported that it was 'even betting' that the disagreement would cause the fight to be called off. Ultimately, the two sides tossed a coin to decide, with Cribb's team winning and duly nominating Thistleton Gap, where the borders of the counties of Lincolnshire, Leicestershire and Rutland intersected. This point of contention finally settled, both factions made their way towards the appointed site of combat; Cribb took up residence at the Bull Inn, between Grantham and Stamford, while Richmond and Molineaux were ensconced in the Coach and Horses in Stamford, before moving on to the New Inn at Greetham.

The tension was palpable, as were the undertones of racial tension and loathing amid the gathering swell of fans and spectators. 'The prejudice against the black colour seems to exist as much in the country as in town,' noted the *Morning Post*, adding that while Molineaux's residence 'remains unnoticed', Cribb had been receiving a steady stream of well-wishers 'of the first consequence in the country'. The message was clear: England and the Fancy were squarely behind Cribb, with the survival of the nation's self-esteem resting on the champion's broad shoulders. Any outcome other than a Cribb win was too dreadful for most to envisage. When Molineaux and Richmond marched to the ring in front of thousands of baying spectators, there would be few, if any,

Englishmen at Thistleton Gap or at home eagerly awaiting news of the contest, who were directing anything other than utter antipathy and ill will towards the 'black pugilists'.

18

Richmond's Ruin

The crowd that flocked to Thistleton Gap on Saturday 28 September 1811 for arguably the most eagerly awaited sporting spectacle of Georgian times was estimated to number between 15,000 and 20,000. The multitude arrived from all directions and in every conceivable form of transport. 'From the barouche to the donkey, every mode of human conveyance was in use,' wrote one observer, who noted that some of those without transportation had trekked for 20 miles or more to gain a glimpse of the action. Surrounding the ring on its elevated stage, every section of society was represented, from the 'Peer, on the coach-box, to the Pickpocket'; rows of standing spectators were nearest to the stage, behind which were huddled 'innumerable horsemen, mingled with every species of carriage, from the chariot to the dust cart'. Astonishingly, most of those on horses stood 'circus-fashion' rather than sit on their saddles, so eager were they for a clear view. There was little danger of them falling and injuring themselves, 'for the living mass was so closely wedged, that once fixed, there was no moving'.

Just before midday, the seconds and bottle-holders made their way to the stage – John Gully and Joe Ward representing Cribb, with Richmond and Bill Gibbons supporting Molineaux. The four men stripped the top layer of their clothing and put jackets on while they waited nervously for the 'principals'. Cribb arrived first, gliding through the heart of the heaving, sweating, cheering multitudes. Clad in a huge brown coat and boots, such was the champion's air of self-assured insouciance that he might have been a farmer out for an afternoon stroll, rather than a prizefighter about to face the most important afternoon of his life. When he reached the stage, Cribb hopped up with 'great gaiety' before making his 'obeisances to the spectators'. Cribb's confidence was unsurprising for he enjoyed pretty much every advantage it was possible for a sporting competitor to enjoy; not only were the crowd almost exclusively supporting him, but his training regime in Scotland had been one of the most scientifically executed and well-funded sporting enterprises ever. Capt. Barclay, who had masterminded his preparations, had every reason to have been meticulous, having staked as much as he possibly could on a Cribb victory. Astonishingly, Barclay stood to win the vast sum of £10,000 if his man won, while he faced financial ruin if he was vanquished.

For all Molineaux's pre-fight bluster that he was 'seven times the man' who fought Cribb the first time, many observers discerned that the pressure of the occasion, coupled with his comparative lack of patronage and support, seemed to adversely affect the American. 'He [Molineaux] came to the fight unsupported by friends of note; while the champion had all the flash-men in his train,' remarked a local reporter, while *The Times* argued that Molineaux exuded 'despondency' throughout the contest. The paper also hinted at widespread anti-Molineaux fervour throughout the country by noting: 'The Black's prowess was regarded by Crib's friends with a jealousy which excited considerable national prejudice against him.' The *Stamford Mercury* reinforced the impression the challenger was ill at ease, observing that 'from his first appearance on the stage', Molineaux 'seemed in a continued state of agitation'.

Whatever anxieties were afflicting him, Molineaux put on a good show during the pre-fight theatrics, following Cribb to the ring in his blue jacket and nankeen trousers, before jumping over the ring railings and eying his foe with a 'vengeful sulky look'. He started the fight well too, drawing first blood by making Cribb's mouth bleed in the second round, and in the same stanza nearly closing his opponent's eye with a ferocious cluster of punches. The 'fury' Molineaux exhibited in the third round was sufficient to cause 'alarm' among Cribb's supporters, with *The Times* remarking that, at this point, 'to an ordinary spectator, the Moor was winning the fight in a hurry'. In the fourth round, things looked even grimmer for Cribb; his head was 'disfigured' and he was bleeding from 'every organ'.

However, during the fourth round, as he manfully absorbed the challenger's best shots, Cribb remained composed enough to flash a knowing smile to the crowd. Such confidence was borne of two factors: Cribb's awareness of his freakish ability to absorb physical punishment, and his knowledge that he had never been in finer physical condition, weighing as he did around a stone less than in the first fight, and a full three stone less than when he had been at his most corpulent.

Molineaux maintained his advantage in the fourth and fifth rounds, clubbing Cribb to the ground in both, but during the course of the sixth the contest swung dramatically in the champion's direction. Most observers credited the turnaround with the fact the under-trained challenger's reserves of stamina were depleted. For example, *The Times* remarked that Molineaux was 'fatigued by want of wind,' and, as a result, adapted his tactics to those of boxing on the retreat, moving away from Cribb's attacks in the manner that his guru Richmond was so expert in. The *Hull Packet* suggested an alternative interpretation for Molineaux's sudden distress though, claiming that an earlier blow he had received to the throat from Cribb had caused 'internal bleeding'. It was, their writer claimed, 'very plain, at times, that he was almost suffocated by the blood rising' in his throat. Whatever the reason for his sudden deterioration, Molineaux was clearly in distress as the sixth round progressed. After failing to block a heavy Cribb blow to his body, he attempted to dance out of range and his demeanour assumed an increasingly frantic air. *The Times* gleefully and somewhat sadistically remarked of Molineaux's retreating tactics that 'no dancing-master ever cut capers more amusing to Crib's friends'.

Cribb, in no mood for mercy, stalked Molineaux relentlessly, flooring the American with a heavy blow to end the round. The seventh round offered Molineaux no respite or relief; Cribb's attacks were now ceaseless as he rained punches 'as violent as can be figured' on Molineaux's neck and throat. Eventually, the challenger slumped to the ground. In the thirty-second break before the next round, Richmond desperately urged Molineaux to rouse himself, but he must have known that his charge's prospects of emerging victorious had reduced to near invisible proportions. With nothing remaining but 'forlorn hope', Molineaux attempted to rally in the eighth, but Cribb trapped his head under his left arm and 'fibbed away' until his foe fell to the ground.

The slaughter continued in the ninth; Molineaux appeared 'dead beat' in the face of Cribb's 'death-like blows', although he did find the determination to mount one final, desperate act of defiance, charging recklessly towards the champion, only for Cribb to calmly deliver a perfectly timed parabola of a left hand which connected with Molineaux's jaw, possibly breaking it.[1] Molineaux 'fell like a log' and there he lay, the gentle rise and fall of his breath barely discernible in his slumbering form as the count began. Thirty seconds passed and victory was Cribb's to claim but, significantly, he waived his right, allowing Molineaux a 'long count' to recover his senses and footing.

By granting this extra respite to his great rival, was Cribb hoping he would end the debate surrounding the probity of the first fight? Was this his way of trying to administer justice, by granting Molineaux an extra chance to recover, such as he had enjoyed at Copthall Common? Perhaps ... although any interpretation of Cribb's actions as a sporting

gesture are undermined by the fact that while waiting for Molineaux
to return to scratch, the champion 'danced a hornpipe about the stage',
an act of triumphalism that delighted the crowd, but further humiliated
Molineaux. This action betrayed the fact that Cribb knew that even if
Molineaux had been granted thirty minutes to recover he would still
have harboured no chance of victory. This was no act of sportsmanship
on the champion's part, but a gesture of wanton sadism that pandered
to the basest elements within the crowd. Cribb had defeated Molineaux
and now, in return for all the barbs that had been hurled in his direction
and the whispers of foul play surrounding the previous fight, the
champion wanted to humiliate the American. When Molineaux finally
rose, the end of the ninth round having seemingly not been enforced,
Cribb floored him again immediately.[2]

There is little in the remarkable life of Richmond for which he should
be reprimanded, but dragging Molineaux back to scratch for the tenth
round – when he had already been knocked down twice in the ninth
– was arguably the most callous act he ever performed, albeit within
the context of a cruel sport. A more charitable interpretation, perhaps,
might be that it was an act of desperation on Richmond's part – a final
gamble by a man whose entire financial future was now in doubt. Such
was Molineaux's debilitated state that Richmond and Gibbons had
to lift him up 'as they would a lump of lead' before leading him back
to the centre of the ring 'as they would a child' for the tenth round.
Unsurprisingly, Molineaux soon fell 'from distress'. Yet again, the thirty
allocated seconds between rounds elapsed and, once more, Cribb gave
'away another chance about time' in favour of allowing Molineaux to
continue. In the eleventh round of what now more resembled a public
execution than a sporting contest, Molineaux's senses were soon 'hit
out of him' and he was again knocked down. This time there was no
way that Molineaux could continue – unless Richmond propped him
up and moved his fists for him like a puppet – for he could hardly move,
let alone stand. The fight was over and Cribb's victory was greeted with
boundless enthusiasm by the crowd, including shouts 'which rent the
skies'.

In the forbidding face of the full power of the English sporting
establishment, Molineaux's challenge had lasted just over nineteen
minutes, more than half an hour less than the fight at Copthall
Common. His bedraggled body was hauled back to his corner, where
Richmond looked on as a surgeon bled him. Eventually, Molineaux
managed to 'crawl to his chaise', his 'body bent like an S' and was
returned to his lodgings, where he lay 'disabled' and received further
treatment. Meanwhile Cribb and his chief second Gully performed a
Scots reel dance of celebration in homage to Barclay's patronage.

For Richmond, who had lost virtually everything he possessed brokering the fight, defeat represented the bitter ruination of his long-held dreams of scaling the summit of English pugilism. Unlike at Copthall Common, Richmond and Molineaux had not been cheated at Thistleton Gap, but their worthy and glorious ambition to annex the English Championship was ultimately revealed to be a vain and futile hope. The symbolism was clear; the nature of the struggle for acceptance by black citizens in England during the early part of the nineteenth century was a harsh and unforgiving one; enterprise, talent and ambition had their limits – and when the establishment closed ranks, it was a well-nigh impossible task to defeat such forbidding odds. In the estimation of Mendoza, Molineaux had beaten Cribb 'three times' at Copthall Common but still had not been declared the winner. This being the case, what chance did Molineaux really have at Thistleton Gap, when Cribb was at his peak of fitness and the American was past his?

The patriotic reports in the English press unsurprisingly revelled in Cribb's victory. With war against France delicately poised, Cribb's success raised the spirits of the entire country. 'I am convinced that many a noble soul among the 15,000 present on the occasion has burn'd for glory in the field of war by observing the honor attending Molineux and Cribb,' claimed one letter writer to the *Stamford Mercury*, who styled himself 'John Bull'. 'What indeed could be more grateful to the Champion himself, or more likely to raise emulation in the youthful breast, than his triumphant entry into the Metropolis in a barouche and four, decorated with ribbons, and cheered by the constant acclamation of thousands?'

One of the *Mercury*'s own correspondents was not convinced by such arguments, bemoaning as the 'disgrace of this age of frivolity' the fact that the fight had 'excited more attention than the impending conflict between Lord Wellington and Marmont, upon which, perhaps, depends the fate of more than one gallant nation'. However, such curmudgeonly sentiments were in the minority, Cribb's triumph was soon not only being analysed and dissected in newspapers, but also being celebrated in folk songs and poems, commemorated in Staffordshire pottery and illustrated in popular prints which flew off the shelves. The issues of *The Sporting Magazine* featuring the contest proved wildly popular, selling hundreds more copies than any previous edition. The fight was, quite simply, a phenomenon.

One fascinating characteristic of many post-fight reflections was that journalists, no doubt relieved the contest had been devoid of serious controversy, made a great show of emphasising the 'fair play' Molineaux had been shown. *The Times*, for example, repeated a claim from the local Lincolnshire press that 'no one can say, that in this battle, Molineaux had not fair play shewn him'. This was true, but did the fact the second contest had been without controversy really nullify the stench surrounding the first fight? Of course not, nevertheless the events of Copthall Common were conveniently forgotten in the rush to acclaim Cribb as a national hero. Despite the questionable taste of his sadistic showboating towards the end of the contest, Cribb proved magnanimous in victory. The day after the fight he visited Molineaux in Grantham to check on his rival's recovery, and in a speech made after a dinner in his honour at Gregson's he sought to downplay the racial dimension of the two men's rivalry, instead insisting his sole motivation was nationalism. ''Tis true I have milled the black!' he remarked. 'And I hope Gemmen, that any foreigner, black or white, that comes to Old England to mill John Bull, will never fail to get a good milling from the Champion of England!'

Others were less successful at keeping a lid on their sneering attitude towards Molineaux and his background. 'If the *black boxer* had beaten the Champion,' joked the *Chester Chronicle*, 'It is claimed that it would have been proposed to [Prime Minister] Mr [Spencer] Perceval to send him out Ambassador at the court of Hayti.'[3] Others delighted in the fact that Molineaux's pre-fight boasts had proved hollow: 'The Black … is said to have declared that "he would kill Crib if he could"', claimed the *Hereford Journal*. 'This savage expression has greatly diminished the commiseration which his fate would have otherwise excited.' A handful of commentators were a little more sympathetic towards Molineaux, expressing distaste with Cribb supporters' fanaticism. 'We would suggest … that the cries of exultation, which proceeded from the champion's numerous friends when the advantage seemed on his side, must have had the effect of cowing the Baltimore man,' one observer wrote. 'We think, in decency and generosity, they ought to have been omitted … It ought not to be forgotten that Molineaux was a stranger.'

Despite the crushing disappointment of defeat, Molineaux remained an object of curiosity for the English public. On returning to the Horse and Dolphin on 3 October, a huge crowd surrounded Richmond's residence, eager for a glimpse of the vanquished challenger. As a gesture of goodwill, and in recognition of Molineaux's role in a stunning sporting spectacle, Jackson even rallied the Fancy and collected forty-nine guineas and sixteen shillings and presented the purse to the beaten man. Ironically, money soon became a subject of contention between Molineaux and Richmond, as resentments that had festered before the fight now exploded. Soon, the duo were arguing about Molineaux's training, who was to blame for losing the money that Richmond had invested and anything else they could find to differ on.

Molineaux, his body sore and pride badly dented, publicly denounced Richmond and Belcher for what he claimed was their failure to properly prepare him. 'He complains vehemently of the treatment he has received from those who styled themselves his friends – particularly the persons to whose care his training was entrusted,' the *Stamford Mercury* reported less than a week after the fight, adding that Molineaux claimed he had been '*sold*' by Richmond and his other backers, a ridiculous accusation which implied they had laid wagers against him. Newspapers eagerly reported Molineaux's complaints, with the *Manchester Mercury* claiming that 'the worst part of his [Molineaux's] training was the Northern tour, which, although it filled his pockets ... subjected him to indiscretions not suitable to a man who was about to fight for £600'.

Such talk received short shrift from Richmond. As far as he was concerned, Molineaux had been an unknown, penniless novice when he first met him and was now a national celebrity. From Richmond's point of view, the way he was now behaving was an example of rank ingratitude. A counter-rumour soon circulated, of which Richmond was most likely the source, concerning Molineaux's unprofessional preparation for the fight. The claim, doubtless intended to damage Molineaux's reputation and deter other potential patrons from supporting him, was that on the morning of the fight Molineaux had consumed 'a boiled fowl, an apple-pie, and a tankard of porter, for his breakfast'. As accusations and vitriol passed between the two men, the Fancy debated whether Richmond had exploited Molineaux or vice versa, a discussion that would continue for years. Egan's assessment of the falling out between the two men was the most apt and accurate:

RICHMOND acquired considerable notoriety from his patronage of *Molineaux*; and, as far as we can learn, from the most impartial sources, his generous behaviour to that pugilist, who came to him an entire stranger, destitute of friends or money, received a very different return from what might have been expected: difference of opinion, however, may exist as to this subject, but it is certain Molineaux was indebted for that patronage and attention ... entirely to his introduction by RICHMOND.

As a result of their disagreements, the two men swiftly parted company, although it is unclear if Molineaux left the Horse and Dolphin of his own volition or if Richmond threw him out. Certainly it appears that their relationship had completely dissolved by late October, when Molineaux publically announced that he was willing to fight any man except Cribb, a challenge which was pointedly delivered via Jackson, and not Richmond. It seemed that the two men could not even stand to be in each other's company; Molineaux appeared at a benefit for Mendoza and Bitton in November 1811, hosted a benefit of his own at the Fives in December and appeared at a benefit for Cribb in January 1812, but Richmond appeared at none of these events.

Despite the absence of Richmond's guiding hand, Molineaux managed to make a decent living for himself in the months after Thistleton Gap. He travelled the country and exhibited his boxing skills in Chichester among other locations. With an unlikely ally in the form of Jack Powers, he even visited Oxford University to teach students for a week or so, before being ushered away by 'the Vice-Chancellor and some of the proctors', an enterprise that stirred memories of Richmond and Belcher's visit to Cambridge in 1807. Molineaux was willing to try any enterprise that might earn him a few guineas; he seconded a local fighter in Somerset in April 1812 and even wrestled at the annual Exeter wrestling festival in August, an embarrassing episode which merely proved that he had 'less powers with toe than the fist'. Nevertheless, the American earned sufficient income from such engagements to be able to pay for a servant to accompany him on his travels, a fact which greatly amused one observer who declared that unlike most 'great men', Molineaux's servant was neither 'a *Black* nor a Frenchman', but a white man. Occasionally, rumours swirled of an impending return to the ring, such as in April when it was claimed that Molineaux had found a new backer in the Isle of Wight who was willing to fund a third match against Cribb for 300 guineas aside. However, talk of such a fight was fanciful; as the *Kentish Gazette* pointed out, it was 'against the *etiquette* of pugilism to challenge a man a third time, who has beat an antagonist twice.' Besides, Cribb had continually stated his reluctance to ever throw a punch in anger again.

Meanwhile, Richmond was absorbed with keeping himself out of the bankruptcy courts and trying to ensure he had enough money to feed his family. Tax records indicate that he was forced to give up the Horse and Dolphin sometime in 1812, confirming *Bell's Life in London*'s assertion that 'the defeat of Molineaux was the cause of poor Bill's retirement from the Prad and Swimmer'.[4] In January, Richmond returned to the north, exhibiting his skills at the Theatre Royal in Manchester for two nights alongside Tom Belcher, with whom he also appeared at the Burton Hunt races in April. Despite his financial difficulties, Richmond also continued to spar for the benefit of others, including an appearance at Jackson's charitable sparring exhibition for British prisoners being held in France at the Fives on 7 May. This event raised the handsome sum of just over £132 and was patronised by over twenty 'noblemen' and many members of the House of Commons, who just four days later would be stunned by the assassination of Prime

Minister Spencer Perceval. *The Sporting Magazine* observed that Richmond's performance 'gave satisfaction', while condemning the selfishness of absent pugilists 'Bitton, Dutch Sam, Mendoza &c' who it claimed were in the 'habit of repeatedly soliciting public favours' yet 'did not condescend to make their appearance for this national object'. As the sparring season drew to a close in July, Richmond also appeared at events in honour of Belcher and his old antagonist Powers.

After leaving the Horse and Dolphin, Richmond settled with his family into new lodgings at No. 6 Whitcomb Street, the address which appears on an 1813 baptism record for Bill and his wife Mary's children Henry and Betsy, who were baptised at St Martins-in-the-Field on 24 May. It is unclear exactly when Henry and Betsy were born; it is possible they were twins, as the joint baptism suggests, although such a dual ceremony could also have been a money-saving measure given the financial pressure the family were under. On the baptism record, Richmond's occupation was recorded as cabinet maker, although his main source of income remained the lessons he offered in pugilistic and gymnastic instruction. None of his new pupils dazzled in the same way that Molineaux had though; for example, in November 1812 Richmond was forced to pull his slight but skilled protégé William Fuller out of a contest against Jay after just fifteen minutes, so superior was the latter's weight and strength. For the rematch the following year, Richmond's poor run of luck continued – he switched sides and seconded Jay, only for Fuller to use Richmond-esque tactics of 'hitting and getting away' in order to secure a remarkable win.

In early 1813, the dispute between Richmond and Molineaux flared up again in public circumstances. As Molineaux prepared for a fight with Jack Carter, his first contest since Thistleton Gap, Richmond had him arrested for an unpaid debt, said to be around £150. The arrest was vindictively timed just before the Carter bout, although Molineaux was bailed, allowing the fight to go ahead. How the matter of the debt was ultimately resolved is unclear; the *Chester Chronicle* claimed that it had, in fact, been settled a year earlier 'by arbitration', and criticised Richmond for continuing to pursue the matter.[5]

When the Molineaux-Carter fight took place on 2 April in Gloucestershire, around 6 miles from Banbury, there was a huge crowd of around 20,000 in attendance, even though 'from the arrest of the Black, and the uncertainty of the fight, but few from London were present'. Richmond provocatively seconded Carter and, truth be told, the grudge between the former friends made for more exciting discussion than the fight, which was a miserable affair. The tone was set before the first punches were exchanged, with Carter betraying his nerves by enquiring, if the victor was set to gain 100 guineas, what the loser would receive. Richmond's reaction was to gnash his teeth and shrug his shoulders, while Gregson, Carter's patron, despairingly declared: '*never talk of losing, boy* – thee must win, the *chance* is all in thy favour!' The reason for Gregson's confidence was abundantly clear and rested on the fact that Molineaux's physical deterioration was pronounced. As early as the fourth round, Molineaux was 'open mouthed for want of wind' and after the seventh he looked ready to quit when Carter almost beat him out of the ring. It was only thanks to the intervention of his seconds including, ironically, Joe Ward – who had seconded Cribb twice against the American – that Molineaux was convinced to carry on. For the next ten rounds, though, he looked weary and out of sorts. In the twentieth, he again looked ready to concede, only to be 'temporarily refreshed' by some gulps of brandy provided by his corner.

Suddenly, before the start of the twenty-fourth round, the fight ended in bizarre circumstances, with Carter unexpectedly collapsing on Richmond's knee and lying 'senseless', for 'nearly half an hour'. Some observers claimed he had suffered a delayed reaction to a blow to the side of the head, or that his collapse was engendered by an ear injury he had picked up in the twenty-first round that had been bleeding ever since. Whatever the reason, it was a highly unsatisfactory conclusion to a poor contest. Unsurprisingly, rumours soon spread that Carter had 'sold' the fight. Richmond, always unscrupulously honest and fiercely opposed to fight fixing, was furious to have been connected with such a farce, while the press' assessment of the event was damning; in the estimation of the *Morning Post*, the fight had been devoid of 'violent hitting' and both men had 'seemed to wish to break away before delivery' of their punches. Molineaux's performance, in particular, was lambasted. 'The Black has fallen off,' the *Stamford Mercury* noted. 'He seemed to want strength and animation, and did not appear in general to punish when he hit. The battle has lost him much of his popularity.'

Richmond's popularity had also nosedived; the acclaim he had gained when vanquishing Maddox having been eroded through his association with the previously feared and now mocked Molineaux. Adding insult to injury was the fact that in their account of the Richmond-Molineaux feud, the *York Herald*, the local newspaper of Richmond's former hometown, dismissively described him as an 'inferior second rate pugilist'. At this point, Richmond seems to have resolved to stop looking backwards by relinquishing his bitter fixation with the money owed to him by Molineaux and instead decided to focus on rehabilitating his own reputation. The most obvious way to do so was to return to the ring; the only problem was that Richmond was now past his fiftieth birthday – an age which conventional wisdom held was insanely advanced to be contemplating a pugilistic comeback. Mind you, as his life amply demonstrates, Richmond was never one to bow to conventional wisdom.

19
Richmond Reborn

Richmond's comeback bout would prove a landmark event in the history of pugilism, becoming the first contest to be fought under the banner of boxing's first governing body, the Pugilistic Club. The PC's foundation was an attempt to rid the sport of its frustratingly notorious reputation. Pugilism's many participants and supporters passionately believed that boxing was an elevating pastime, essential in breeding a fighting spirit among all right-thinking and patriotic Englishmen, and thus preventing the rise of effetism – a quality traditionally linked by the English to the French, of course. As Egan declared, the 'practice of boxing through the means of the prize-ring is one of the corner stones towards preventing effeminacy from undermining the good old character of the people of England.'

Horseracing and cricket were sports that had made moves towards greater central governance of their rules and administration, and John Jackson believed boxing should follow suit. Thus the aim of the Pugilistic Club was not only to ensure sound financial governance and the sporting probity of major fights, but also to add a veneer of respectability to a sport hitherto regarded by many as something of a rogue activity. Annual subscriptions from its 120 or so founder members ensured that the PC would not only act as a guardian of the sport, but was also in a position to promote its own fights.

The establishment of the PC could not have come at a better time for Richmond. During his association with Molineaux, he had become isolated from his fellow pugilists, who had mainly rallied to Cribb's cause (Tom Belcher being a notable exception). Although Richmond may have harboured grievances about how he and Molineaux had been treated before, during and after the two Cribb contests, he correctly discerned that his continued economic survival and status within pugilism depended on him re-establishing his position within the sport's elite. For both practical and economic purposes, then, affiliating himself with the PC was the perfect opportunity to reintegrate within the pugilistic firmament.

Richmond's decision to join the PC symbolised the end of his spell as a pugilistic revolutionary; his association with Molineaux had seen him challenge the sport's established structure and rock it to its very foundations, but post-Molineaux he would readopt the pragmatic and integrationist approach that had characterised his initial rise from slavery to sporting stardom. Richmond's approach has its critics; over the years some historians and academics have attempted to demean Richmond by characterising him as some kind of placid 'Uncle Tom'-type figure. For example, the academic Dr Ruti Ungar claimed that Richmond was a 'docile and unthreatening' figure, dismissing him as a 'timid' man who, in a servile manner, conformed to 'prevailing perceptions of appropriate behaviour for a Black man'. Ungar also drew an unflattering contrast between Richmond and Molineaux, lauding the latter as an 'independent spirit' with an 'individualistic nature'.

Not only does Ungar's interpretation undervalue the pivotal role Richmond played in mentoring Molineaux, but it also demonstrates a lack of understanding of the complexity of daily existence within Georgian England for black citizens. The reason that Richmond was able to survive and thrive for such an extended period was precisely because he was an arch pragmatist, adopting and adapting his survival strategies to the changing circumstances and social contexts that he faced throughout his life. He initially won his freedom and built his career, first as a cabinet maker and then as a pugilist, through an eye for social networking and advancement, his ability to conform to the accepted social conventions of English society allowing him to win favour with first Earl Percy and then Lord Camelford. Once Richmond had attained a position of prominence and celebrity, and had met a fellow black man in Molineaux who he believed capable of winning the championship, it became clear that his willingness to conform was not all encompassing. While promoting Molineaux's career, Richmond redefined himself as a pugilistic revolutionary, identifying himself more readily and with greater reference to his ethnic background; for example, through the 'black pugilists' tours across England that he masterminded. His decision to abandon pragmatism for a more militant expression of 'black challenge' to the existing white pugilistic hegemony was probably motivated by two forces: firstly, Richmond's sense of ethnic pride, but also his sharp eye for a commercial opportunity. It was with this more radical philosophy that Richmond masterminded Molineaux's two challenges to Cribb. However, after Molineaux's defeat in the second contest and the dissolution of the two men's partnership, Richmond faced severe financial difficulties and discerned that reversion to his former pragmatic philosophy was necessary. Far from being representative of a 'docile' nature, this was an eminently sensible decision. Indeed, any other approach would have most likely spelt poverty for both Richmond and his family.

It is also crucial to note that although Richmond may have largely conformed to the conventions of Georgian society by adopting the customs of a typical English gentleman, he always refused to adopt the servile demeanour of a victim or a slave. As was frequently shown throughout his life, Richmond was utterly unwilling to accept racial insults, and there were frequent occasions when he answered such epithets not with equanimity or meek surrender, but with force and physical resistance; he challenged Frank Myers to bare-knuckle combat when Myers insulted him and his female companion in York in the 1790s; he confronted a spectator who insulted him during his contest against Carter in 1808 and he refused to accept or countenance the persistent slurs hurled at him by Powers. When Molineaux was cheated out of victory against Cribb, Richmond also ensured that the public were made aware of his plea for racial tolerance through his appeal for Molineaux's colour not to 'operate to [his] prejudice'. Were any of these the actions of a 'docile and unthreatening' man? Of course not – they were the actions of a refined gentleman who possessed pride and self-esteem enough to defend his honour and ethnic identity with his wit and intellect, but also physically when necessary.

Yet Richmond's sense of ethnic pride was also tempered with an admirable self-control. He realised that to respond physically to every single slur or example of racism within a society where black people were regularly abused or discriminated against would be impossible, and would probably have resulted in him being engaged in confrontation virtually every day. He therefore imposed sensible limits upon his patience and acted consistently within these boundaries. Viewed in the context of his life as a whole, Richmond's decision in 1814 to become one of the founding members of the PC can be seen as symbolising a return to his pragmatic roots. A crucial factor in his decision was also the fact that the PC were able to offer purses for contests using members' subscriptions. For a black boxer such as Richmond, who had always struggled for patronage, this was an attractive prospect, particularly as he was planning a return to the ring.

Richmond was, in fact, the first boxer to benefit from the club's establishment, with his 50-guinea comeback contest against Jack Davis, known as 'the navigator', being the first spectacle to be fought under the PC's aegis in May 1814. A further benefit of being part of the PC was that both Richmond and Davis were paid in advance for their training expenses, as indicated by receipts carefully prepared by John Jackson and signed by both men.[1] Davis was a lively competitor, and therefore a risky choice of opponent. Described by Egan as 'fine, tall, powerful, young, athletic', he had '*thumped* his way into notice, by *sarving* seven or eight customers with tolerable ease' and was viewed by some as a possible future champion. Davis' promise, coupled with Richmond's advanced age and four years of competitive inactivity, made for an intriguing match-up. Most of the Fancy couldn't decide who would emerge victorious, with the pre-match betting first favouring Richmond, before the odds moved to even and then narrowly shifted in Davis' favour as the fight approached; the *Morning Chronicle* also tipped Davis to prevail.

The fight was set for 3 May in Coombe Warren, Kingston-upon-Thames and the Pugilistic Club did their utmost to create as grand a spectacle as possible. Members of the PC were dressed in the club's blue coats and yellow kerseymere waistcoats, including buttons with the club's initials engraved on them, while the 25-foot ring looked particularly splendid, the club having invested in a handsome new set of ropes and eight stakes with iron tops, also with the letters 'PC' emblazoned on them. Meanwhile, PC-appointed officials patrolled the ringside area, dark blue ribbons in their hats designating their authority. A mood of festivity prevailed, not only because of the excitement surrounding the fight, but also because of the mood of nationwide exultation that still prevailed following Napoleon's April abdication of the thrones of France and Italy and his subsequent exile to Elba. It looked like the long years of war were finally at an end and England was in the mood to acclaim its heroes – the very same day that Richmond faced Davis, it was announced that the Prince Regent had conferred the title of Duke of Wellington upon Arthur Wellesley, the hero of the Peninsular War.

Davis entered the ring first, bowing extravagantly, his lithe 12-stone 10-pound frame glowing with musculature. Richmond followed, weighing a trim 12 stone 2 pounds and, according to Egan, looking 'more like a man of thirty than what he actually was'. It was such a sunny day that the boxers tossed a coin to decide whose corner would be in the shade. Richmond won, and the fight commenced, with both men receiving warm applause; if the Fancy had harboured any resentment against Richmond for backing Molineaux's 'black challenge' then it appeared to have been forgiven amid the warm glow engendered by the weather and Napoleon's surrender, as well as the excitement surrounding the first bout organised by the PC.

In the opening round, Richmond's competitive rust was obvious as his usually impeccable judgement of distance and timing proved surprisingly poor. Davis took advantage, pressing forward and landing a sharp punch to Richmond's temple that promptly floored him. The next three rounds were tightly contested, but Davis retained a narrow advantage; Richmond's smart and stinging punches may have caused Davis' face to start bleeding, but the Navigator's advantage in physical strength was obvious from the fact that Richmond was floored at the end of each of these rounds.

The fifth saw Richmond begin to gain the ascendency, though, as he showed 'much daring and science'. After a close rally, Richmond retreated nimbly, smashing Davis with a smart counter-attack, before also landing a terrific shot on his opponent's mouth, flooring him heavily. The sixth was another dominant Richmond round, and by the seventh Davis was showing 'weakness and symptoms of losing'. The Navigator's punches were now hurried and his demeanour increasingly frantic, as he pursued the retreating Richmond around the ring and was picked off by a rattling shot to his jaw, which jarred his senses.

Davis rallied in the eighth, but a precise and heavy Richmond blow to his ear in the ninth floored him again. The tenth and eleventh rounds saw Davis knock Richmond down twice, once via a heavy throw, but a comprehensive twelfth round shifted the contest comprehensively in Richmond's favour: firstly, the veteran's dancing, retreating style befuddled Davis who swung wildly, missing his elusive target with regularity. Once Richmond had manoeuvred Davis into a state of near exhaustion, he set his feet and unleashed a devastating right hand. The effect of Richmond's raw knuckles on Davis' face was gruesome, as they 'separated the upper lip of his antagonist from the nose'. Blood spurting horribly from the wound, a distressed Davis fell heavily and, although he made it to scratch for another round, his spirit had been broken. Another heavy knockdown marked the end of the contest and the rebirth of Richmond's pugilistic career was complete.

It was, for the fifty year old, a hugely emotional moment; the last four years – encompassing the dramatic events at Copthall Common and Thistleton Gap, his bitter split with Molineaux and the loss of the Horse and Dolphin – had been turbulent to say the least. By defeating Davis, Richmond had not only re-emphasised his pugilistic credentials with a stunning seventh victory in succession, an undefeated run now stretching more than six years, but had also reinforced his own sense of self-worth and self-esteem. No wonder that he allowed himself the luxury of an ostentatious and defiant gesture of celebration at the end of the fight by leaping over the 5-foot-high ring ropes in one mighty bound to accept the acclamation of the gasping crowd.

At an age when many pugilists were either dead or overfed and florid elder statesmen of the sport rather than active participants, Richmond had provided eloquent evidence of his evergreen skills. His remarkable victory won notices redolent of the adulatory reception he had been given when vanquishing George Maddox in 1809. According to the *Salisbury and Winchester Journal*, the contest 'afforded a striking specimen of what a man upwards of 50 (like Richmond) of first-rate science, could do against a fresh man under 30, of superior weight, length, and strength'.

The restoration of Richmond's reputation was further emphasised the following month. As part of the celebrations relating to the signing of the Treaty of Paris, various members of European royalty who had allied themselves with Britain against Napoleon were welcomed to London, including King Frederick William III of Prussia and Czar Alexander of Russia. On 17 June, Frederick William and his sons William and Frederick were among the members of the group who visited Lord Lowther's rooms in Pall Mall for breakfast and a display of sparring from 'the most celebrated pugilists' from across the country. Organised by Jackson, Richmond was present, alongside Cribb, Tom Belcher and several others. 'There was some excellent sparring, which afforded the highest entertainment and delight to the illustrious spectators,' noted one journal. Among the other extravagant events mounted to celebrate the 'Glorious Peace' and the centennial of Hanoverian rule was a recreation of the Battle of Trafalgar in the Serpentine in Hyde Park. Accompanying this event were a wide array of tents, stalls and booths housing refreshments, entertainments and amusements, including the ever-enterprising Richmond, whose displays of his pugilistic, acrobatic and gymnastic skills made him 'one of the most successful sutlers in this huge camp'. To be present at such a high-profile national occasion was a significant honour for Richmond, and indicated that the racial tensions that had surrounded Molineaux's challenge for the championship had abated.

Although Richmond had been welcomed back into the pugilistic fold, the ideological arguments surrounding abolition and race in Britain and the wider world were far from over. Ironically enough, the terms of the Treaty of Paris had provoked much criticism among prominent abolitionists, who hoped the treaty would encompass an international agreement outlawing slavery. Such ambitions were thwarted, however, and abolitionists viewed the article within the treaty which gave the

French government five years to cease trading in slaves as unduly lenient. Richmond's presence at events such as the visit of European Royalty indicated that while English society was not ready to embrace a black champion, the sport of pugilism remained one of the more inclusive preserves of Western civilisation.

Such inclusivity was not universally welcomed by everyone within the Fancy but it was endorsed by pugilism's most noted wordsmith, Pierce Egan, who promoted an admirably liberal vision of the sport, in which men were judged on fighting merits, rather than by reference to social or ethnic background. For example, the poetic song 'A Boxing We Will Go', a popular ditty of uncertain authorship re-printed by Egan in *Boxiana*, imagined a series of pugilists confronting Napoleon ('Boney'). Significantly, this military alliance of boxers included 'native' Englishmen in Cribb and Gully, but also a Jew (Mendoza) and a black (Molineaux). By explicitly endorsing a vision of a multicultural society in which different ethnic groups fought together against foreign foes, Egan was endorsing a patriotic vision of Britain far more progressive than the majority of his contemporaries could conceive:

> If Boney doubt it, let him come,
> And try with Crib a round;
> And Crib shall beat him like a drum,
> And make his carcase sound.
> Mendoza, Gulley, Molineaux,
> Each nature's weapon wield,
> Who each at Boney would stand true,
> And never to him yield.

Egan's 1812 essay on Richmond, one of the earliest third-person biographies of a black celebrity ever written, was also striking in its forward-thinking sentiments, albeit somewhat clumsy in its articulation of its author's liberal views. Throughout, Egan made it clear that he regarded any form of prejudice as contemptible, writing: 'It [is] wrong and beneath the character of an Englishman, to abuse any individual for that he could not help – either on account of his COUNTRY or his *colour*.' He also made a noble attempt to urge readers to ignore the colour of Richmond's skin, quoting from Joseph Addison's 1712 play *Cato*, a popular pro-liberty text, and referring to Shakepeare's *Othello* to support his point:

> It cannot be denied to him, that he wears a *head*; and although its *colour* may not prepossess the *million* in its favour, yet the liberal part of mankind will acquiesce with the sentiments of *Desdemona*, that

"the visage" may be *"seen in the mind!"*
Tis not a set of features, or complexion,
The tincture of a skin, that I admire;
Beauty soon grows familiar to the lover,
Fades in his eye, and palls upon the sense.

Furthermore, in lauding the 'intelligent, communicative, well-behaved' aspects of Richmond's character, Egan succeeded in challenging the offensive stereotypes that were routinely affixed to blacks during Georgian times. For example, Egan's laudatory comments about Richmond's intellectual capacity contrast dramatically with the 'study' conducted by William Charles Wells which was presented to the Royal Society in 1813 in which he concluded that 'the woolly hair and deformed features of negroes are connected with want of intellect'. Egan ended his profile of Richmond by emphasising the impartial, inclusive philosophy underpinning *Boxiana*:

> BOXIANA will do his duty – and as far as the infirmities of human nature can be admitted - neither colour, strength, patronage, or any other consideration, shall tempt him to swerve from IMPARTIALITY.

Despite Egan's willingness to embrace non-white boxers and his refusal to stereotype them, the debate surrounding the extent to which a black pugilist such as Richmond was 'accepted' within English society is not a straightforward one. Egan may have lauded him but, as we have seen in previous chapters, the language used to describe Richmond in the English press oscillated wildly from scornful to respectful. Reports of Richmond's early fights, before he established his reputation, were notable for their use of insulting racial epithets, giving way to a more respectful tone as his status within pugilism grew. However, during his association with Molineaux, who was regarded as a dangerous threat to white dominance of the championship, Richmond's public reputation seemed to suffer. Once his association with Molineaux ended, though, it appears that Richmond was treated with renewed respect once again.

The thesis that Richmond was more harshly treated when he and Molineaux were threatening to wrest the title from Cribb's grasp is lent extra weight if we consider various contemporary artistic representations of him.[2] The most famous rendition of Richmond is the popular etching *A Striking View of Richmond* published by Robert Dighton in March 1810, and therefore drawn after his victory against Maddox and before his association with Molineaux.[3] Significantly, this print, as well as Dighton's alternative pencil and ink portrait of Richmond held by the Royal Collection,[4] is devoid of the offensive tropes and stereotypes that characterise many Georgian artists' conceptions of black subjects. The over-exaggerated lips, nose and squashed head often used to denigrate and dehumanise blacks are all conspicuous by their absence in Dighton's rendering of Richmond.

Instead Dighton's rendering of Richmond is characterised by an air of upright nobility and dignity. Furthermore, within the print there is a surprising and atypical lack of symbolism to suggest Richmond's status as a former slave, or imply that he is in any way anything less than a noble or heroic figure. Many artists of the period would typically render black subjects in bare feet, wearing some form of 'exotic' dress or within an unusual or foreign landscape, as a means of suggesting their 'primitivism' or 'otherness'. Dighton, though, places Richmond within the simple context of a typically green English landscape, while he is dressed in the traditional boxing uniform of the day and is wearing shoes. The only apparently exotic adornment is the yellow sash with red dots that he wears around his waist, which in actual fact is representative of an English custom, whereby pugilists would wear their own unique 'colours' into the ring, and fix them to the post in their corners. Although Richmond's facial features look marginally more exaggerated in the more widely known etching, Dighton's rendition of Richmond is remarkably realistic and complimentary, as opposed to the satirical caricature one might have expected; even the dramatic title *A Striking View of Richmond* is praiseworthy in tone, with the double meaning of the word 'striking' suggesting that Richmond is not only a powerful and fearsome boxer, but also an admirable and handsome man.

In contrast, in both George Cruikshank and Thomas Rowlandson's prints of the second Cribb-Molineaux contest, both Richmond and Molineaux are rendered in a far less flattering light, with absurdly exaggerated physical features and facial expressions that render them grotesque. These works were produced after Dighton's print and reinforce the impression that once Richmond was perceived as being 'in opposition' to the established order, artists were more likely to emphasise and mock his ethnic background, in order to provide a contrast with Cribb's more heroically rendered white vision of 'Englishness'.

The conflicting interpretations and representations of Richmond rendered by contemporary artists and writers demonstrate the wildly differing attitudes to his ethnic background that he would have encountered on a daily basis. Richmond was simultaneously both feted and reviled, indicating that the course of life for a black celebrity in England in the early nineteenth century was seldom smooth. An unusually nimble nature was a perquisite for a black man to successfully traverse the turbulent ethnic politics of the Georgian era. In this respect, Richmond's pugilistic style – with its clever footwork and desire to avoid the lunges of his opponents before launching devastating counter-attacks – stands as an enduring metaphor for the pragmatic philosophy which enabled him, against all the odds, to both survive and thrive in a society that seldom paused to offer a black man comfort or kindness.

20

Richmond Retires

While Richmond was relaunching his pugilistic career and performing for royalty, his former protégé Molineaux was in freefall. Remarkably enough, although he and Richmond were now bitter enemies, Molineaux seemed to bear Tom Cribb no ill will, even selling tickets for benefit events held by the champion who he frequently referred to as a 'good fellow' and 'brave man'. In the period since their epic battles, Molineaux had not been short of female admirers but, as Egan explained, his physical capabilities had entered a period of rapid decline:

> It is not surprising ... that the charms of the softer sex should warmly interest the attentions of the lusty *Moor* ... Pleasure was the order of the day with him, and the *stews* of the metropolis tended not only fast to ease him of his *blunt*, but to undermine that terrific overwhelming impetuosity, so prominently possessed and so conspicuously displayed by MOLINEAUX in his terrible combats with the mighty Cribb. The consequences of this line of conduct were obvious, and even the *iron*-like frame of the *Black* seriously felt the dilapidating effects of intemperance!

At the end of May 1814, just weeks after Richmond-Davis, Molineaux returned to the ring for the first time since his farcical victory against Carter. The American was now based in Scotland, where pugilism was gaining a foothold but was still not as popular as in England, and was matched for a 100-guinea purse with William Fuller. As had become customary for a contest involving Molineaux, it proved a controversial bout. An attempt to stage the contest on the lawns of Bishopton House near Glasgow on 27 May was thwarted after ten minutes when the sheriff-substitute of Renfrewshire, accompanied by several constables, halted the fight. Four days later, the bout was rearranged and passed off without interference on the Drymen Road, around 12 miles from Glasgow. Only two rounds were fought but the length of them – twenty-eight minutes and forty minutes – was remarkable.

Conscious of his diminished stamina, Molineaux displayed cautious tactics contrary to the furious attacking style he had exhibited against Cribb. The first round ended with Molineaux knocked down and the second round was desperately close, with both men shipping significant punishment. After thirty-four minutes of the second round, Molineaux was distressed and 'shaking violently'. However, while his stamina was questionable, his bravery was not; somehow he pulled himself together and engaged Fuller in a fierce rally near the latter's corner. As the two men exchanged punches, Fuller suddenly fell. An incensed Molineaux protested, claiming that Fuller's second Joe Ward had pulled him down just as Molineaux had been about to strike him with a potentially fight-ending blow. It seemed a flimsy protest, but the judges agreed and Molineaux was declared a very unsatisfactory winner. Such a contentious decision would probably have caused a riot in England, but the Scottish spectators, inexperienced and unversed as they were in the rules and customs of pugilism, accepted the decision with equanimity. The *Caledonian Mercury* was merely relieved the contest had been terminated before either man suffered serious injury, noting that 'if the battle had been much more protracted, the infliction of punishment would have become extremely disagreeable'.

Although he had secured a second successive victory, Molineaux's precipitous decline was obvious and the Fancy knew he was ripe for the taking. In a sad twist of fate Richmond was present to see the last rites applied to Molineaux's career ten months later. For a while a contest between Molineaux and George Cooper, a former bargeman who had opened a gym in Edinburgh, had been rumoured and, on 10 March 1815, it finally took place in Lanarkshire. Cooper, reckoned by Egan to be a 'consummate boxer', was yet another fighter who had benefited from Richmond's tuition. The chance to pit his wits against Molineaux proved too delicious for Richmond to pass up and he eagerly accepted the offer to lead Cooper's corner. Appropriately enough, the fight took place against the most dramatic of historical backdrops; as Molineaux was preparing for what would prove his final battle, Napoleon, having escaped from exile in Elba, was in the process of marching on Paris and reseizing the French throne; both great warriors were about to be defeated by time, fate and their considerable hubris.

As soon as Molineaux and Cooper stripped, the American's physical deterioration was manifest, with one journal slyly noting, 'it was evident to the knowing ones, that Cooper had made good use of his time when training, and that the black had not'. Despite a spirited display in the opening three rounds, by the fourth Molineaux was exhausted. In the fifth, Cooper 'gave him three facers' which 'made the claret fly' – a savage salvo which proved the prologue to a sustained assault against the increasingly forlorn American. Time and again, Cooper floored Molineaux, yet on each occasion the latter bravely returned to scratch. In the tenth round, the punishment Molineaux absorbed was frightful, a series of punches doubling him up before he fell and his head collided with a ring post, leaving him dazed as well as bloody.

The eleventh round was Molineaux's final hurrah. Somehow, tremendous fighting talent that he was, he delved into the recesses of his fading talents and conjured perhaps the most perfectly timed punch of his career, detonating it flush on Cooper's face after he had been driven on to the ropes. For a few incredible moments it looked like Molineaux may have secured a sensational victory, but Cooper eventually rose, and Richmond ushered him back to scratch. In the following round it was clear that Molineaux's desperate effort had drained him of his last vestiges of energy and Cooper knocked him off his feet with three heavy punches. As Molineaux awaited the thirteenth round, blood pouring from his battered face, he defiantly called for a swig of brandy. The Fancy knew the end was nigh; the betting – in a colourful metaphorical flourish – was now 'the Bank of Scotland to a China orange on Cooper'.

After two more rounds and two more heavy knockdowns, a battered Molineaux finally conceded after the fourteenth; he had 'had his belly full', not only of the contest but also, it seemed, of pugilism. It was a desperate end to a remarkable career. We can but wonder, as Cooper accepted the congratulations of Richmond, whether the latter felt a twinge of regret for Molineaux's fate, or whether he merely harboured a feeling of grim satisfaction to see his estranged former pupil comprehensively beaten. Whatever Richmond's feelings, it was clear that his and Molineaux's careers were now on dramatically contrasting trajectories; while Molineaux prepared to return to a life of dissolution and excess – which would terminate three years later in a dingy barracks in Galway – Richmond's career was about to soar to new heights.

As Britain triumphed in the Battle of Waterloo on 18 June and basked in the news of Napoleon's humiliating retreat and abdication, Richmond's position within the pugilistic sphere was loftier than ever. Exactly a month later, he was among the pugilists who sparred at the Fives Court in aid of those widowed or orphaned by the events at Waterloo. It was a truly grand occasion and *The Sporting Magazine*'s account of proceedings positively swelled with patriotic pride: 'The pugilists, noted in the London ring, volunteered their services upon this national occasion of charity, and the court was filled with the first respectability. The setting to was of longer duration than usual, the pugilists being anxious to do all in their power to assist the general cause of humanity.'

The same issue of *The Sporting Magazine* confirmed that Richmond was already in training for his next contest against a man more than two decades his junior named Tom Shelton, an unstable canal worker with a depressive streak and a dangerous penchant for alcohol and gambling. Shelton's eccentric nature was best summed up by a bizarre series of events in September 1812: by the end of a day's drinking in Hampstead, Shelton had gambled away all his worldly possessions, whereupon he risked the only thing he had left – namely his life – on the roll of a dice. The luckless Shelton lost that wager too and, bound by a twisted sense of honour, tried to hang himself on a street lamp. His first attempt failed, so he tried again, at which point a passing police officer intervened. Although the policeman succeeded in preventing Shelton's suicide, he received two black eyes and a broken nose for his troubles.

Thereafter, Shelton threw his hat into the prize ring, competing in three contests, winning two while losing a tight bout to the accomplished Harry Harmer. Despite this defeat, Shelton was seen as one of pugilism's rising stars. He was also one of many boxers to have received advice and instruction from Richmond, who seconded him in the Harmer contest in April 1815. However, by the summer the two men had fallen out and a grudge match was duly brokered for 1 August. It was an eagerly awaited contest between pugilists both reckoned by the *Morning Post* to be 'first raters'. Pre-fight betting was brisk and, according to *The Sporting Magazine*, around 10,000 spectators swarmed to Moulsey Hurst in eager anticipation of a first-rate spectacle. After Shelton inflamed his right knee in training, Richmond was made narrow favourite, although during the contest Shelton appeared to suffer no ill effects from the injury.

The pre-fight posturing positively crackled with tension, with Shelton initially refusing to accept Richmond's proffered hand for the customary pre-fight courtesy. Cribb, in the ring to second Shelton, was disgusted with his charge's lack of sportsmanship and threatened to walk out if Shelton did not relent, forcing him to finally accept Richmond's hand. Cribb's gentlemanly intervention was to prove a turning point in his relationship with Richmond, which would improve dramatically over the succeeding years, to the point that the former enemies became firm friends. That was all in the future though; for now, Richmond was about to face arguably the toughest fight of his illustrious career.

Both men began the fight anxiously, their punches falling short of their targets. Richmond connected with a well-timed body shot, but Shelton countered with a smart left that crashed into Richmond's eye, drawing blood. Shelton pushed his advantage, knocking Richmond down, hitting him again as he fell to the turf. As Richmond prepared for the second round it was alarmingly obvious that Shelton's left hand had occasioned severe damage to his eye, which had swollen rapidly and was closing fast. Clearly concerned that the injury would prove an insurmountable handicap if the contest became a battle of attrition, Richmond gambled on a quick finish. He raced out at the beginning of the second round, shocking Shelton with his aggression and landing a sledgehammer of a right-hand; the 'claret flew copiously,' and Shelton 'went down ... much *amazed*'. Richmond maintained his attacking approach in the next round, as he sought to 'speedily get judgement in this Chancery suit'. However, Shelton ducked under Richmond's rapier right, had the better of the ensuing rally and knocked him down.

By now Richmond's eye was 'completely in darkness' and he was in severe peril. The fourth and fifth were dominated by Shelton, who was also now a five-to-two ringside betting favourite. Richmond roared back in the sixth, though, landing 'another of his terrible right handed hits' to level Shelton. The *Morning Post* could not resist indulging in an extravagant military simile, reflecting that Shelton 'went down like *parlez vouz* men at Waterloo, as *elegantly roared* out by a Bermondsey lad in his extacy of joy'. The flattering comparison between Richmond and a British soldier was an apt symbol of his pugilistic renaissance.

The fight now settled into a grim pattern, with neither man able to stay ascendant for long. Both combatants were 'much punished' in the seventh round and by the eleventh they were exhausted. Ultimately, it was the consistent sharpness and destructiveness of Richmond's right hand that proved decisive; in the thirteenth and eighteenth rounds this punch found its target with devastating effect, occasioning heavy Shelton knockdowns. In the face of such relentless precision, the younger man grew desperate; when Richmond fell in the twenty-first round, Shelton punched him in the side of the face despite the fact he had been on the ground for more than a second, an illegal manoeuvre that provoked earnest discussion between the umpires. It was finally decreed that the fight should continue and Richmond, with the benefit of his vast experience, shrugged off Shelton's gamesmanship. In the twenty-second round he coolly levelled his man with a heavy blow, and in the twenty-third he applied the *coup de grâce*, another 'heavy hit upon his adversary's eye' producing so much blood and such a disorientating effect upon Shelton that he failed to make it back to scratch in time for the next round.

As he had done after his contest against Davis, Richmond leapt over the ropes to celebrate another remarkable triumph and a handy purse of 70 guineas. As the crowd rose to acclaim him, the emotional pugilist decided it was the perfect way to end his fighting career and promptly announced his retirement. Egan was among those to pay eager tribute:

> From the above victory, the *man of colour* added another laurel to his wreath ... Impetuous men must not fight RICHMOND, as in his hands they become victims to their own temerity. The right hand of the *man of colour* is truly dreadful; and two hits from it, well applied, have produced sufficient severity, in some instances, to decide a contest ... It is ... singular to state, that it has been observed, by the best judges in the *Fancy*, when speaking of RICHMOND, that "the older he grows, the better pugilist he proves himself." He is an extraordinary man.

As Richmond settled into retirement a new generation of black pugilistic talent was emerging; in 1816, emboldened by the exploits of Richmond and Molineaux, at least five new black boxers entered the sporting sphere. Three of them, in particular, made a noticeable impact on the sport: Sam Robinson, Joseph Stephenson and Harry Sutton. Robinson was an American who hailed from New York and had enjoyed a colourful past, with several newspapers claiming he served under Lord Nelson during the Battle of the Nile prior to becoming a labourer in Westminster. Accounts of Robinson's pugilistic background vary somewhat, with some claiming he was trained by Richmond for a period, while others state he was always under the tutelage of Tom Oliver. By early 1816, Robinson had picked up some impressive, if low-key, wins before he was matched in March against a navigator named Butcher. Robinson won a thrilling forty-four-round contest, as well as plaudits for his sportsmanship in twice refusing to hit his opponent when he was trapped in the ropes. This victory secured a high-profile contest against Jack Carter before a huge crowd at Moulsey Hurst in April. Carter won with ease to halt Robinson's rise and, as a result, Robinson was then matched against Stephenson, who was being tutored by Richmond and also had a loss to Carter on his record.

Little concrete information exists about Stephenson's past although it has been claimed that he was born in Havre de Grace, Maryland and escaped to England after murdering his slave master, before serving as a steward on a British ship during the 1812 war with the United States. The Robinson versus Stephenson contest, which took place at Coombe Warren in May 1816, was the first significant contest between two black pugilists, with *The Sporting Magazine* describing it as a 'nouvelle exhibition'. Robinson outclassed Stephenson in an hour and twelve minutes, winning 40 guineas for his trouble. At the same gathering, 'two vagabond blacks' also fought, while Caleb Baldwin engaged in a contest against yet another black pugilist, named Bristow, who was seconded by Richmond and went on to fight several more contests.

After his victory against Stephenson, Robinson took on Carter again, losing to him in an odd 'timed contest' that Carter had wagered he would win before thirty minutes were up. Robinson then participated in yet another 'all-black' contest, this time against one of the 'vagabond blacks' referred to above, Harry Sutton, who was arguably the most accomplished of the new generation of black pugilists. Sutton had been born in Baltimore before ending up in Deptford, London where he worked as a corn runner at a granary. In the wake of his impromptu debut after the Robinson-Stephenson bout, Sutton linked up with Richmond and was duly matched against Robinson in Doncaster in September 1817. It seems that Richmond and Harmer acted not only as Sutton's seconds for this bout but also as the fight's promoters, with spectators charged 3s to enter the paddock where it took place. Sutton was lucky to escape disqualification after hitting Robinson with a 'dreadful *foul blow*' in the opening round, but thereafter dominated and secured victory after twenty-five rounds.

The following year Robinson drifted north and had several bouts in Scotland, while Sutton won a tough contest against Ned Painter in July 1817. However, Sutton lost a rematch a few months later and thereafter his forays into the prize ring were more sporadic. His only other fight of note was a victory against 'Massa' Kendrick, another black boxer, in 1819, after which he made ends meet by touring Scotland and Ireland before he returned to London and fell ill with asthma. Richmond made a collection at the Fives Court to lend Sutton a helping hand, yielding £7, but it was ultimately to no avail – early in 1823 Sutton passed away. Richmond publicly announced the sad news at the Fives before generously organising a benefit for his widow.[1]

Although none of the black pugilists who fought in the late 1810s and early 1820s achieved the same level of fame as Richmond or Molineaux, they nevertheless made an important contribution to the sport's development, even if they were often patronised or viewed as an amusing novelty; the *Weekly Dispatch*, for example, frivolously noted in 1817 when an Irish boxer failed to show up for a planned fight that 'it is said to be the intention of the FANCY, to send immediately out to America for a ship-load of Blacks'.

As well as serving as the inspiration for the emergence of a new generation of black pugilists, Richmond's reputation was now so elevated that he was widely regarded as a respected elder statesman of the sport. A constant presence at virtually all the major fights, he was often called upon to perform significant ceremonial roles. For example, in February 1817 the future Tsar Nicholas I of Russia, then a mere Grand Duke, visited Coombe Warren in the company of Lord Yarmouth for the Fisher-Crockey fight, and the honour fell to Richmond to introduce the visiting Royal to Fisher, who won the contest. Two months later, when a lone magistrate turned up at a planned fight on Twickenham Common to inform the Fancy that he would not allow the contest to proceed it was Richmond and Harry Harmer to whom he addressed his plea for safety and understanding. Showing remarkable grace, despite the pressure of a disappointed crowd that perhaps numbered 20,000, the two pugilists reassured the magistrate that 'his mandate should be obeyed, and he was as safe as under the protection of a regiment of hussars'.

It was highly appropriate, given the frequent appearances he had made at benefits for other boxers over the years, that Richmond's own accomplishments were recognised with an event in his honour on 17 April 1817 at the Fives Court, to which the 'Corinthian order ... flocked in groupes'. Richmond had only recently recovered from what Egan described as a 'severe' attack of rheumatism, but he was in an exuberant mood, delighting the crowd with his gymnastic defensive moves and dancing feet when sparring with Oliver. Egan wrote that he performed 'all the pirouettes of a Des Hayes or an Oscar Byrne at the Opera, to the no small amusement of the spectators'. Oliver joined in the festive mood, quipping to the crowd: 'I never could hit *lily white* but on the back!' Cribb also appeared, further indicating the thaw in previously icy relations between the champion and his former foe. The event ended with Richmond taking a bow and making a well-received speech of thanks.

In July, Richmond was present at a more sombre occasion – the funeral of his old mentor Earl Percy, who had died suddenly of rheumatic gout aged seventy-four at his London residence on the Strand. Since his military days, Percy's life had remained defined by an over-riding sense of generosity and humanity – in 1815, for example, when corn prices had fallen dramatically, he had slashed rents for his agricultural tenants in Northumberland by 25 per cent, and he was also renowned for his regular gatherings at Alnwick to which he invited local tenants and trades-people. Richmond was among the many mourners at an extravagant funeral, alongside the Archbishop of Canterbury and Lord Gwydyr to name but two prominent guests. As Percy's remains were deposited in the family vault, the solemn anthem 'Man That is Born of Woman' was sung. For Richmond, still healthy but now well into his sixth decade, the lyrics were an apt reminder of his own mortality – death having now claimed from among his friends and colleagues

Lord Camelford, Henry Pearce, Jem Belcher and Earl Percy – as well
as a reminder that every day was precious, every experience should be
savoured and every opportunity grasped:

Man that is born of a woman is of few days, and full of trouble. He
cometh forth like a flower, and is cut down: he fleeth also as a shadow,
and continueth not.

21

Richmond's Crowning Glory

To add to the sense that death was stalking Richmond's former comrades and friends, Molineaux's dramatic life ceased in the summer of 1818. After his sojourn in Scotland, and defeat against Cooper, Molineaux had resurfaced in Ireland. Controversy had dogged him even there, with a planned contest against a fighter named McGlown collapsing in December 1815 when the American withdrew, apparently concerned that he would not receive fair play from the crowd. Molineaux was subsequently arrested, while a furious McGlown stole his sparring gloves and 'fighting dress', declaring he would only return them when (and if) Molineaux met and beat him in the ring. Thereafter, Molineaux's drinking increased and his physical condition deteriorated as he suffered, most probably, from the effects of consumption.

For the last few months of his life, his former magnificent physique was, in the words of Egan, reduced to 'a walking skeleton'. Movingly, he was 'maintained by charity' and 'very humanely attended' to by 'three people of his colour' in Galway in a room occupied by the band of the 77th regiment. He died in the same room on 4 August 1818 and a funeral was held three days later after the regiment initiated a subscription in his honour. There wasn't enough money left to erect a planned tombstone in his memory, though, and today his grave's likely location in the cemetery of St James' church in Murvue, eastern Galway is unmarked.

Although Molineaux's death was widely reported, most newspapers went no further than briefly reciting the basic facts of his life and career. It was left to the *Chester Chronicle* to provide a more fitting epitaph in the form of a detailed obituary, elements of which later appeared in *Boxiana*. The *Chronicle* rightly pointed out the considerable impact Molineaux had exerted on English pugilism, noting that he had been 'viewed by the English boxers with jealousy, concern and terror'. Quoting

Bill Gibbons, the *Chronicle* somewhat patronisingly speculated that had Molineaux possessed an 'English heart' he would have been 'completely invulnerable'. The obituary also struck a wistful note, recalling how in his pomp Molineaux had 'electrified the best judges of the Prize Ring'.

Several hundred miles away, Richmond was apparently unmoved by Molineaux's death (outwardly at least, for we can never know what thoughts occupied his private moments). As usual, the continuing soap opera of the prize ring was dominating his attention, rather than any sense of regret for the errors of the past. For a couple of years, Richmond had observed with amusement, and no little disdain, the return to pugilistic prominence of Jack Carter, whose bizarre collapse against Molineaux had been forgiven by the Fancy now he had embarked on a winning run. Richmond was resolutely unimpressed, though, particularly with the fact that, after three victories against Stephenson and Robinson, Carter had styled himself as the 'king of the blacks'. When Carter also defeated the highly-rated Tom Oliver in October 1816, some among the Fancy argued – citing Cribb's five years of inactivity – that the champion should fight Carter or else pass recognition of the title to him. Carter himself, with typical bravado, agreed and began referring to himself as 'champion' on the flimsy basis that Oliver had challenged Cribb, who had refused, and that he had then beaten Oliver.

Cribb weighed up the merits of a Carter bout with his customary care and his resolution never to fight again momentarily wavered – indeed, the *Morning Chronicle* claimed that a Carter-Cribb contest only floundered due to Cribb's request for a 300-guinea-a-side stake, which Carter's backers could not muster. Considering Cribb was now thirty-six and 17 stone, it was probably to the benefit of his reputation that the contest failed to come off. In the meantime, Carter continued to crow, earning an amusing rebuke from Richmond, who when informed Carter had defeated 'all the blacks', wittily retorted that he had, in fact, beaten 'all but one' and offered to come out of retirement to face him for 200 guineas.

Richmond and Carter did eventually square off, but it was in a purely informal manner, with no money at stake. In November 1818, Carter had returned to London after a tour of Europe and his boastfulness about his 'prowess' and his 'challenge to fight any man in the world' soon grated with his pugilistic colleagues. On the evening of 12 November in a tavern in Chancery Lane, Carter's boasting was so insufferable that he was ejected from the building by several of his fellow pugilists, Richmond among them. From the street an incensed Carter roared: 'Is there any among you that dare to face Jack Carter singly?' Richmond promptly 'answered in the affirmative', and an impromptu contest was arranged in the tavern yard, with Tom Belcher on hand to support and assist Richmond.

In the first round, the men exchanged a few 'random hits' before Carter wrestled Richmond to the ground and refused to let go. Several bystanders dragged Carter off a fuming Richmond, whose coat buttons popped off in the ensuing fracas. After a second round 'full of bustle', Richmond settled matters in the third, landing a jackhammer of a right hand upon 'Carter's upper works' which floored him 'like a shot'. When Carter finally recovered he admitted, 'I've been finely served out this evening,' before slinking away 'weeping over the stupidity of his fracas'. As for Richmond, with typical nonchalance, he returned to the tavern to continue socialising.

A few days later, a resentful Carter publicly complained to the spectators at Tom Spring's Fives Court benefit that Richmond and Belcher had 'taken advantage of him' while 'in a state of inebriation' before offering to fight both men in one ring for £200. An unrepentant Belcher replied that he would rather fight Carter there and then for 2*d*, prompting the fuming Lancastrian to storm out of the arena, boos and hisses from the crowd ringing in his ears. Richmond then ascended the stage, to cheers and applause, quipping that he had 'hitherto beat all his men singly and he should not now have anything to do with co-ship'. As more cheers echoed around the arena, Richmond added that, although he was now fifty-five years old, he would remain willing to give Carter another beating should he 'behave to him again in the same way as he had done on that evening'. This was the cue for yet more applause and a shout from one spectator of 'Well done, old one!' The disgruntled Carter, incidentally, would go on to lose a contest against Tom Spring the following year, thus ending his tenuous claim to the championship.[1]

If the Carter set-to was a surreal way for Richmond to end his fighting career, then events of the next three years would provide a more fitting platform for recognition of his considerable achievements. In March 1819, Richmond once again displayed his sparring talents for visiting royalty, exhibiting his skills at an event organised by John Jackson in Grosvenor Square for the visiting Archduke Maximilian Joseph of Austria-Este. Richmond's sparring session with Jack Randall was the 'finale' of the event, which was greeted with 'thunders of applause', while the visiting Archduke was suitably impressed by 'the manliness of the English character'.

The same month, *Tom Crib's Memorial to Congress* by Irish poet Thomas Moore was published, a satirical take on the previous autumn's Congress of Aix-La-Chapelle in which the political negotiations between Britain, Austria, Prussia and Russia – concerning matters as varied as the end of the military occupation of France and the international slave trade – were reimagined as a boxing match. Richmond's iconic status as a symbol of black emancipation was aptly represented by Moore giving him the appellation of 'Emperor of Hayti', as well as his inclusion in Moore's verse pleading with British Foreign Secretary Lord Castlereagh for 'fair play' to be shown to 'the Lily-Whites' so that 'us, poor Blacks' would not 'fare as ill/As if we were but pigs, or Irish!'

In representing Richmond as challenging the political status quo, Moore's work proved somewhat prophetic, for as 1819 progressed there were signs of a burgeoning radicalism within the pugilistic community, with relations between the sport and the political establishment becoming unusually strained. These were, of course, turbulent times; the Peterloo Massacre at St Peter's Field in Manchester on 16 August had provoked indignation and fear in fairly equal measure. The poor economic state of Britain since the end of the Napoleonic Wars had left the nation ravaged by discontent and a new enthusiasm for radicalism, as well as a desire for greater suffrage, now existed among many sections of society. Peterloo, so named in an ironic allusion to the victory at Waterloo four years earlier, occurred when a demonstration due to be addressed by the famous radical Henry Hunt was disrupted by a fatal cavalry charge initiated by a local magistrate who issued orders to arrest Hunt and other radicals. The cavalry plunged into the crowd of 60–70,000 protestors with total disregard for public safety, killing between eleven and fifteen civilians and injuring approximately 400 to 700. As news of the events spread, the predominant reaction among the general populace was fury, while a nervous government, fearing armed rebellion, initiated a rapid crackdown, imprisoning many leading figures of the radical movement and introducing the 'Six Acts' legislation, which decreed that any meeting for the purpose of radical reform was a treasonable act.

In the wake of Peterloo, an intriguing letter, most likely a satirical missive, appeared in the *Morning Post*, purporting to be written by 'J. Sneak', a 'radical reformer' who referred to Hunt as 'friend Hunt' and claimed he was writing on behalf of an unnamed radical 'Committee'. The letter described a new vision of parliamentary politics, including greater suffrage and parliamentary representation more in keeping with the needs and desires of ordinary people. 'Sneak' suggested a series of 'popular' and 'independent' names as candidates for these new parliamentary seats. Among them were familiar radicals, such as William Cobbett, and Sir Charles Wolseley. Additionally, and intriguingly, the name of 'Richmond, the black' was also cited as a candidate for Tottenham.

Although almost certainly a satirical jest by an opponent of radicalism rather than a serious proposal, the letter raises several questions. Does the inclusion, for example, of Richmond's name indicate that he was a known advocate of the radical reform movement? For a man with seemingly no other recorded connections or affiliations with any political movements, save for his brief association with Richard Brinsley Sheridan, it seems somewhat unlikely. A more logical explanation seems to be that his name was referred to because of his status as a black celebrity, as a way of mocking the inclusive views of many radicals.

Interestingly, though, there is firm evidence that the Peterloo-provoked 'Six Acts' were highly unpopular within the pugilistic corps. As the acts were making their way through parliament in late December, the leading pugilists of the day held a meeting to discuss their concerns about parliament's actions at Tom Belcher's public house. The gathering was described in a detailed report in the *Westmorland Gazette*:

> It appears that the Bills now before Parliament, which are intended to impose certain restrictions upon public meetings, and to prevent training, except in the manner by law established, has excited alarm in the minds of other persons than those who are disposed to embark in political discussions. The 'Fancy' have felt that their liberties too are proposed to be infringed, and in common with other classes of the community have felt themselves called upon to assemble and to express their feelings.

Cribb took the chair and Richmond was among those to speak out against the proposals. The *Gazette* transcribed his words using patronising syntax that misrepresented the well-spoken Richmond in a demeaning manner as a stereotypically uneducated black man, but the pro-libertarian thrust behind his sentiments was still clear:

> Richmond said, that in de country he come from, dere was no law against milling – every man was allowed to fight if he liked – and dat was what he called a fair stand up sort of Liberty. Dey had talked of the Lord Chancellor, and dat - and he had heard of bribery and corruption – he could only say, as he'd give his Worship twelve lessons any time, if he'd not let dese bills pass.

Interestingly, a 'pugilistic reporter', almost certainly Pierce Egan, was also present at the meeting and made a long-winded speech, which provoked an objection from Harry Sutton who felt his allusions to *Othello* were offensively framed. In the event, the 'Six Acts' passed parliament, but were only enforced sporadically and were eventually dropped and repelled. They ultimately had little discernable effect on pugilism, with the sport continuing to operate much as before.

By 1820, Richmond's focus had fully returned to sporting matters. In February his customary wit was in evidence when he seconded a hapless local against Bill Abbott in an impromptu bout at Epsom Downs. When the 'yokel', who Pierce Egan nicknamed 'Johnny Raw', had his senses scrambled at the end of the first round, Richmond scraped him off the floor. The confused local turned to his second and asked him, confusion writ large across his face: '*Who done that? What's that for? Where am I?*' With a broad grin, Richmond replied: 'Why, you are in the Court of *Chancery*; and let me say, you are not the first man that has been *bothered* by its *practice*.'

Later that month, on 29 February, the Royal Tennis Court in Great Windmill Street started to host sparring exhibitions, sometimes in direct opposition to the Fives, and Richmond was given the honour of having the first benefit at the new venue. The *Morning Post* admiringly noted that the Tennis Court was 'of considerably larger dimensions than the Fives-court', and that Richmond's benefit was a huge success, claiming 'most probably it never was, nor ever will be again, so crowded'. Interestingly, the *Post* also noted that the majority of spectators were 'gentlemen whose faces are not known in the prize ring', indicating Richmond's popularity extended far beyond the usual confines of the Fancy. Richmond's sparring session with Tom Belcher was the finale to a very successful event.

By 1821, Richmond was also leasing training rooms at the tennis court, which Egan reported in the third volume of *Boxiana*, were 'well attended', possessed 'good *character*' and did 'not want for the patronage of numerous *Swells*'. Boxing's most noted wordsmith also took the opportunity to laud Richmond's numerous virtues, remarking,

> we know of no pugilist better calculated to teach the *science* than RICHMOND; not only from his superior knowledge of boxing, but from his acquaintance with men and manners, and civility of deportment on all occasions. He is full of anecdote: and the *milling* talents of the various professors of the art of boxing he is able to descant upon with considerable judgment. In short, *Old* BILL is justly entitled to the appellation of a very interesting feature in the Sporting World.

It was somewhat appropriate that in the year these words were written the greatest personal honour of Richmond's life also occurred when, along with seventeen other pugilists,[2] he was invited to perform an official role at George IV's coronation. This considerable achievement owed much to John Jackson, who had been enlisted by the new monarch, via Lord Gwydyr, to assemble a group of ushers for the coronation festivities, as well as to Richmond's own insistence, at a meeting to discuss the proposals, that 'gentlemen of colour should be represented'. George's desire for a group of pugilists to provide some 'muscle' at his coronation was partly borne out of his awareness of his public unpopularity, as well as the likelihood that his estranged wife Caroline might try to gain admittance to the event. It was also, however, a reflection of the lofty status and widespread fame that top pugilists enjoyed in England, as well as George's affection for the sport. When he had been Prince of Wales, the new king had been an enthusiastic patron of pugilism, attending several contests and, it was said, brokering some too, although he had reportedly sworn never to attend another boxing match in person after seeing a man killed in a bout near Brighton in 1788. The Prince had continued to gamble on boxing after this incident, although his elevation to the position of Prince Regent had forced him to curb any public patronage of the sport. Nevertheless, he remained a keen fan of pugilism and was, as *Fistiana* explained, 'a constant reader of the sporting papers', who was 'familiar with the names of all the men who in succession obtained celebrity or notoriety'. Interestingly enough, it was later said of George that he possessed 'an unconquerable antipathy to blacks being near his person', and that he had vetoed the idea of a black drummer being a member of the Royal Band. Yet, where Richmond was concerned, the King clearly had no reservations about him being present at his coronation celebrations; quite simply Bill's considerable reputation appeared to override any personal prejudices the new King harboured.

In a gesture redolent of the new monarch's extravagance, the pugilists were dressed as pages in retro Tudor-Stuart costumes George himself had designed. On the self-confident frame of a man of style and refinement, such as Richmond, the 'scarlet frock-coats trimmed with gold lace, blue sashes, ruffs, white small-clothes and stockings, [and] black shoes with crimson rosettes' looked splendidly ostentatious; the same could not be said for some of the other pugilists, who shuffled around in a somewhat uncomfortable and embarrassed fashion.

Although it is unclear if they were present in Westminster Abbey for the coronation ceremony itself, the politician Grantley Berkeley later claimed that the pugilists in general, and Richmond, Josh Hudson and Peter Crawley in particular, played a crucial role in blocking Caroline's carriage as it approached the Abbey, noting that 'Richmond the black' was among the 'most active in impeding the progress of the royal carriage'. Caroline did eventually reach the doors of the Abbey and was turned away, William Cobbett claiming that she was 'thrust back by the hands of a common prize-fighter' – an assertion that other accounts fail to support.

Having stayed overnight at Westminster Hall, the pugilists' primary responsibility was supervising the doors at the coronation banquet by checking the tickets of guests as they arrived and directing them to their seats. *The Times* were somewhat disapproving of the presence of such 'notorious persons' at an official state occasion. 'The persons present in the hall had, singularly enough, a full opportunity of seeing Cribb, Richmond and [Jack] Randall,' the paper reported, before adding disparagingly that the pugilists had possessed 'a mimic air of official confidence'. It was also not to *The Times*' liking that Cribb, at one point, had used an ale jug to refresh his companions 'with an invigorating beverage'. It was, the journal lamented, a 'strange' tribute to the 'real champion' (i.e. the new King) to have 'these fellows' given the responsibility of combating 'misdoers'.

The pugilists' duties did not end on the day of the coronation itself, but also extended to the following Monday, when Westminster Hall was opened so that the public could see for themselves the opulent glory of the banquet's location. Several thousand visitors took advantage of the opportunity and 'Cribb, Belcher, Spring, Oliver, Richmond, Carter, Owen &c' were all 'in attendance at the door,' according to the *Morning Post*, who were rather more appreciative in their tone than *The Times*, declaring that the pugilists' 'united strength of arms' prevented 'any sort of rush or danger from occurring'. Furthermore, the *Post* argued that the pugilists' 'knowledge of society prevented any improper characters' from entering. 'Not the slightest accident occurred,' the paper concluded, indicating that George's decision to rely on his pugilistic heroes had been an inspired one. Certainly the King was delighted with the pugilists' steadfast attention to their duties. Lord Gwydyr sent each of them a letter of thanks on behalf of the King, also enclosing the letter the Home Secretary Lord Sidmouth had sent him. The missives ran as follows:

WHITEHALL, 21 July, 1821.
MY LORD, – I am commanded by His Majesty, to express to your Lordship His Majesty's high approbation of the arrangements made by your Lordship in the department of the Great Chamberlain of England, for the august ceremony of His Majesty's coronation, and of the correctness and regularity with which they were carried into effect.

To the exemplary manner in which these duties were performed by your Lordship, and by those officers who acted under your Lordship's authority, His Majesty is graciously pleased to consider that the order and dignity, which so peculiarly distinguished the ceremony, are in a great degree to be ascribed; and I have to request that your Lordship will communicate to the persons referred to the sense which His Majesty has condescended to express of their services.
I have the honour to be, my Lord,
Your Lordship's most obedient, humble servant,

SIDMOUTH

GREAT CHAMBERLAIN'S OFFICE, 22 July, 1821.
SIR, – Having received His Majesty's commands, through the Secretary of State for the Home Department, to communicate to you, sir, His Majesty's gracious approbation of the manner in which you discharged

your duty on the 19th of July, I know no way so effectual of executing these most gratifying instructions, as by inclosing you a copy of the original document. Permit me at the same time to add, how sensible I am of your attention to the very imperfect directions I was enabled to furnish you with, and that the arrangements, which have been with so much condescension noticed by your King, are in a great degree to be attributed to the loyalty, judgment, and temper, exhibited by you at His Majesty's coronation.

I remain, sir,

Your faithful and obedient servant,

GWYDYR.

As a symbol of appreciation, the pugilists were also awarded a single, gold coronation medal between them, designed by the Royal Mint's chief engraver Benedetto Pistrucci. It is estimated that only around 1,000 of these medals were minted and it was said that Gwydyr had received the medal 'from the hands of his majesty expressly for the boxers'. The medal couldn't very well be split eighteen ways, so the pugilists raffled it at an extravagant dinner held to mark their 'steady conduct' – paid for by Gwydyr – which took place at Cribb's on 6 August. Tom Belcher won and resolved he would not part with the medal 'till death'.

Richmond may not have had a gold medal to show for his endeavours at the coronation, but as he sat at dinner – surrounded by his pugilistic comrades and with a mood of warm conviviality pervading the room – his incredible journey from slavery in a rural Staten Island parsonage to the rarefied heights of English society was complete. No wonder he enthusiastically drank to the King's health four times; all things considered, representatives of the British Crown – from Earl Percy to George IV – had treated Richmond well.

22

'The Joys of the Days That Are Gone'

In retrospect, George IV's coronation proved the last hurrah of pugilism's greatest age. Thereafter the sport entered a period of gradual decline, both in influence and popularity, as well as probity. Part of the reason for this slump was the lack of an active champion – by 1821, Cribb had hogged the title for almost a decade without defending it since the second Molineaux contest. In January, it looked like the champion might make a sensational comeback to face Bristolian Bill Neat. However, the contest fell through and, in April, Cribb announced that he had 'resigned' the crown and was passing it to Tom Spring, his 'adopted boy'. Spring had defeated some decent fighters – Tom Oliver, Jack Carter and Ned Painter among them (although Painter had beaten him in a rematch) – but the title being handed to him like an heirloom left a sour taste. Besides which, Cribb's farewell proved interminable, his retirement only becoming official in May the following year when a benefit and dinner were held in his honour. Spring would not be widely recognised as champion until he defeated Neat in 1823 and, although he proved his mettle in a pair of popular contests against Irishman Jack Langan in 1824, the days when a bare-knuckle contest seemed to unreservedly occupy the national attention were coming to an end.

Where once pugilism's somewhat shambolic organisation and frequent controversies had seemed a reflection of the sport's charmingly ramshackle nature, the stench of foul play now pervaded, with allegations of fight-fixing and gambling coups growing. In 1822, a contest between Jem Ward and Bill Abbott caused a scandal when Ward threw the fight. Richmond, who was seconding Abbott, was among the disgusted ringside observers.

However, it was the events of 1824 that proved to be a turning point for the sport, leaving the *Weekly Dispatch* to lament, 'Alas the golden age of pugilism is gone.' The execution of Jack Thurtell for murder in January provided a useful opportunity for pugilism's opponents to give the sport a public kicking. Thurtell was the son of an affluent Norwich businessman who had travelled to London, become a heavy gambler and sought to fix several fights. With two accomplices he had killed a man in a dispute over a game of cards. According to *The Times*, Thurtell's 'plunge into crime' had been 'occasioned by his predilection for prizefighting', sentiments which many other moralists rushed to concur with.

Events in the prize ring itself merely added ammunition to the anti-pugilistic cause; the first Langan-Spring contest in January ended sourly, with Langan objecting to the fact his seconds had conceded on his behalf. 'Molineux's treatment was fair play, in comparison to mine,' he grumbled. Although the rematch in June, like the first fight, attracted a huge crowd, corruption in pugilism was becoming more widespread and gradually wrecking the sport's reputation. In October, a contest between Jack Martin and Jem Burns caused a stink when it collapsed, amid revelations Martin was planning to lose on purpose, while in January 1825 Justice Burroughs' stand against pugilism in the Surrey courts brought Ned O'Neal and Burns to court on charges of breach of the peace, effectively ending the sport's longstanding association with the popular venue of Moulsey Hurst. 'Something rotten in the state of Denmark,' remarked the *Morning Chronicle* of the Martin-Burns farce, adding that 'Tom Cribb, Tom Spring, Bill Richmond, Tom Belcher and other members of the old school ... expressed their disgust at such scenes.'

The 'old school' were part of the problem though. Although their honesty was not in doubt, it did not help that they were more concerned with lucrative exhibitions that lined their own pockets, rather than the development of pugilism as a whole. From one perspective, this was eminently understandable – they had a living to make after all – but it was also indicative of a short-sighted desire for immediate profit for the few at the expense of what might have proved greater long-term rewards for the many had pugilism maintained its position at the pinnacle of the sporting and social scene. Gradually the public tired of seeing the same faces at the Fives or at the tennis court and it was to nobody's advantage that pugilists began to hold competing benefits, sometimes on the same day, souring the perception of the sport and relationships between boxers – Richmond and Tom Belcher's friendship, for example, was never quite the same again after the men held rival events on the same day in June 1824.

Hastening the sport's decay, Jackson closed his rooms in Bond Street the same year and the Pugilistic Club was dissolved in 1825. Meanwhile, the Fives Court and Richmond's former pub the Horse and Dolphin were both pulled down not long after as part of the gradual process of redeveloping the local area to make way for the eventual construction of Trafalgar Square. In a further symbol of pugilism's decline, in 1825 the disgraced Jem Ward acceded to the championship crown vacated by the retired Spring by defeating Tom Cannon. As the *Chester Chronicle* noted sadly: 'A good, fair fight or two might do wonders towards restoring the credit of the prize ring. At present, there is not much chance.'

Richmond maintained his dignity as best he could as pugilism's reputation and profile slumped. The *Morning Post* made clear the esteem in which he was held by stating he was 'a respected individual ... tried and approved as a good man in private', while Richmond's appearance in William Maginn's satirical novel *Whitehall* – in which he was described as 'the hero of a hundred combats' – was a further indication that he retained a high level of public recognition and respect. As he grew older, Richmond searched in vain for a new black boxer to assume his mantle. One of his more intriguing pupils was a New York-born man named Green, who 'exceedingly resembled Molineux' and even claimed to be the cousin of the former title challenger. Richmond introduced his new charge at the Fives Court in July 1824, announcing that the time was 'not far off' when he would quit boxing for good. He expressed his desire to 'bequeath' to Green 'all his sable honours'. However, arranging a contest for his latest protégé amid the state of *ennui* that had enveloped the Fancy proved impossible and Green disappeared as quickly as he had emerged, seemingly without throwing a competitive punch.

Although the prize ring offered him scant comfort as the 1820s advanced, Richmond did find time – rather movingly – to bury his enmity with his old rival Cribb and the two men gradually became firm friends. This rapprochement had most likely begun in 1815 when Cribb had forced Shelton to shake Richmond's hand and, by the mid-1820s, Richmond was often to be found in Cribb's public house, the Union Arms on Panton Street, conversing with his former rival and exchanging tales of pugilistic derring-do.

In May 1825, Richmond even ended up in court on a charge of assault after rushing to the defence of Cribb's dog, Billy.[1] Richmond was called before a magistrate at Bow Street after Mr Teasdale, 'a Chemist and a Druggist', claimed the retired pugilist had struck him in the mouth and loosened his teeth. Teasdale recounted how he had been walking towards Whitcomb Street when his own dog, a mastiff, began fighting with Billy, at which point he kicked Cribb's dog in the belly to separate them. The passing Richmond, seeing the kick but not what had preceded it, had then, according to Teasdale, struck him a backhanded blow on the mouth, causing a 'torrent of blood'.

Contesting this, Richmond stated that he had been concerned that Billy was 'overmatched' and 'outweighed' by Teasdale's dog and, therefore, when he saw Teasdale kick him he had believed it was 'not fair play'. Amusingly, Richmond explained to the magistrate, Mr Minshull, that he was 'always an advocate' of fair play, whether it be 'between man and man, or dog and dog'. Richmond insisted that he had merely lifted his hand to push Teasdale back and, in doing so, had inadvertently struck him. The *Morning Post* provided a transcript of the next section of proceedings:

> Mr. MINSHULL – he swears you struck him.
> Richmond – I never strike but with my doubled fist, and if I had done so in this instance I should have knocked his teeth out.
> Mr. Teasdale – You did loosen them, and I know by the feel that your fist was doubled.

Cribb was called as a witness and testified he had not seen the blow in question. Richmond offered to apologise and Cribb 'endeavoured to intercede for his sable friend', but the magistrate cut him off, declaring that 'the law must take its course'. Minshull concluded that the assault had been committed on the 'spur of the moment' and was 'entirely without malice or premeditation'. Richmond was bailed and it is unclear how the somewhat bizarre case was concluded.

The following year, Richmond and Cribb again teamed up, this time for altruistic purposes, as they arranged a benefit at the Royal Tennis Court in July for those weavers who had suffered during the power-loom riots of 1826. Unrest had broken out in several northern industrial towns after power looms were introduced and replaced traditional handlooms, thus threatening many weavers' livelihoods. It was but one of many expressions of public unrest during the post-Napoleonic period, and Richmond and Cribb's sympathy for the weavers, many of whose leaders had been arrested, indicates that something of the radical spirit of 1819 still lingered within both men. Sadly, the benefit was a failure, raising only £7 after expenses were deducted. Barely any leading pugilists agreed to spar and Richmond, who was 'orator' for the day, closed the event by expressing his 'regret that his brother pugilists had, with their character, lost their feelings'. It was a second failure in just three months for Richmond, whose own benefit event in May had been so poorly attended that he lost money.

Although *Bell's Life in London* reported that his new sparring rooms in St Martin's Lane were being met with 'deserved encouragement', the numbers of pupils requiring Richmond's services as a gymnastic instructor were soon falling. This was partly a consequence of pugilism's dwindling popularity, but also a symptom of a general economic downturn which had swept the country since the 'Panic of 1825' when the London stock market had crashed, sending many banks out of business. In an effort to diversify and expand his business interests, Richmond sunk his dwindling funds into establishing a butcher's business at No. 73 St Martin's Lane early in 1827.

An April benefit event that Richmond organised was also poorly attended, while in November he was embroiled in further legal proceedings, although this time of a somewhat comic nature. On this occasion Richmond was the complainant, as he sought counsel from the Lord Mayor at Mansion House to have a six-legged ox returned to his possession. Richmond explained to the principal clerk, the famed wit Francis Hobler, that the ox had been the prize in a raffle at which he had asked another man, named Jackson, to throw for him. Jackson had consequently thrown the highest number in the competition, however two men named Benson and Hildyard, who had organised the raffle, had kept possession of the ox. Apparently there had been an offer to re-raffle the ox and split the profits with Jackson, but Richmond had declined, insisting the ox was worth £50. He joked that he intended to exhibit it at his next benefit 'as it was a greater curiosity than the gloves'.

Hobler summoned the 'detaining parties' and the case stretched into a second day, with Cribb present to lend support to his 'black brother in arms'. Benson admitted that he had possession of the ox, explaining that Jackson was also claiming ownership of the animal, thus placing him in a quandary. To general hilarity, Hobler pointed out that the raffle had been illegal anyway and recommended the ox was given to Richmond, warning that once the matter got 'into the hands of the lawyers, your ox will soon be devoured'. Richmond left 'cheered with the hope of getting his six-legged prize', although it is unclear if he ultimately got his hands on the animal or not.

Sadly, the comic circumstances of the 'ox trial' were a rare moment of levity in the final years of Richmond's life. On 8 January 1828 he was arrested for an alleged assault of John Webb, a charge for which he was bailed on 14 January. It is unclear what the nature of the assault was, or what the ultimate outcome of the case was, but it can't have helped Richmond's peace of mind.

Such was the state of Richmond's financial desperation that he even considered a return to the professional ring, despite the fact his sixty-fifth birthday was fast approaching. Throughout the summer of 1828, a publican named Stephen Ford, who ran the Beaufort Arms in Bath, had issued a series of pugilistic challenges via the letters page of *Bell's Life,* and Richmond replied to one of Ford's invitations thus in a letter printed on 25 May:

SIR – I noticed in your Paper, a short time since, a challenge from a publican of the name of Ford, at Bath, offering to fight any publican for £50, or £100. He says, he is an old man; now I am still older, being sixty-five years of age, and if Massa Ford means what he says, I shall fight him for £100, or as much more as he likes, halfway between London and Bath; or at Bath, if he will pay my expenses down. I shall be ready to make a deposit of £85, at any house and time he may appoint in London.

Yours, BILL RICHMOND

Taking into account his ongoing financial struggles, it seems unlikely that Richmond would have been able to raise an £85 deposit. Nonetheless, a week later, *Bell's Life* reported that Ford had accepted Richmond's challenge and would soon appear in London to make the match. However a further letter published at the end of June – this time written by Ford - made it clear that the match had still not taken place:

SIR – Seeing in your Paper, some weeks back, a challenge given to Stephen Ford by Bill Richmond, the Black, to fight him for £100, or as much more as he liked, I sent to his friend Frank Redmond, to say that I would meet him at Cheltenham, on the 17th or 18th, and fight him for £200, and to allow himself for his expenses. I was at Cheltenham, expecting to see Bill Richmond, but he never appeared. I am now ready to fight him at Bath Races, on the same terms, on the 3d, 4th, and 5th of July next,; and if he can't post the blunt, I will fight him for a bellyful or a glass of gin, and allow him £5 for a good thrashing. Or I will fight any man in the kingdom of my age, for £500, let him come from where he will.

STEPHEN FORD

For all of Ford's fiery rhetoric, the editor of *Bell's Life,* Vincent George Dowling, was unimpressed, defending Richmond and remarking drily of Ford's missive:

Mr. Ford is a little too bounceable – if he had meant fighting, there was a regular mode of answering Richmond's challenge. Serious matches are not made and fought at two or three days' notice.

A week later a pugilistic colleague of Richmond's, who signed his name 'G. W.' and addressed his letter from boxer Josh Hudson's public house the Half-Moon Tap, joined the debate, pointing out that Ford had previous form as a pugilistic irritant, recalling how he had travelled to London years before to challenge then champion Henry Pearce, despite the fact Pearce wasn't in London at the time, only to be soundly 'licked' in a trial against another pugilist. 'G. W.' also claimed that when Richmond and Molineaux had visited Bath races in the lead-up to the Molineaux-Cribb rematch, Ford's insults had so infuriated Richmond that he had stripped and offered to fight the publican there and then – only for Ford to flee.

'G. W.' and Ford's correspondence continued for several weeks, each letter more tiresome than the last as their squabble became mired in claim and counter-claim. Richmond clearly felt the whole matter was now beneath his considerable dignity and wisely declined further comment. In the meantime, he seconded the last black fighter of his career, his 'new black' losing, somewhat ignominiously, on a foul against Bill Franklin in Hertfordshire on 15 July for a paltry £5 purse. At the same time, Richmond's butcher's business was unfortunately in the process of collapse; in December, *Bell's Life* commented sadly that Richmond 'after buffeting the vicissitudes of life with industry and perseverance' was now 'hard up'.

When his butcher's shop finally closed, late in 1828 or possibly early in 1829, Richmond was left with 'not a feather to fly with'. Heartbreakingly, the day the business was dissolved, he wandered down the street and bumped into an old friend, who was shocked to see a 'tear running down his iron cheek'. Asked what the cause of his grief was, Richmond replied, 'I have had all my goods sold ... and where to go I know not; I am without a bed to rest my unhappy head upon.' A benefit at the Tennis Court was duly organised in May to try and support 'poor Richmond' who, the *Morning Chronicle* noted, 'needs a helping hand'. The event seems to have been successful enough to ensure that Richmond staved off bankruptcy and was able to secure lodgings for himself and his family in Tichburne Street. By August, though, it was clear that Richmond was again in desperate financial straits, with *Bell's Life* reporting that he was 'as black as ever, and in want of a friend'. A further benefit for 'poor old Richmond' took place at the Red Horse pub in Bond Street in October, suggesting that the last few months of his life were strained and poverty-stricken.

Although his number of pugilistic pupils had declined and he had plunged into poverty, it is striking that Richmond continued to make a significant impact on those who he did tutor. *The Times* newspaper's Italy correspondent, Michael Burke Honan, met Richmond in the year before his death and in his memoirs recalled in detail the advice and instruction that his 'old master' had imparted. Honan's account of his time training with Richmond speaks eloquently of the latter's gentlemanly character and precise teaching methods. For example, Honan recalled the scientific way that Richmond would dispense his technical instructions while he was sparring:

> Keep quiet, sir, and when you hit, hit hard! Spring from the point of your foot, middle your man with the left, and catch him under the butt of the ear with the right; let your shoulders go with the blow, let the whole weight of your body follow, and only deliver at the point.

However, it was Richmond's vision of pugilism as an essentially defensive art that made the biggest impact upon his eager pupil. Honan's account of Richmond's explanation of this philosophy is an eloquent document of the values by which Richmond sought to live his life:

> As he [Richmond] used to say: 'A gentleman, sir, only uses his hands to defend himself, and not to attack; we call the pugilistic art, for that reason, the noble science of defence. Depend on it, sir, you can never give, without receiving, and the very worst spoon can mark you a black eye. "Keep quiet, sir," that is the golden rule, it will save you from many a licking.'

Movingly, Honan noted that 'those were the last words of the black, as I only came into his hands a year before his death'. Appropriately enough, in the week leading up to his death in December 1829, Richmond did fulfil one final professional pugilistic engagement, seconding a fighter named Appleby to victory against his opponent Noyes in what was described as 'the best fight seen in Bristol for some years'. No doubt Richmond – described in the enthusiastic report of the contest as 'that rare good 'un' – was thrilled with the 'gallant fight' in which the two pugilists matched each other 'hit for hit'.

A few days later, on the evening of Sunday 27 December, Richmond was back in London and visited Cribb at the Union Arms, as had become his regular custom. The two men, as usual, swapped affectionate stories and Richmond left 'in the most cheerful manner' at around 11 p.m. However, around an hour after returning home to Tichburne Street, he was 'attacked with a violent fit of coughing'. His wife Mary called for medical assistance, but by the time it arrived at 2 a.m. on Monday morning it was too late – Richmond 'was a corpse'.

Despite being in his sixty-seventh year, the sudden and distressing nature of Richmond's passing came as a shock to his family and pugilistic comrades. Tributes soon appeared in dozens of national and local newspapers and, without exception, the published obituaries were extravagant in their praise, if a little ham-fisted in their references to his ethnic background; so while Richmond was somewhat patronisingly referred to as a 'perfect black', the 'hero of the "black work"' and the 'well known man of colour', he was also, more pleasingly, hailed as a 'pugilistic hero' and 'the celebrated boxer'.

The obituaries in the *Weekly Dispatch* and *Bell's Life* were particularly glowing, pointing out the 'great celebrity' Richmond had earned as a 'game and honest boxer and a scientific teacher of the art of self-defence'. Both journals praised Richmond's sense of self-discipline, emphasising that when he had left Cribb's on the night of his death he had been 'perfectly sober'; indeed, the *Dispatch* noted, 'he was remarkably abstemious ... seldom taking more than a glass of sherry and water'. Meanwhile, *Bell's Life* referred to Richmond's pride in his ethnicity, commenting that he 'was never offended on being called a *black*; but rather pleased with his *colour*, as if it tended to obtain for him *notoriety* in the sporting world'.

The *Dispatch* obituary closed on a nostalgic note, as it mourned not only Richmond's passing and his 'gallant' nature, but also the expiration of pugilism's greatest era:

> The latter days of this gallant veteran were clouded with poverty; but he still maintained a respectable appearance, and his conversation and manners were admired by all who met him at the house of his old friend, Tom Cribb, where he still delighted to 'fight his battles o'er again,' and converse on 'the joys of the days that are gone'. Bill has left behind him the reputation of a brave and honest man – he flourished as a boxer in those days when *gentlemen* backed pugilists, and *crossing* was hardly known.

The theme of Richmond's unimpeachable honesty was taken up by the tribute paid to him by the Fair Play Club, a high-profile if rather ineffective organisation, which had been established in 1828 in the vain hope of eradicating fight fixing and other dubious practices from pugilism. At a meeting soon after Richmond's death, the Fair Play Club chairman hailed Richmond's bravery and argued that 'his memory we all with sincerity prize'.

Unfortunately, the avalanche of kind words and admiring obituaries did little to alleviate the most immediate and unfortunate consequence of Richmond's death – namely that it had left his widow, four children and several grandchildren in a 'state of destitution'. It was left to Cribb to leap to their aid; the former champion initiated a collection at the Tennis Court during a benefit for Dutch Sam the day after Richmond's death and also opened a benevolent subscription. Jackson collected additional money for the Richmond family and a benefit event for the 'widow Richmond' was scheduled for 9 February, although the hastily organised event was, sadly, destined to be 'not very fully attended'. Cribb then spent several hours carefully penning a eulogy in Richmond's honour, which he planned to deliver at the funeral on Monday 11 January at St James's churchyard in Piccadilly. However, when the day of the ceremony finally dawned the former champion was suffering from a severe attack of gout and was unable to attend.

In Cribb's absence, the funeral was a low-key affair, Richmond being quietly 'followed to his grave by his children and grand children, and by his old companions in arms, Tom Spring, Jem Burn, Ned Neal, Josh Hudson, Edward Baldwin, and Tom Gaynor'. History has not recorded whether any of these pugilists, or anyone else, stepped forward and spoke in Cribb's stead as Richmond's coffin was lowered into the cold earth, or whether the final stages of the ceremony merely unfolded in solemn silence.

However, one of those present at the funeral, referred to as an 'Old Pal' of Richmond, did compose a reflective verse entitled 'Tears of the Fancy' which described the funeral and was later published in *Bell's Life*. The conclusion of the poem stands as a permanent epitaph to the unlikely fact that a black man who had once been a slave in Staten Island succeeded in finding fame and respect in England, within the occasionally maddening, but always generous-hearted embrace of the Fancy:

> Then farewell, Bill Richmond! Thy praise I will sing;
> And a more honest boxer never fought in the Ring;
> Farewell to the black work/farewell to the chaunt;
> No more to the fair ones to act the gallant –
> May thy soul rest in peace, all unspotted with crime,
> And at the last trumpet be ready to 'Time!'
> P.S. A tribute is due to the gallant and brave,

Who followed the body of Bill to the grave.
Tom Cribb would have wept o'er his coffin, no doubt,
But, alas! he was tied hand and foot by the gout;
Tom Spring and Tom Gaynor, with hearty goodwill,
Were present to pay the last duties to Bill;
And jolly Josh Hudson, Ned Neal, and Jem Burn,
United in dropping a tear on his urn ...

23

'You All Lov'd Richmond Once'

Although Cribb was unable to deliver his planned eulogy at Richmond's funeral, *Bell's Life in London* published it in full. Since its original publication it has, to the best of my knowledge, never been reprinted. Indeed, for the best part of 200 years, Cribb's tribute to his friend lay dormant in an obscure corner of a dusty archive – unremembered, unrecognised and unremarked upon. Then, one day in the summer of 2003, I was lucky enough to discover the issue of *Bell's Life in London* containing Cribb's 'oration' in the British Newspaper Archive in Colindale. On reading his words I was so inspired that I resolved, there and then, to write a biography of Bill Richmond. A decade later the oration warrants reprinting in full:

TOM CRIBB'S FUNERAL ORATION OVER BILL RICHMOND

Friends, Fancy Coves, and Millers, cock up your ears,
I come to bury Billy, not to wake him.
The roguery of men lives after them,
The good is soon forgotten as themselves;
So let it be with Richmond. Some have told you
That Billy was a black and ugly nigger;
If it were so, it makes no odds at all;
For, from our perch we all in turns must tumble.
Here, by desire of Billy's better half
(And, Heaven knows well, poor thing! she's badly off,
So are her young-'uns - wery badly off!),
Come I to speak at Blacky's funeral.
He was my friend, always a trump to me:
But people say he was a foreign nigger,

As if the colour always made the man. -
He hath stood many glasses in my bar,
Tho' he was free to sluice his gob for nothing:
Did this in Bill look *niggardly*?
When a poor cove has begg'd, Billy has tipp'd;
These niggers have got bowels like ourselves.
But yet we're told he was a jumping Yankee,
And we must hear folks taunt a man that's down.
You all do know, when he was turn'd adrift,
How oft I wish'd to lend him half a crown,
Which always he refus'd - Was this dishonest?
And yet, forsooth, they call a man a nigger,
Who was as right in conduct as a trivet. -
I am not here to say that Bill was white;
But here I stand to give the Devil his due.-
You all lov'd Richmond once - not without cause -
Then drop a tear in memory of a brave un.-
O, Pugilistic glory is no more!
And men are sold like cattle. - Bear with me,
My heart is slumbering in that shell with Billy,
And I must pause till it come back to me.-
If you have tears, prepare to pipe your eye.
You all know these white kicksies: I remember
The first time Billy ever drew them on -
'Twas on a summer evening, in my crib -
That day he took his shop in Martin's-lane.
Look how that front is stain'd with porker's blood-
See what a rent behind old Time hath made:
A street row led to this unseemly slit,
And, as the snowy garment gap'd across,
The dowlas shirt of Billy was display'd,
As rushing out of doors to be resolv'd
If there was such a precious gap or no.
I come not, friends, to waste your time with chaff -
I am no orator, like Harry Holt;
But as you know me all, plain, blunt Tom Cribb,
That loves my friend, and that's the time of day,
Why I am here to speak a bit about him.
I never had the power to spin a yarn,
Gammon, nor blarney, nor a string of words
To come it strong - I only speak right out,
Shew you poor Billy's young and hungry kids,
And beg a trifle for them. Do not withhold it -

> For, like the bread you cast upon the waters,
> Assuredly it shall, and no mistake,
> Return and bless you after many days.

Viewed through the prism of modern sensibilities, Cribb's work is painfully clumsy in its handling of Richmond's ethnicity. Nevertheless it remains one of the most profoundly moving speeches I've ever encountered, as well as a wonderfully artful and elegant reworking of Mark Antony's eulogy for Julius Caesar as written by William Shakespeare. Part of the affecting nature of the piece is, of course, the knowledge that Cribb never got to deliver it; that the words were only ever printed and not spoken; that Cribb never got the chance to brandish in church Richmond's blood-stained trousers ('kicksies') during the section where he recounts an anecdote concerning Bill's time as a butcher.

Another factor which makes the eulogy so touching, I think, is that it was written by 'plain, blunt Tom Cribb', one of the toughest, most manly men who ever walked the face of the earth, yet when he writes about Richmond, Cribb is uninhibited, unabashed and unashamed in expressing affection and love for his friend. 'You all lov'd Richmond once,' he emphasises, a sentiment which could seem like a trite rhetorical flourish but, coming from Cribb, who also admits that his 'heart is slumbering in that shell with Billy', it achieves a profound poetic grandeur. There is also something unusually inspiring about the vision of friendship that Cribb elucidates between himself and Richmond, a friendship that was able to develop, thrive and endure despite the barriers engendered by their births in different continents and their possession of contrasting skin colours during a period of history when ethnicity overwhelmingly defined a man's station and status in life. Lest we forget, the two men had also formerly been the most bitter of professional rivals, so the oration can also be seen as an eloquent example of the redemptive power of reconciliation.

Furthermore, despite its embarrassing stumbles ('I am not here to say that Bill was white'), Cribb's speech also succeeds in doing something quite remarkable: namely, directly challenging the barriers and prejudices that were so prevalent in Georgian England. When Cribb wrote his eulogy, the abolition of slavery in the British Empire was four years away, and the Emancipation Proclamation by Abraham Lincoln still thirty-three years in the future. Yet, years in advance of these landmark events, Cribb was making a brave call for all human beings to be judged by their characters and actions and not their ethnicity; to modern ears the phrase 'these niggers have got bowels like ourselves', is utterly offensive, but Cribb's rejection of the idea that 'colour always [makes] the man' is both honestly expressed and inspiring. In the face of death, Cribb points out that all men, no matter what their 'colour', will one day succumb to the same fate and 'tumble' from their 'perch'.

The eulogy is also a vivid and valuable source in terms of what it tells us of Richmond the man, as opposed to Richmond the pugilist. The portrait Cribb paints of Richmond is of a man of honour ('as right in conduct as a trivet'), as well as a man who inspired loyalty and devotion in others ('always a trump to me'). Less flatteringly, Richmond also emerges as somewhat stubborn and with a possibly misguided surfeit of pride, resulting in an insistence on always paying his own way ('He hath stood many glasses in my bar/Tho' he was free to sluice his gob for nothing'), as well as a refusal to accept pity or charity ('when he was turn'd adrift/ How oft I wish'd to lend him half a crown/Which always he refus'd'). These lines raise the possibility that the poverty Richmond and his family endured in the final months of his life was partly a result of his bloody-minded refusal to accept help from others. However, although his sense of pride may have been misguided, Richmond, to his credit, emerges as a man who harbours considerable compassion towards others, as Cribb points out: 'when a poor cove has begg'd, Billy has tipp'd.'

It is made clear in Cribb's conclusion to his eulogy, which echoes *Ecclesiastes*, that the former champion believes that charitable acts never go unrewarded, on earth at least, for the eulogy is unusual in that it is devoid of any allusions to life after death. Cribb expresses a lack of faith in the perspicacity of posterity though, bemoaning the fact that 'the roguery of men lives after them/The good is soon forgotten as themselves'.

In this case though, Cribb's pessimism was misplaced for, since his death, Richmond's reputation has both endured and grown. In the remaining decades of the nineteenth century, he remained a renowned and oft-referred to figure; his 'ghost' regularly appeared in the dramatic verses featured in the pages of *Bell's Life* – usually bemoaning the decline of pugilism and fair play – and among the many famous writers to reference Richmond were William Makepeace Thackeray in his *The Four Georges* lectures in 1855 (later published in book form), and Arthur Conan Doyle in his 1896 novel *Rodney Stone*, who hailed him as 'the first born American to win laurels in the British ring.'[1] Meanwhile, George Borrow, in his much admired 1851 novel-cum-memoir *Lavengro*, referred to Richmond as 'the most dangerous of blacks', including him among his roll call of pugilistic heroes of whom he claimed wistfully: 'what were the gladiators of Rome, or the bull-fighters of Spain, in its palmiest days, compared to England's bruisers?'

Throughout the first few decades of the twentieth century, Richmond's name inevitably faded somewhat from public consciousness, but his lofty position in boxing history was solidified, with pugilistic reference works continuing to cite him as an important innovator and one of the great sportsmen of the bare-knuckle era. From the 1980s onwards, though, Richmond's fame and reputation have accelerated to new heights and his socio-historical significance, as opposed to his purely sporting importance, has become increasingly recognised, particularly in Great Britain. Booker Prize winning English novelist Alan Hollinghurst made Richmond one of the 'icons' admired by his character Charles Nantwich in his 1988 novel *The Swimming Pool Library*, while Scottish author George MacDonald Fraser's superlative 1997 novel *Black Ajax* brought to vivid life the careers of Cribb, Molineaux and Richmond for a whole new generation. The Juniper TV documentary *Bareknuckle Boxer*, which aired on British television in May 2003, advanced Richmond's reputation even further by focusing on his whole career, as opposed to merely his role in the Cribb-Molineaux contests. Richmond also featured in a sketch on the popular BBC children's series *Horrible Histories* in 2010, while one of the programme's writers, the historian Greg Jenner, wrote a lengthy and well-researched article about his career for *BBC History Magazine*, which was published in 2013 to celebrate the 250th anniversary of his birth.

Richmond's profile has taken longer to rise to prominence in the United States, perhaps due to his Loyalist association with the British Army during the War of Independence and the persistent (albeit untrue) rumours linking him with Nathaniel Hale's execution. Nevertheless, Richmond did gain belated recognition in the land of his birth in 2005, when he was finally inducted into the International Boxing Hall of Fame within the 'pioneer category', a full fourteen years after Cribb's induction and eight after Molineaux's.

Regardless of his wider historical reputation, Richmond remains a personal inspiration for many writers and artists on both sides of the Atlantic. In his native Staten Island, Deacon Geri Swanson has written about Richmond and the importance of America coming to terms with the legacy of slavery, while local historians Nick Dowen and Barnett Shepherd oversaw an issue of the *Staten Island Historian* devoted to Richmond. In New Jersey, another Richmond fanatic, Jerry Leibowitz, is currently writing a novel about his life, while in London the Ghanaian artist Godfried Donkor has, since the early 1990s, produced many acclaimed works of art featuring representations of Richmond.

Donkor's explanation of how Richmond has inspired him is an apt summary of his value as a beacon within black history. 'A lot of my work examines hidden and absent histories,' Donkor told me. 'I take heroic figures who weren't represented in their time or adequately in the history books and recreate and represent them now. Bill is a great subject. His life was remarkable – not only did he manage to survive life as a slave in America but also, through his wits, his skills and his intelligence, he came to England and set himself up as a man of means when it was very difficult for black people to do so. He was a celebrity in his own right and he also part promoted two of the greatest contests in sporting history – the first unofficial world championship boxing matches if you like. And after all that he ended up at George IV's coronation. He was a hero of heroes, a true renaissance character and the first black man to mix among other great sportspeople as equals.'

Richmond's ever-growing reputation makes it clear that his death should not be perceived as tragic, for his achievements were too remarkable and varied to merely be defined by the final poverty-stricken months of his existence. As the first black sportsman to capture the public imagination, as well as an innovator of pugilistic technique, Richmond's place in sports history is assured. Ultimately, though, as Donkor suggests, Richmond is a historical figure of vital importance not because of what he achieved in terms of sporting excellence – for, as worthy and admirable as these achievements are, they are not, in isolation, truly 'historic' – rather, Richmond is important because he achieved these things during an era when racism was so ingrained within society that for a black person to attain the levels of success that Richmond did required formidable powers of determination and enterprise. He was a beacon within the black British community when that community was still nascent and under siege from the forces of slavery and prejudice and, in achieving all he did, Richmond proved the innate human capacity to transcend circumstance, social standing and background. In short, Richmond showed us that even the chains of slavery need not shackle a man's mind or spirit, and he proved that skin colour was no way to judge, label or constrain a man.

Unsurprisingly, in terms of assessing Richmond's social, historical and cultural significance, his contemporary obituary writers singularly failed to do him justice. The truth is that a black celebrity in Georgian England was seen as an oddity, a freak or an accident, not as a harbinger of the fundamental social change and revolution to come. Ironically, the most useful Georgian source in terms of putting into perspective Richmond's achievements as a black man within a white-dominated society is a highly objectionable and racist letter published a mere fortnight after his death. The writer of this letter, who styled himself 'John Bull', claimed that a world where you would find 'a coal black judge', or a 'sable bishop', or a 'black lawyer' was 'impossible', as was the idea that black people could ever 'become equal participators' in society. 'The black is an inferior being to the white,' 'Bull' asserted. 'He is doomed to be so.' The letter even cited the example of Richmond, claiming that a black man such as him, with the capacity for 'conversation and manners', was a 'wonder' and a 'splendid exception'.

The limitations of the collective Georgian mentality were such that most people, this letter writer included, could not conceive of the fact that Richmond's achievements, far from being a one-off freak occurrence, would in time (and given improved social mobility and inclusivity) become the norm. The reality that white-dominated Western society would have to eventually recognise the inevitability of assimilation, equality, migration and immigration was a truth that Richmond's near contemporary Ignatius Sancho articulated in a letter written in July 1777, appropriately just a month after the young Richmond had arrived in England with Percy. They are words that might have been addressed to Richmond himself, just as his journey through English society was about to begin:

> We will mix, my boy, with all countries, colours, faiths. See the countless multitudes of the first world, the myriads descended from the ark, the patriarchs, sages, prophets and heroes! My head turns at the vast idea! We will mingle with them, and try to untwist the vast chain of blessed Providence, which puzzles and baffles human understanding.

Although he has now been dead for approaching 200 years, Richmond's spirit endures and resides, like a strand of unbroken DNA, throughout the lives of his sporting and political contemporaries and heirs as well as within the hearts, minds and consciousness of those who consistently refuse to kowtow to society's conception of who they are, where they come from or what they can achieve. Richmond's countless spiritual brothers, sisters and descendants – including Sancho, Olaudah Equiano, Jack Johnson, Joe Louis, Muhammad Ali, Rosa Parks, Martin Luther King, Angela Davis, Malcolm X and Barack Obama, among many others – all share Richmond's most essential and admirable quality, namely an unwillingness to be contained or constrained by their ethnic background.

It is for these reasons that the appellation of greatness can worthily – and without hyperbole – be attached to the name and life of William Richmond.

Epilogue
St Martin's Parish Workhouse, Castle Street, London, 1 March 1858

The building on the junction of Castle Street and Hemmings Row had seen better days. A gloomy structure with the forbidding air of a prison rather than a charitable institution, the St Martin's workhouse was an irregular, four-sided building surrounding a small central courtyard. There was something macabre but somehow appropriate about the fact the building rested on what had previously been a 'well-stocked' burial ground, as for the residents living within the cramped and unsanitary interior, the ghosts of the past – whether they comprised bitter regret or warm reminiscence – were the only constant companions during the long days and lonely nights of workhouse life.

Mary Richmond, Bill's widow, had lived in the workhouse for at least five years and had now outlived her husband by nearly thirty years. How many memories of Bill and their marriage she was still able to conjure we can but guess. However, given her physical frailty, infirmity and advanced years – she was now eighty-four – it seems a fair conclusion that such memories had inevitably decayed, although it is preferable to nurse the fervent hope that the 'joys of the days that are gone' provided Mary with some much-needed comfort in her final years.

At one time, the St Martin's workhouse had been a well-regarded institution which offered free bed and breakfast to penniless migrants and job seekers passing through London, as well as doubling up as a district hospital which mainly catered for the poor and the needy. However, after the designation of St Martin's as a Poor Law Parish in 1835, conditions had gradually deteriorated. A report in *The Lancet*, published in 1865, seven years after Mary's death, remarked disapprovingly of the 'gloomy darkness' of the cramped wards and the fact there was 'no proper system of subsidiary ventilation', as well as noting that when the weather was cold, the closed windows created a 'very offensive' atmosphere. As for the washing facilities, they were described as 'extremely deficient', and the water closets as 'decidedly bad'. All in all, the journal concluded, the 'inmates' at St Martin's had to endure 'things which we suppose no man of the commonest sense or feeling could bear to inflict, unless he were a "guardian of the poor"'.

On 1 March, after rising from her 'lumpy and comfortless' bed, Mary awoke and ate breakfast, most likely stale bread and butter or, perhaps, water gruel seasoned parsimoniously with spice and sugar. Not long afterwards, she passed away, and with her expired the most recent familial link I have yet found to Bill Richmond, the location of whose genetic inheritance is, sadly, unknown – lost somewhere in the folds of time.

What became of the four children and the grandchildren mentioned in reports of Bill's funeral is a mystery. One factor that makes any ancestors so hard to trace is that, in the wake of the Slave Trade Act of 1807 and the Slavery Abolition Act of 1833, the number of black immigrants to Britain entered a period of decline for around 100 years. The high proportion of black men compared to black women meant that 'inter-marriages', such as that between Mary and Bill, were relatively common but this, in turn, led to a decline in the black population throughout Victorian times. By the early twentieth century the majority of children born with black heritage were probably completely unaware that they even possessed any black ancestors.

Extensive searches of public records have found no inarguable traces of William, Hannah or Betsy beyond the bare details already recounted. Of Henry, known as 'Young Richmond' a little more is known, for he attempted to follow in his father's footsteps and become a boxer, as well as a pugilistic instructor, in which endeavour it was later claimed by J. Ewing Ritchie that he tutored Prince George of Cambridge, a grandson of King George III. At the benefit for 'the widow Richmond' in February 1830, Henry sparred against 'Young Dutch Sam', rumoured to be the illegitimate son of the great Sam Elias, to widespread acclaim and 'repeated cheers'. *Bell's Life in London* confidently predicted that 'time and study' would place Henry 'among the stars'.

After several more sparring engagements, Henry wrote to the journal in September to launch his pugilistic career and announce his willingness to take on all-comers:

To the Editor of Bell's Life in London
SIR – Anxious to follow the steps of my respected father and having already obtained some favour in the character of a teacher of the art of self-defence, I am desirous of illustrating my acquirements practically; and, with that feeling, I am prepared to make a match with Jackson (the pedestrian), Ned Stockman, or any 10 st. novice, for from £25 to

£50. I shall be prepared to attend any appointment that may be made at Mr Cribb's, the Panton Arms, Haymarket.

Yours, &C, Henry Richmond

There was long-standing tension between Stockman and the Richmonds. Back in 1824, Bill had argued that Ned, known as 'the lively kid', should be 'excluded from the Select' of the prize ring due to the 'bad company' he kept. Perhaps this explains why at an April 1830 exhibition at the Tennis Court a set-to between Stockman and Young Richmond had been unusually vicious, with Stockman earning 'disapprobation' by 'substituting throwing for sparring'. A contest between the men never materialised, though, after a disagreement over how much Richmond weighed, and Henry did not make his pugilistic debut until May 1831 when he fought Jack Adams, having already forfeited once against the same opponent. In technique, Richmond showed promise, with *Freeman's Journal* reporting that 'the young *snow ball* proved himself a true "chip of the old block"'. However, 'youth, and light sparring habits, were against him', and Adams triumphed after thirteen rounds and twenty-one minutes. The purse for the contest was just £5.

Despite *Freeman's* view that Henry could have been a contender if he got more 'meat on his bones', he also lost his second contest against Byng Stocks in October 1831 and a planned contest against Bob Coates early in 1832 appears to have never taken place. Henry's next major appearance in the press came in March 1832, when he again wrote to *Bell's Life*, this time to deny a report claiming he had married on the Isle of Wight and take issue with the journal's description of him as 'black', claiming 'I must have a few more dips before I can be called black'.

Although his eloquent writing style suggested he had inherited his father's sharpness of mind, Henry unfortunately seemed to lack Bill's gentlemanly manners. A few days after the publication of this letter, Henry was involved in an unsavoury incident when he lifted the skirts of a young woman 'above her knees' on London Bridge and became embroiled in a brawl with a man who remonstrated with him. The case came to court in April and Henry was found guilty of assault, fined ten pounds and warned if he didn't pay he would be imprisoned. The court recorder assessed the offence as 'very scandalous'. Henry then disappeared from public view for nearly a decade, before making one final appearance in an August 1841 newspaper when a boxer named Bill Haymon, who was based in Birmingham, claimed to have twice been 'hoaxed in the appointments of Young Richmond' and stated that he would not stand for 'any more of his chaffing'. Thereafter Henry's fate, like that of his siblings, is unknown. It is possible that one or more of the Richmond children or grandchildren emigrated and there are rumours of Richmond descendants in Idaho in the United States, but I have not managed to substantiate these.

If the few details of Henry's life inspire disappointment, given his father's honourable nature and considerable achievements, then it is undoubtedly worth emphasising that Mary should be hailed as a hero of this story. For most of this book, she has been an anonymous figure, languishing in the shadowy margins of my narrative. Indeed, it speaks damningly of the lack of rights and status afforded to women in the nineteenth century, that the personal history of this white Georgian woman has left less of a historical trace than that of her black husband.

Although we know little about Mary and Bill's relationship that is not speculative, one minor detail of the Richmonds' domestic life has survived which hints that their marriage was a settled one. In the report of the 'ox case' in 1827, Bill specified that the reason he could not take part in the raffle was due to the fact he needed to be at home because his 'son was sick'. There is something very moving about the fact that Bill was adamant a social engagement should be second priority behind tending to his son; it is a detail that suggests a level of fatherly devotion from which we can infer the existence of a calm familial context. Furthermore, I cannot shake the feeling that without Mary's support and love, it would have been much harder for Richmond to achieve the incredible things he did.

As a consequence of the state of extreme poverty that Bill's death had left Mary in, she was first admitted to the St Martin's workhouse in 1838. She was discharged on 23 April 1839 to 'nurse her daughter' although whether this was Betsy or Hannah is unclear. Exactly how long Mary stayed with her daughter (and where) is also unknown but in 1841 – while Henry was in the Midlands failing to make good on his pugilistic appointments – Mary was back in the workhouse, possibly as an in-patient, having been recorded as being a 'pauper' there in the June census.

On 11 November 1842 she was listed as having been re-admitted and was recorded as 'old, infirmed or disabled'. This re-admittance suggests that her children were absent, dead or living in poverty themselves, or a mixture of all three circumstances. The records for 1843 paint an even bleaker picture: Mary's calling is listed as 'washing and charing', but it is also recorded that she is 'wholly' disabled. Movingly, the reference to her profession indicates she had been trying to support herself by working, but that her disability meant she was no longer able to. Strikingly, among the names on the workhouse register, it is clear Mary was admitted as a charitable gesture in lieu of her infirmity, as opposed to the variety of anti-social behaviour patterns cited as the reasons for many other admissions. The 1851 census also records Mary as being resident in the workhouse, as well as being either blind or deaf and dumb.

For the last few years of her life, Mary remained in a state of infirmity, distress and probable confusion in the workhouse before her aforementioned death. The bare details on her death certificate, which label her 'occupation' as 'widow of William Richmond Cabinet-maker' are frustrating in their simplicity and utter failure to provide her with a fitting epitaph. Having said that, with so little information existing about her, is it even possible to write for Mary a worthy and honest epitaph?

Probably not, in which case perhaps a simple wish will suffice; namely that Bill Richmond's incredible life and achievements, and Mary's existence and devotion to him, should never be forgotten. Some form of permanent memorial to Richmond's life would be a good start, for while there are currently heritage plaques commemorating the careers of Daniel Mendoza, Tom Cribb and Tom Sayers among other boxers, there is – in neither England nor America – any form of public memorial to Bill Richmond.

Postscript

Although there is still no publicly funded memorial to Bill Richmond, in August 2015, at a launch event for this book, a copy of Dighton's famous print *A Striking View of Richmond* was unveiled at Shepherd Neame brewery's Tom Cribb pub on Panton Street, London. Formerly the site of the Union Arms public house, where Cribb and Richmond spent many hours together, Bill now resides on the wall alongside other pugilistic heroes, including Cribb himself. If you ever visit the pub, you can drink to Bill's memory.

Bill Richmond Ring Chronology

Fight no.	Date	Opponent	Source	Location	Result	Purse	Duration
	Late 1780s/ early 1790s						
1	Unknown	George 'Docky' Moore	B	York racecourse, Knavesmire, Yorkshire	Won	Unknown	25 mins
2	Unknown	Unnamed soldier of Inniskilling Dragoons	B	York racecourse, Knavesmire, Yorkshire	Won	Unknown	Unknown
3	Unknown	Unnamed soldier of Inniskilling Dragoons	B	York racecourse, Knavesmire, Yorkshire	Won	Unknown	Unknown
	(Fights 2 and 3 probably took place on the same day)						
4	Unknown	Unnamed blacksmith	B	The Groves, York, Yorkshire	Won	Unknown	Unknown
5	Unknown	Frank Myers	B	The Groves, York, Yorkshire	Won	Unknown	Unknown
	1804						
6	23 January	George Maddox	M	Wimbledon Common, Surrey	Lost	12 gn.	9 rds
	1805						
7	12 April	'Whipmaker' Green	B F H	Islington Fields, Middlesex	Won	Unknown	10 mins
8	21 May	Youssop	M	Blackheath, Kent	Won	10 gn.	6 rds / 15 mins
9	8 July	Jack Holmes	M	Cricklewood Green	Won	50 gn.	26 or 28 rds / 35-50mins*
10	8 October	Tom Cribb	M	Hailsham, Sussex	Lost	25 gn.	90 mins
	1808						
11	14 April	'Westcountryman' Carter	M	Epsom Downs, Surrey	Won	Subscription purse (15 gn.)	25-29 mins
12	11 June	Atkinson	B F H	Golder's Green, Middlesex	Won	Subscription purse	20 mins
13	6 September**	Unnamed baker	B	Willesden Green, Middlesex	Won	Unknown	2 mins
	1809						
14	11 April	Isaac Wood	M	Coombe Wood, Surrey	Won	100 gn.***	23 rds / 40 mins
15	11 August	George Maddox	M	Between Margate and Reculver, Kent	Won	100 gn.	52 mins
	1810						
16	1 May	Jack Power (room fight)	M	Holborn, London	Won	20 gn.	7 rds / 15 mins
	1814						
17	3 May	Jack Davis	M	Coombe Warren, Surrey	Won	50 gn.	13 rds / 20 mins
	1815						
18	1 August	Tom Shelton	M	Moulsey Hurst, Surrey	Won	70 gn.	23 rds / 23 mins****
	1818						
19	12 November	Jack Carter (street fight)	M	Chancery Lane, London	Won	None	3 rds

Overall record: 19 fights, 17 wins, 2 losses
Total known ring earnings: 415 gn.

Sources:
B - *Boxiana*
F - *Fistiana*
H - *The Hand-book to Boxing*
M - Multiple contemporary newspapers (as well as the above sources)

* *Boxiana* claims this fight lasted twenty-six rounds, *Fistiana* and *The Hand-book to Boxing* state twenty-eight. Newspaper reports do not specify how many rounds were fought, and all sources disagree on the timing.

** *Boxiana* specifies that this fight took place at Willesden Green in 1808. The only contest recorded at that location in 1808, according to *Fistiana* and *The Hand-book to Boxing*, was on this date between Chas Brannan and Renny. I would therefore suggest that this is the most likely date for Richmond's contest against the baker.

*** Some sources claim the purse at stake was 200 guineas, which seems unlikely.

**** Multiple sources state this fight was for 50 gn. plus a subscription purse of a further 20 gn. Nearly all newspapers specify the contest lasted twenty-three minutes, however *Boxiana* claims twenty-nine-and-a-half and *Fistiana* twenty-nine.

Acknowledgements

Researching and writing this book has taken over a decade, and there are many people to thank. I owe a huge debt to my wonderful historical researcher Kristina Bedford. Not only did she discover countless nuggets of information about Bill's life, but she also made countless constructive suggestions about my manuscript as it progressed. I must also thank Kristina for putting me in touch with Michael Barton, whose military research proved invaluable.

Trevor Von Eeden is also deserving of heartfelt thanks, both for his wonderful illustrations and also for the consistency of his encouragement and advice.

Deacon Geri Swanson guided my work in many fruitful directions. She also introduced me to Nick Dowen and Barnett Shepherd, who were similarly helpful. The support of these three Staten Islanders has been unstinting and I will never forget the happy afternoon I spent with them eating pizza and talking about Bill Richmond. Also in the USA, I must thank Dennis Genovese, who showed me around St Andrew's church, and Jerry Leibowitz, for his abundant support and kindness.

Closer to home, I would like to thank my publishers, Amberley, especially Jenna Whittle and Jenny Stephens. I must also thank several friends, principally Rowland Stone, Richard Evans and Graham Rye, as well as Daniel Stone, Nicholas Ashton, Paul Gadsby, Craig Holmes, Ben Moser, Lev Myatt, Karen Ryan and James Cartwright. My mother Jenny, stepfather Mike and my sister Zoe have also been hugely encouraging.

To my late father, Gerry, who bought me *Black Ajax*, the book that ignited my interest in Richmond, I also owe a debt of thanks.

For sharing their expertise, as well as for their own contributions in ensuring Bill Richmond's name and those of other fistic heroes are not forgotten, producer David Caldwell-Evans and artist Godfried Donkor also warrant my appreciation, as do the wonderful writers Greg Jenner and David Snowdon.

I am also thankful to Christopher Hunwick, Sandra Blake, Arthur

Landon, Sara Giles, George Percy, Matt Laing, Kate Alderson, Chris Lamb, Nigel Baker and Graham Houston from *Boxing Monthly*, Sam Harrison, Raymond Newman, Lesley Abernethy, Margaret Scott and Adam Chill.

Above and beyond everybody else, though, I would like to thank my wife, Kemi, for her truly humbling love and support. She is the perfect partner.

To close, I would like to extend an invitation to anyone out there with further knowledge of Bill Richmond's incredible life to get in touch with me. Indeed, I live in hope that one day an email will pop into my inbox from one of his descendants.

That, for me, would complete the story.

Luke G. Williams, Summer 2015

Except where otherwise stated, the illustrations in this book are original works by Trevor Von Eeden and may not be reproduced without the permission of the author.

The author and publisher would like to thank the following people/ organisations for permission to use copyright material in this book: *The Royal Collection* for *A Striking View of Richmond* by Robert Dighton, as used on the front cover (Royal Collection Trust/© Her Majesty Queen Elizabeth II 2014); Godfried Donkor for *The Olympians IV* (© Godfried Donkor); the J. Paul Getty Trust for *Bust of a Man* by Francis Harwood (Digital image courtesy of the Getty's Open Content Program) and The Derbyshire Record Office for *Rural Sports, A Milling Match* by Thomas Rowlandson (reproduced with permission of Derby Local Studies and Family History Library; Original illustration held by Derbyshire Record Office, D5459/4/32/2). The image of the back cover of this book is *The Close of the Battle or the Campion Triumphant* by George Cruikshank (Author's Collection).

Every attempt has been made to seek permission for copyright material used in this book. However, if we have inadvertently used copyright material without permission/acknowledgement we apologise and we will make the necessary correction at the first opportunity.

Notes

Prologue

1. This would equate to over £10 million today.
2. Versions of this etching are reproduced on the front cover and in the selection of images in the centre of this book.
3. Egan's authorship of the first volume of *Boxiana* has been disputed with some claiming it was the work of several writers under his editorship. On publication it was credited to 'one of the Fancy', however for ease of reference, I will credit it to Egan.
4. Usually spelt 'noyau' – a French liqueur made from the pits found in peach kernels that possesses an almond-like flavour. Richmond's penchant for such a drink adds to the impression he was a man of sophistication.

1: The Strange Mystery of Bill Richmond's Birth

1. Wilson misquotes Egan, who stated 'Cuckold's Town', not 'Cuckold's Point'.
2. At one point during his narration in *Black Ajax*, Richmond declares: 'I'm half white, what they call dingy Christian.' Fleischer cites the 'editor of a British publication' who refers to Richmond as a 'mulatto'.
3. Seton converted to Catholicism in 1805 and established the first free Catholic school for poor children in the United States. She died in 1821 and was canonised in 1975.

2: 'Humanity Adorns All His Actions'

1. Macintyre is suspected to have fabricated reviews on the Internet Movie Database of silent films the only known copies of which have been long lost, claiming to have seen prints held by 'private collectors'. Given the erratic nature of his career, his work must be treated with the utmost scepticism. He died in June 2010. T. J. Desch Obi's article *Black Terror: Bill Richmond's Revolutionary Boxing* cites correspondence with Macintyre in which he claimed the Percy material came from the 'public record office'.

2. Musters for the *Mercury Packet* have not survived, but numerous newspaper accounts, as well as letters between Sir William Howe and Lord George Germain, confirm Percy travelled to England at this time. It seems unlikely that Richmond would have travelled at a later date or on a different vessel.

3: An Education and 'a Complete Milling'

1. For example, Hogarth's *Taste in High Life* (1746) and Hancock's *Tea-bowl and saucer* (1756–57).
2. Fleischer, founder of *The Ring* magazine, is an utterly unreliable historian; his claim that Richmond fought Moore on 25 August 1791 illustrates his shortcomings. Moore was, in fact, dead by this point, while Fleischer claimed the contest took place during York's Ebor race meeting – a festival that did not begin until 1843.

4: Black Britain and Bill's Better Half

1. Some historians claim the black population in England was much smaller; for example, Norma Myers maintains there were just 5,000 black citizens in London at the beginning of the nineteenth century.

5: 'A Turbulent, Rakehelly, Demented Existence'

1. The Vancouver expedition incorporated visits to five continents and would last four and a half years, producing substantial cartographical results.
2. The Pitt and Vancouver row would rumble on until the latter's death in May 1798.
3. Camelford had been appointed acting master and commander of the *Favourite*, in preference to Peterson. This seems to be the source of loathing between the pair.
4. Camelford may have also been responsible for the death of a man who was killed in Barbados after an argument between Camelford and the captain of another ship resulted in a wild melee. The victim was allegedly shot by one of Camelford's crew and then stabbed in the buttocks by the Lord himself.
5. Henning's work was not published until 1902, so the original source for this assertion is unclear.
6. Gregson was a Lancastrian boxer who often recounted pugilistic incidents in entertaining albeit hyperbolic verse, making him the unofficial 'Poet Laureate' of the Fancy.

6: Richmond Is 'Dared to the Field'

1. Harvey calculated that between 1793 and 1815 there was a rise of 64.5 per cent in the number of prizefights and 85.6 per cent in the expenditure spent/wagered on these events.

2. Like all the bouts in this book, my account of the contests at Wimbledon is drawn from contemporary sources rather than later retellings, which are often full of errors and fictional flourishes. For example, Egan describes these fights in detail but makes the error of describing the Maddox versus Richmond contest as being only three rounds long, an assertion contradicted by nearly all contemporary accounts, which state the fight lasted nine rounds. *The Sporting Magazine* of January 1804 also makes the error of describing the fight as ending in the third round, which is probably where Egan's account originated.

3. The lineage of the English Championship is open to debate, however this contest was certainly regarded as a 'title' bout. *The Times*, for example, remarked: 'The conqueror was to be proclaimed *Champion of England*, as Belcher never *lost* the title, but *resigned* it.' The question of the title's lineage would be settled definitively when Belcher made a comeback and was defeated by Pearce.

4. *The Morning Chronicle* claimed the Maddox-Seabrook contest lasted two rounds - other sources say three.

5. Estimating how much this, or any of the other sums referred to in this book, is equivalent to in modern terms is problematic. Nevertheless, by way of a basic comparison, Arthur Young estimated that the average weekly wage in 1770 was around seven shillings four pence, while the average farm-worker's wage in 1811 was around fourteen shillings, four pence. A guinea was worth just over a pound, so a six-guinea purse, although small, was still more than many manual labourers would earn in a week. Later in his career, when fighting for fifty guineas or more, Richmond was earning purses in one fight which were the equivalent of a year's wages or more for some professions.

7: Exit Camelford, Enter Cribb

1. Tolstoy speculates that Camelford may have been part of a plot to assassinate Napoleon and suggests Simmonds was an agent of a French conspiracy to prevent the assassination by enticing Camelford to his death.

2. Egan claims Richmond only seconded Cribb in the latter of these contests. It seems he has solely drawn on *The Sporting Magazine* as his source for 'Black Sam' and not Richmond being the second for the Cribb versus Maddox contest. However, this account is contradicted by the *Morning Chronicle* and the *Morning Post* which both identify Richmond as Cribb's second. *The Times* also mentions 'Black Sam' seconding Cribb. The likelihood is that 'Black Sam' was another nickname for Richmond. The name does not recur again in Egan or any other contemporary sources and should not be confused with Dutch Sam, who was also in attendance.

3. Given an absence of contemporary evidence concerning this fight, it remains unconfirmed. *Fistiana* and *The Handbook to Boxing* both

claim it took place on 12 April 1805, however Egan describes the contest as Richmond's 'first public set-to in London', implying it took place before Richmond's loss to Maddox. Given other inconsistencies in Egan's biography of Richmond it is likely he made an error.

4. Possibly a politically incorrect corruption of the surname Pick. Although other sources claim his name was Heathapeake.

8: 'The Crowd Were Very Clamorous Against the Black'

1. Curiously, the *Morning Chronicle* refers to Richmond as 'George Richmond'. The same error is made throughout Oxberry's *Pancratia*.
2. There is debate surrounding when Jews were officially 'allowed' back into England. Cromwell raised the idea of re-admitting them at the 1655 Whitehall Conference, although he met with opposition. After this conference, scholars seem to be in broad agreement that Cromwell informally and unofficially allowed Jewish immigrants to come to England, which they did from 1656 onwards.
3. By way of comparison, Henry Pearce and John Gully would fight for a total of 1,000 guineas the same year.
4. The *Morning Post* claims 'Old Cribb', presumably Tom, served as one of Holmes' seconds. However, no other journal mentions this.
5. The *Morning Post* claimed the fight lasted forty-five minutes, *The Sporting Magazine* specified thirty-nine, while the *Morning Chronicle* stated thirty-five.
6. *The Sporting Magazine* maintained the cut occurred in the tenth round. However, both the *Morning Post* and *Morning Chronicle* specify the first round.

9: Bitter Tears for Bill

1. Cribb's recent biographer Jon Hurley claims he was drunk before and during the Nichols fight, although his source is unclear. Attempts by Cribb's supporters to remove the Nichols loss from the mythology of the Black Diamond's career would earn the censure of Egan, who claimed: 'the friends of the CHAMPION acted injudiciously in withholding the name of Nichols' from the names on his fight record.

10: 'The Dexterity of His Coup de Main'

1. The *Bury and Norwich Post* claimed Berks was deported to Botany Bay. However, Egan claimed that 'through the great exertions and humanity of Mr. Jackson ... BERKS ... obtained the situation of a non-commissioned officer in one of his Majesty's regiments on foreign service.'
2. There are frequent examples of Sheridan's support for abolition. In 1789, the Drury Lane Theatre, which he managed, mounted a production of the anti-slavery play *Oroonoko*.

3. The location of the fight had to be moved seventeen miles to Sir John Seabright's Park in Hertfordshire, due to the intervention of magistrates.
4. Not to be confused with Jack Carter, a pugilist from Lancashire.
5. The description of the heckler is intriguing. Does the description 'china-eyed' mean that he was Oriental? Does 'Brown' refer to his surname or skin colour? Was Richmond being heckled by a fellow black man?
6. Egan's chronology of Richmond's career in 1808 and 1809 is problematic. He claims the fight with Carter took place on 14 April 1809, yet newspapers clearly state 14 April 1808. The logical explanation is that Egan made a typographical error, which would also explain why he recounts details of the fight on page 444, before the Wood fight on page 445, even though his stated date for the Carter fight is five days *after* the Wood contest. See the ring chronology elsewhere in this book for further details of this and Richmond's other bouts in 1808.
7. Accounts vary concerning whether the injury was to Belcher's arm, wrist or hand. Some claim Belcher broke two fingers when a wayward punch connected with a ring post.

11: 'Native Valour'

1. Watermen, or bargemen, worked on the river transporting customers along or across it.
2. There is some confusion concerning the purse. The *Bury and Norwich Post* maintains 200 guineas were at stake, while the *Morning Chronicle* claimed 100. The latter seems more likely.
3. Maddox's first major contest was estimated by Egan to have taken place in 1776, others claim 1792.
4. From the poem *Zelinda* by Edmund Waller.

12: The Molineaux Myth

1. Percy's gift was initially a loan, however on the day construction of the new theatre began, he wrote to the theatre's manager John Kemble and made it a gift instead.
2. Hockley-in-the-Hole in Clerkenwell, London was a venue famed for bear and bull baiting.
3. London Land Tax Records for 1809 and 1810 reveal that Richmond began to pay Land Tax in 1810, enabling us to pinpoint this year as when he assumed the position of landlord. The original site of the Horse and Dolphin is now occupied by the National Gallery.
4. According to records held at the London Metropolitan Archives.
5. Henning's book is a reprint of a series originally published in the *Licensed Victuallers' Gazette*, probably in the 1890s.
6. Fleischer claimed his account was based on 'proper research', yet he

does not refer to a single specific source, instead relying on vague attributions such as 'one of the London papers of the time'.

7. Fleischer claims this man was Randolph Peyton, possibly referring to Peyton Randolph, a prominent planter and public official who also served as the first President of the Continental Congress. However Randolph died in 1775, so any connection with Molineaux is impossible.

8. A vast sum, which strains the credibility of this account.

9. This is unlikely. Pinckney was the United States 'Minister to Great Britain' from 1792-1796, and no other account mentions Molineaux arriving in England so early.

10. In 1810, *The Sporting Magazine*, *Kentish Gazette* and *Leicester Journal* all claimed Molineaux was twenty-six.

13: Molineaux 'Threatens to Mill the Whole Race of Fighters'

1. The other possibility is that 'Lilly white' here refers to Molineaux; however it seems unlikely that Richmond would consider matching Molineaux with a boxer as accomplished as Belcher in his debut, or that Molineaux would have been considered favourite.

2. Gell's imitation of Belcher's Bristolian speech patterns; he had a somewhat patronising habit of writing sections of his letters in his own approximation of Jem or Tom's 'voice'.

3. The same sentence was used in, among others: *The Times*, *Morning Post*, *Kentish Gazette*, *Northampton Mercury*, *Hampshire Chronicle* and *Leicester Journal*.

4. This probably apocryphal exchange is from various sources, notably Henning.

14: England's Anxiety

1. Barclay was in Scotland, having been invited to become Master of the Turriff Hunt.

15: 'Old England For Ever'

1. Cribb's tussle against Richmond also contends for this accolade, although it was not a title bout and Richmond was arguably considered more English than American.

2. Not all accounts even claim the fight lasted forty-four rounds. Oxberry, for example, maintains it ended after thirty-three and Egan thirty-four. Earlier reports in *The Times*, *Chronicle*, *et al* all state forty-four though.

3. Henning claims Apreece acted as referee, with Lord Archibald Hamilton and Colonel Barton as umpires.

4. Egan here cites the Bill Ward incident examined in chapter 10.

16: 'The Antipathy Against a Man of Colour'

1. On 10 January 1811, the *Morning Post* and *Morning Chronicle* reported that Richmond had appeared at Bow Street on a charge of 'violently assaulting John Hart' on the night of the fight between Molineaux and Cribb. Reports of the outcome of the case do not appear in newspapers in the succeeding weeks, and records at the London Metropolitan Archives are incomplete for this period. Given that Richmond's movements are referenced in newspapers throughout the rest of the year, it seems likely that the charges were dropped. If Richmond had been found guilty, he probably would have only had to pay a fine.

18: Richmond's Ruin

1. Most reports claim Molineaux's jaw was broken, however the *York Herald* claimed this was 'incorrect'.
2. How this squared with the convention that a round was declared over once one combatant was knocked down is unclear. Nevertheless, several reports do clearly state that in both the ninth and eleventh rounds Cribb knocked Molineaux down, only to cede his right to victory. Perhaps, therefore, it would be more accurate to say that the fight lasted thirteen rounds rather than eleven.
3. Haiti became an independent republic in 1804 as a result of a slave rebellion against the French.
4. Richmond is listed as resident in St Martin's Street and paying London land tax in 1812, but not 1813, indicating he left the Horse and Dolphin in 1812.
5. The *Cheltenham Chronicle* claimed the story of the arrest was 'erroneous'. Whatever actually happened, it is clear Richmond made some sort of financial claim against Molineaux during the lead-up to the Carter contest.

19: Richmond Reborn

1. These receipts sold at auction for $2,390 in 2009 and represent the only known and confirmed signature of Richmond in existence, except for that on the Marriage Bond of William Richmond and Mary Dunwick, which is most likely his.
2. Intriguingly, perhaps the best likeness of Richmond that might exist is a bust in the Getty Museum that the Getty does not recognise as being of Richmond. Although the literature associated with this bust claims it is a work of Francis Harwood in 1758, Jerry Leibowitz advances a convincing thesis that it was actually produced later and that Richmond was the subject. Leibowitz's fascinating investigation into this matter can be located at www.idiscoveredamerica.com. An image of this bust can be found in the illustrations in the centre of this book.

3. An image of this print is located in the illustrations in the centre of this book.

4. An image of this print is on the front cover of this book.

20: Richmond Retires

1. It is often stated that Sutton fell out with Richmond, although the fact the latter helped him when sick and informed the Fancy of his passing indicates a rapprochement.

21: Richmond's Crowning Glory

1. If recognition of the title of English Champion should have passed to anyone since Cribb last fought, Richmond arguably had the best claim; he had not lost a contest since his 1805 set-to with Cribb and, if we also take the Carter 'contest' into account, by 1819 he was undefeated for an incredible fourteen years and nine bouts, albeit with several periods of inactivity.

2. The eighteen pugilists were: Richmond, Tom Cribb, Tom Spring, Tom Belcher, Jack Carter, Ben Burn, Harry Harmer, Harry Lee, Tom Owen, Joshua Hudson, Tom Oliver, Harry Holt, Peter Crawley, Dick Curtis, Ben Medley, Bob Purcell, Philip Sampson and Bill Eales. Not many of the pugilists were mentioned in newspaper reports, so the fact Richmond was name-checked in virtually every one indicates his considerable reputation.

22: 'The Joys of the Days That Are Gone'

1. Billy was said to have killed over 10,000 rats and to have never lost a dog fight. On his death in 1829, several newspapers ran obituaries of him. Apparently, his stuffed corpse ended up as a permanent resident on the bar of Cribb's pub.

23: 'You All Lov'd Richmond Once'

1. Less pleasingly, the physical description of Richmond by Conan Doyle indicated that casual racism remained endemic within England, even sixty-seven years after Richmond's death: 'A little way down the room,' recounted Conan Doyle's eponymous narrator, 'I saw the black face and woolly head of Bill Richmond, in a purple-and-gold footman's livery - destined to be the predecessor of Molineaux, Sutton, and all that line of black boxers who have shown that the muscular power and insensibility to pain which distinguish the African [and] give him a peculiar advantage in the sports of the ring.'

Bibliography

While researching this book, many thousands of sources have been consulted. This partial bibliography merely includes a brief list of those that were most useful. A full bibliography and complete references is at: www.billrichmond.blogspot.co.uk.

Archives/online archives

Ancestry.co.uk; Alnwick archives; Borthwick Institute for Archives, University of York; British Library; Britishorigins.com; British Newspaper Library/Online Archive; Derbyshire Record Office, Matlock; Findmypast.co.uk; London Family History Centre; London Metropolitan Archives; The National Archives.

Books

Bolton, Charles Knowles (ed.), *Letters of Hugh Earl Percy from Boston and New York, 1774-1776* (Boston: Charles E. Goodspeed, 1902)

Brailsford, Dennis, *Bareknuckles: A Social History of Prize-fighting* (Cambridge: Lutterworth Press, 1988)

Dowling, Vincent George, *Fistiana* (London: W. Clement, Jnr, 1841)

Egan, Pierce, *Boxiana or Sketches of Ancient and Modern Pugilism Volumes 1-V* (London: George Virtue, 1812, 1818, 1821, 1828, 1829)

Fryer, Peter, *The History of Black People in Britain* (London: Pluto Press, 1984)

Henning, Fred, *Fights for the championship: the men and their times* (London: Licensed Victuallers' Gazette, 1902)

McManus, Edgar J., *Black Bondage in the North* (New York: Syracuse University Press, 1973)

Miles, Henry Downes, *Pugilistica: The History of British Boxing* (Edinburgh: John Grant, 1906)

Oxberry, William, *Pancratia, or a History of Pugilism* (London: W. Oxberry, 1812)

Papas, Phillip, *That Ever Loyal Island: Staten Island and the American Revolution* (New York: New York University Press, 2007)

Shattuck, Gardiner H., *Episcopalians and Race* (Lexington: The University Press of Kentucky, 2000)

Swift, Owen, *The Hand-book to Boxing* (London: Nicholson, 1840)

Tolstoy, Nikolai, *The Half-Mad Lord* (London: Jonathan Cape, 1978)

Newspapers / journals

Bath Chronicle and Weekly Gazette; Bell's Life in London and Sporting Chronicle; Bell's Weekly Messenger; Blackwood's Edinburgh Magazine; Bury and Norwich Post; Caledonian Mercury; Cambridge Chronicle and Journal; Carlisle Patriot; Cheltenham Chronicle; Chester Chronicle; Chester Courant; Cobbett's Weekly Political Register; Coventry Herald; Daily Universal Register; Derby Mercury; Freeman's Journal; Gaines Mercury; Guardian; Hampshire Chronicle; Hampshire Telegraph; Harper's Weekly; Hereford Journal; Hull Packet; Ipswich Journal; Kentish Gazette; Lancaster Gazette; Leamington Spa Courier; Leeds Intelligencer; Leicester Chronicle; Leicester Journal; Liberator; London Chronicle; London Gazette; London Standard; Manchester Mercury; Morning Chronicle; Morning Post; Newcastle Courant; Norfolk Chronicle; Northampton Mercury; Oxford Journal; Police Gazette; Royal Cornwall Gazette; Royal Gazette; Salisbury and Winchester Journal; Scots Magazine; Sheffield Daily Telegraph; The Spirit of the Times; The Sporting Magazine; The Sportsman's Magazine; Staffordshire Advertiser; Stamford Mercury; Sussex Advertiser; Star; Sussex Advertiser; The Times; Weekly Dispatch; Westmorland Gazette; York Herald.